GENTILITY IN EARLY MODERN WALES

THE SALESBURY FAMILY, 1450–1720

by

SADIE JARRETT

UNIVERSITY OF WALES PRESS
2024

© Sadie Jarrett, 2024

All rights reserved. No part of this book may be reproduced in any material form (including photocopying or storing it in any medium by electronic means and whether or not transiently or incidentally to some other use of this publication) without the written permission of the copyright owner. Applications for the copyright owner's written permission to reproduce any part of this publication should be addressed to the University of Wales Press, University Registry, King Edward VII Avenue, Cardiff CF10 3NS.

www.uwp.co.uk

British Library CIP Data
A catalogue record for this book is available from the British Library

ISBN   978-1-83772-096-5
eISBN   978-1-83772-097-2

The right of Sadie Jarrett to be identified as author of this work has been asserted in accordance with sections 77 and 79 of the Copyright, Designs and Patents Act 1988.

This book is freely available on a Creative Commons CC-BY-NC-ND licence thanks to the kind sponsorship of the libraries participating in the Jisc Open Access Community Framework OpenUP initiative.

Typeset by Richard Huw Pritchard
Printed by CPI Antony Rowe, Melksham, United Kingdom

STUDIES IN WELSH HISTORY

Editors

RALPH A. GRIFFITHS   CHRIS WILLIAMS
ERYN M. WHITE

39

GENTILITY IN EARLY MODERN WALES

SERIES EDITORS' FOREWORD

Since the foundation of the series in 1977, the study of Wales's history has attracted growing attention among historians internationally and continues to enjoy a vigorous popularity. Not only are approaches, both traditional and new, to the study of history in general being successfully applied in a Welsh context, but Wales's historical experience is increasingly appreciated by writers on British, European and world history. These advances have been especially marked in the university institutions in Wales itself.

In order to make more widely available the conclusions of original research, much of it of limited accessibility in postgraduate dissertations and theses, in 1977 the History and Law Committee of the Board of Celtic Studies inaugurated this series of monographs, *Studies in Welsh History*. It was anticipated that many of the volumes would originate in research conducted in the University of Wales or under the auspices of the Board of Celtic Studies, and so it proved. Although the Board of Celtic Studies no longer exists, the University of Wales Press continues to sponsor the series. It seeks to publish significant contributions made by researchers in Wales and elsewhere. Its primary aim is to serve historical scholarship and to encourage the study of Welsh history.

For my parents

CONTENTS

SERIES EDITORS' FOREWORD	v
ACKNOWLEDGEMENTS	ix
A NOTE ON SPELLING	xi
LIST OF ABBREVIATIONS	xiii
MAPS	xv
GENEALOGICAL TABLES	xvii
Introduction	1
1. The Salesbury family	21
2. Territorial legitimacy	67
3. Networks of power	109
4. Culture, scholarship and religion	151
5. The wider world	197
EPILOGUE	229
BIBLIOGRAPHY	235
INDEX	251

ACKNOWLEDGEMENTS

It has been a great pleasure to spend time with the Salesburys of Rhug and Bachymbyd over the last few years. The Rhug Estate funded my initial doctoral research on the family and I have thoroughly enjoyed working with the place that the Salesburys called home. I am very grateful to Lord Newborough and the team at Rhug for all their support. My particular thanks to Janice Dale who has continually championed the project and provided me with invaluable assistance.

This book would not have been completed without the help and advice of numerous people. I am indebted to Huw Pryce for all his knowledge and guidance, as well as his comments on a full draft. Shaun Evans first introduced me to the Salesbury family for my PhD and continues to be a hugely supportive mentor. Lloyd Bowen helped to clarify my early thoughts on the book and provided helpful advice on a draft section. Richard Cust, Sharon Howard, Melvin Humphreys, Conor O'Brien, Gwilym Owen, Sara Elin Roberts, Rebecca Thomas and Gruffydd Aled Williams generously answered questions, discussed ideas, or provided sources, and Cath D'Alton produced the maps. I am especially grateful to Ann Parry Owen who advised on my translations of Welsh poetry. The peer reviewer also provided very valuable comments. Needless to say, any remaining errors are my own.

I am grateful to the Economic History Society, the Institute of Historical Research and The Queen's College, Oxford, for funding my postdoctoral research.

This book is dedicated to my parents for all their love and support.

A NOTE ON SPELLING

The Salesbury surname can be spelt in a variety of ways, including Salusbury and Salisbury. Family correspondence from at least the mid-sixteenth century shows that the Salesburys of Rhug and Bachymbyd preferred the 'Salesbury' spelling. Rhug, historically Rûg, is the current English and Welsh spelling of the estate.

When quoting from sources, contractions and superscriptions have been expanded. The original spelling has been kept, with corrections in square brackets where necessary. New Style dating is used throughout. References to women use their fathers' surnames to avoid confusion over marriages.

LIST OF ABBREVIATIONS

Al. Oxon.	Joseph Foster (ed.), *Alumni Oxonienses: The Members of the University of Oxford, 1500–1714*, vol. 2 (Oxford, 1892)
BBCS	*Bulletin of the Board of Celtic Studies*
BL	British Library
BUASC	Bangor University Archives and Special Collections
Ca. MS	Cardiff Manuscript (Cardiff Central Library)
CPR	*Calendar of Patent Rolls*
CRO	Caernarfon Record Office (Gwynedd Archives)
CSP Dom.	*Calendar of State Papers, Domestic*
CSP For.	*Calendar of State Papers, Foreign*
DRO	North East Wales Archives (Denbighshire Record Office), Ruthin
DWB	*Dictionary of Welsh Biography*
EHR	*English Historical Review*
FRO	North East Wales Archives (Flintshire Record Office), Hawarden
Foster, Admissions to Gray's Inn	Joseph Foster (ed.), *The Register of Admissions to Gray's Inn, 1521–1889* (London, 1889)
HMC	Historical Manuscripts Commission
Hughes, 'Noddwyr y beirdd'	Arwyn Lloyd Hughes, 'Noddwyr y beirdd yn Sir Feirionnydd' (unpublished MA thesis, University of Wales, Aberystwyth, 1969)

Jones, Welsh Gentry	John Gwynfor Jones, *The Welsh Gentry 1536–1640: Images of status, honour and authority* (Cardiff, 1998; repr. 2016)
LP	*Letters and Papers, Foreign and Domestic*
NLW	National Library of Wales, Aberystwyth
ODNB	*Oxford Dictionary of National Biography*
RCAHMW	Royal Commission on the Ancient and Historical Monuments of Wales
RWMS	Daniel Huws, *A Repertory of Welsh Manuscripts and Scribes, c.800–c.1800,* vol. 1 (Aberystwyth, 2022)
SA	Shropshire Archives, Shrewsbury
Smith, Salusbury Correspondence	W. J. Smith (ed.), *Calendar of Salusbury Correspondence, 1553–c.1700* (Cardiff, 1954)
THL	The Huntington Library, San Marino, CA
TNA	The National Archives, London
WHR	*Welsh History Review*

MAPS

Figure 1: The estates of prominent early modern gentry families in north Wales.

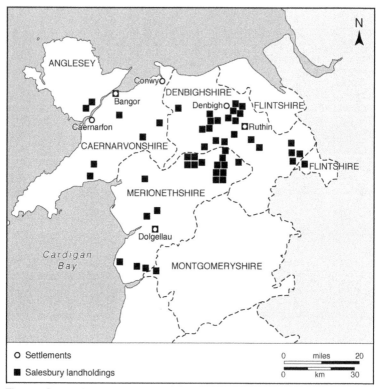

Figure 2: Landed interests of the Salesbury family, c.1470–1720.

GENEALOGICAL TABLES

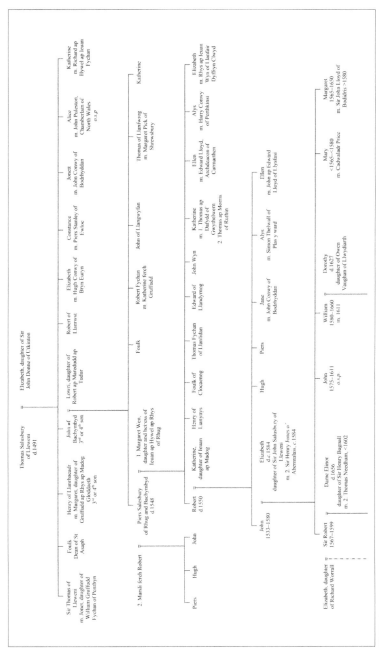

Table 1

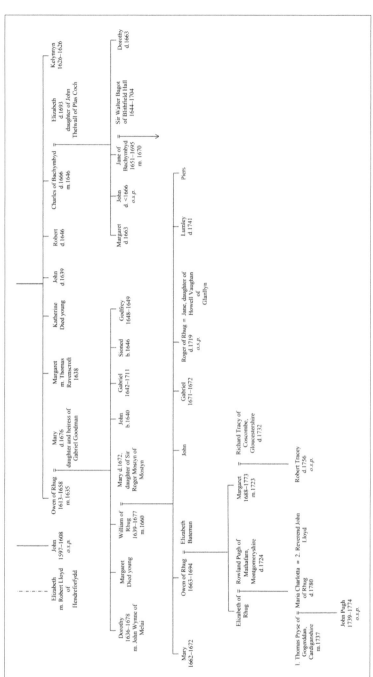

Table 2

INTRODUCTION

The elite families of early modern Wales were acutely aware of their status. It manifested itself in elaborate pedigree rolls outlining their glorious ancestors and the coats of arms emblazoned on their houses. They understood that a Welsh gentry family had a great and noble history, descent from kings and princes, which set them apart from ordinary people and gave the Welsh gentry the right to govern. The family name was paramount and so was the sense that it would continue in perpetuity, forever associated with their patrimony and the great deeds of their family. This book looks in detail at the Salesburys of Rhug and Bachymbyd, one of the leading gentry families in north Wales from the fifteenth to the eighteenth century. It examines how they established themselves as a gentry family and how they fought to maintain their status during a period of significant change in Welsh and British history. In doing so, it illuminates broader aspects of Welsh gentility and the changing nature of early modern Welsh society.

The early modern Welsh gentry is an established and expanding field of study. John Gwynfor Jones (1936–2020) was a prolific scholar on the Welsh gentry and his research forms much of the foundation for this study of gentility in early modern Wales. Although previous research, such as Brian E. Howells's studies of the south-west Wales gentry, recognised regional differences, Jones established the early modern Welsh gentry, or *uchelwyr*, as a unique social class, separate from their English counterparts.[1] Coupled with the work of A. D. Carr on medieval Wales, Welsh gentry

---

[1] Brian E. Howells, *The Gentry of South-West Wales, 1540–1640* (Cardiff, 1968).

studies has burgeoned in recent years.[2] Shaun Evans has developed Carr's work on the Mostyns of Mostyn with a particular focus on how the family cultivated its public image.[3] Robin Grove-White used a case study of Hugh Hughes of Plas Coch to understand how the gentry navigated between English and Welsh society.[4] Sarah Ward Clavier has examined the importance of historical memory in Welsh gentry society, while Lloyd Bowen, as part of his extensive engagement with early modern Wales, has explored the gentry's participation in British politics and the role of status and honour in gentry culture.[5] The existing scholarship on the Welsh gentry, discussed in more detail below, has particularly focused on the gentry's engagement with Welsh culture and society and their participation in English government and political networks. The example of the Salesburys both corroborates and expands on this existing scholarship, presenting the Welsh gentry as an integral part of local communities who fully capitalised on the opportunities presented by union with England.

Studies on early modern Britain have begun to acknowledge Wales's cultural differences. For example, the influential work of Felicity Heal and Clive Holmes on the early modern gentry, *The Gentry in England and Wales, 1500–1700*, is notable for its inclusion of significant amounts of Welsh material, although this is largely used to supplement the English material and highlight

---

[2] A. D. Carr, *The Gentry of North Wales in the Later Middle Ages* (Cardiff, 2017).

[3] A. D. Carr, 'The Mostyn family and estate, 1200–1642' (unpublished PhD thesis, University of Wales, Bangor, 1975); Shaun Evans, '"To contynue in my bloud and name": Reproducing the Mostyn dynasty, *c*.1540–1692' (unpublished PhD thesis, Aberystwyth University, 2013).

[4] Robin Grove-White, *A Prism for His Times: Late-Tudor Anglesey and Hugh Hughes of Plas Coch* (Llangefni, 2020).

[5] Sarah Ward Clavier, *Royalism, Religion and Revolution: Wales, 1640–1688* (Woodbridge, 2021); Lloyd Bowen, *Politics in the Principality: Wales, c.1603–1642* (Cardiff, 2007); 'Information, language and political culture in early modern Wales', *Past and Present*, 228/1 (2015), 125–58.

common characteristics of the gentry in England and Wales.[6] Nevertheless, there is still much to be done and the Welsh gentry remain understudied and largely unincorporated into the wider historiography of early modern Britain. In the words of Sarah Ward Clavier, 'Wales is both too foreign . . . and too familiar to be a major prescription for most English historians'.[7] In providing a case study of Welsh gentility in practice, this book hopes to make the Welsh gentry more accessible and highlight their rich potential to enhance our knowledge of early modern Britain. The family case study is a fruitful means to increase our understanding of early modern society.[8] In her work on the Temples of Stowe, Rosemary O'Day said that 'we need to study more families in detail to understand how families and households functioned within society and either upheld or undermined its mores'.[9] There are natural limitations to a case study and individual families are vulnerable to the charge that they do not fit the norm. Of course, every family is unique in its own way, but they also operate within the constraints and expectations of their own societies. This study of the Salesburys illustrates the constraints and expectations of gentry society in early modern Wales and how they changed between the fifteenth and eighteenth centuries. In a period when the state became increasingly centralised, it highlights the continued strength of regional identities in early modern Britain,

---

[6] For examples of scholarship which acknowledge Wales's cultural differences, see Brendan Bradshaw and Peter Roberts (eds), *British Consciousness and Identity: The Making of Britain, 1533–1707* (Cambridge, 1998); Philip Schwyzer, *Literature, Nationalism, and Memory in Early Modern England and Wales* (Cambridge, 2004); Alexandra Walsham, 'The Holy Maid of Wales: Visions, Imposture and Catholicism in Elizabethan Britain', *EHR*, 132/555 (2017), 250–85; and Felicity Heal and Clive Holmes, *The Gentry in England and Wales 1500–1700* (Basingstoke, 1994). In the last title, the references to Welsh material are extensive, and include the Bulkeley family, pp. 43–4, 52, 73–4, 85, 88, 204; the Morgans of Tredegar, pp. 163, 194; the Mostyn family, pp. 36, 65–6, 75, 82, 90, 280, 376; and the gentry of Caernarfonshire, pp. 11, 14, 174, 278.

[7] Clavier, *Royalism*, p. 2.

[8] For other case-study approaches to the early modern gentry, see John Gwynfor Jones, *The Wynn Family of Gwydir: Origins, Growth and Development, c.1490–1674* (Aberystwyth, 1995); Vivienne Larminie, *Wealth, Kinship and Culture: The Seventeenth-Century Newdigates of Arbury and Their World* (Woodbridge, 1995); Rosemary O'Day, *An Elite Family in Early Modern England: The Temples of Stowe and Burton Dassett, 1570–1656* (Woodbridge, 2018).

[9] O'Day, *An Elite Family*, p. 20.

as well as the enthusiasm of the localities for Britain's developing colonial enterprises.[10]

The Salesburys of Rhug and Bachymbyd were a cadet branch of the Salusburys of Lleweni, but they became a leading family in their own right.[11] John Salesbury, a younger son of Thomas Salusbury of Lleweni, began to establish himself at Bachymbyd from the 1470s. At the time, Bachymbyd was in the marcher lordship of Denbigh and John's burgeoning estate straddled the border of Denbigh and the neighbouring lordship of Ruthin. Fifteenth-century Wales was administratively complicated, but John Salesbury understood how to capitalise on a dual legal system to develop a sizeable holding to support his family. Bachymbyd became the ancestral home of the Salesburys, though they added the Rhug estate, fifteen miles south down the Vale of Clwyd and located in the Principality of North Wales, when John's son, Piers, married Margaret Wen, heiress to Ieuan ap Hywel of Rhug. As a family, the Salesburys navigated shifting and complicated identities. They were barons of Edeirnion claiming ancient privileges from the old princes of Wales; they were respectable politicians and lawyers in London making the most of union with England; they were Oxford-educated scholars who helped to promote and preserve Welsh-language literature; they were proud descendants of Owain Glyndŵr and his rebel forces; and they were soldiers and pirates and poets.

Like many of the early modern Welsh gentry, they were a family of contradictions. Certainly, they were proud Welshmen who spoke, wrote and prayed in Welsh, and they were deeply rooted in the gentry community of north-east Wales. This is perhaps surprising because their paternal ancestors were medieval English settlers who arrived at Lleweni in the lordship of Denbigh soon after the Edwardian Conquest of 1282–3, yet the

---

[10] Michael J. Braddick, *State Formation in Early Modern England, c.1550–1700* (Cambridge, 2000).

[11] For an introduction to the Salusburys of Lleweni, see W. J. Smith (ed.), 'Introduction', in Smith, *Salusbury Correspondence*, pp. 1–13; and Emyr Gwynne Jones and W. J. Smith, 'Salusbury, Salisbury, Salesbury family, of Lleweni and Bachygraig', *DWB* (1959).

Salesburys, and their cousins at Lleweni, became an archetypal Welsh gentry family who embraced the representations of Welsh gentility.[12] They developed their estates; they held local and national offices; they engaged in bardic patronage; they cultivated martial qualities; they educated their children; and they defended their reputation in rivalries with their fellow gentry. The Salesburys and the wider Salusbury kindred transformed themselves from medieval English settlers to early modern Welsh gentry. This adoption of Welsh gentility makes them a useful case study: they recognised, knowingly or not, the political and social advantages of establishing themselves as an elite family in Welsh communities. Other north Wales families, such as the Pulestons of Emral, the Hanmers of Hanmer, and the Bulkeleys of Baron Hill, also originated as English settlers in medieval Wales; thus, the Salesburys were far from unique.[13] The Salesburys lived in north-east Wales, an important heartland for early modern Welsh culture and home to a significant number of gentry families.[14] These included the Thelwalls of Plas y Ward, the Mostyns of Mostyn, the Almers of Almer, the Conwys of Bodrhyddan, the Trevors of Trevalyn, the Davieses of Gwysaney, the Myddeltons of Chirk, and the Lloyds of Bodidris. As a cadet branch of the Salusburys of Lleweni, the Salesburys of Rhug and Bachymbyd also had shared kindred with numerous other cadet branches across north-east Wales, including the Salusburys of Bachygraig, of Plas Isaf, of Llanrhaeadr, of Leadbrook, and of Erbistock. These other gentry families provided competition for the Salesburys, but also opportunities to establish kinship networks, and they had a common desire to maintain their position as a gentry class.

[12] For a study of English settlement in the neighbouring lordship of Ruthin, or Dyffryn Clwyd, see A. D. M. Barrell and M. H. Brown, 'A settler community in post-Conquest rural Wales: The English of Dyffryn Clwyd, 1294–1399', *WHR*, 17/3 (1995), 332–55.
[13] Carr, *Gentry of North Wales*, pp. 157–61; Thomas Richards, 'Bulkeley family, Anglesey, etc.', *DWB (1959)*.
[14] G. J. Williams, 'Traddodiad llenyddol Dyffryn Clwyd a'r cyffiniau', *Transactions of the Denbighshire Historical Society*, 1 (1952), 20–32; Enid Roberts, 'The Renaissance in the Vale of Clwyd', *Flintshire Historical Society Journal*, 15 (1954–55), 52–63.

WELSH GENTILITY

In theory, gentility, or *uchelwriaeth*, was a straightforward concept in early modern Wales. It represented the qualities associated with the *uchelwyr*, literally the 'high men'. In medieval Wales, *uchelwyr* were free men and heads of their households.[15] Although degrees of status existed among free men, most notably between royalty and non-royalty, all free men were noble.[16] They were also descended from other free men, and thus *uchelwriaeth* derived from lineage, rather than land or money. A. D. Carr has highlighted that the *uchelwyr* were leaders of their local communities and negotiated on their communities' behalf with the aristocracy, first the Welsh princes and later the English Crown and the marcher lords. After Edward I's conquest of Wales, English kings depended on the Welsh gentry to reinforce their authority and act as mediators with local communities.[17] With the native Welsh aristocracy largely extinct after the Conquest, the Welsh gentry became their political successors. They absorbed ideals previously associated with royalty and constructed an image of themselves as brave warriors, merciful leaders, generous neighbours, and literary patrons. This was encompassed by the principles of *uchelwriaeth*: lineage, bravery, military skill and, according to Carr, 'a pride bordering on arrogance . . . No one should dare question a man's courage or challenge his status or authority in the community'.[18]

In the late Middle Ages, the Welsh gentry were families that successfully negotiated the complicated political and legal situation in Wales after the Conquest, facilitated by the uncertain place of Wales in the wider framework of government. After the Conquest, Welshmen were barred from holding major offices in the administration of Wales, and Henry IV reinforced the restrictions in 1401 during the Glyndŵr Revolt (1400–c.1415),

---

[15] Thomas Charles Edwards, *Early Irish and Welsh Kinship* (Oxford, 1993), pp. 172–3.
[16] Ben Guy, *Medieval Welsh Genealogy: An introduction and textual study* (Woodbridge, 2020), p. 6.
[17] Carr, *Gentry of North Wales*, pp. 12–21.
[18] Carr, *Gentry of North Wales*, p. 176.

as part of a wider programme of penal laws.[19] Although there were some exceptions, such as Sir Gruffudd Llwyd (d.1335), who was sheriff of Caernarfonshire twice, of Merioneth twice, and Anglesey once, the Welsh gentry generally occupied minor offices and established themselves as reliable deputies; in this way, they could gain significant power, particularly when English lords held major offices *in absentia*.[20] The governance of Wales relied on the Welsh gentry to the extent that the Glyndŵr Revolt did not especially hinder their advancement, despite Owain Glyndŵr relying on the support of much of the gentry.[21] Although Henry IV's post-Glyndŵr legislation was theoretically very restrictive, it is unlikely that it was enforced in full. Indeed, Ralph A. Griffiths suggests that it was 'tempered in practice by a blind eye'.[22] In 1429, for example, Gruffudd ap Nicholas administered Dinefwr Castle on behalf of the absentee constable, Sir Roland Standish.[23] Military service was an important occupation for the Welsh gentry and it could be a source of opportunity for them: Sir Hywel ap Gruffudd became constable of Criccieth in about 1359 in part because of his service to the Black Prince.[24]

Between 1536 and 1543, the so-called Acts of Union transformed the legal and constitutional position of Wales, extending English law and citizenship across the country. They abolished a complicated dual legal system which restricted the ability of elite families to develop estates and delegated responsibility for governing Wales to Welsh gentlemen.[25] For the

---

[19] R. A. Griffiths, 'Wales and the Marches in the fifteenth century', in his *King and Country: England and Wales in the Fifteenth Century* (London, 1991), p. 60.

[20] Carr, *Gentry of North Wales*, p. 40; Ralph A. Griffiths, 'Patronage, politics and the Principality of Wales, 1413–1461', in his *King and Country: England and Wales in the Fifteenth Century*, p. 173.

[21] Ralph A. Griffiths, 'Gentlemen and rebels in later medieval Cardiganshire', *Ceredigion*, 5/2 (1964–7), 143–67; R. R. Davies, *The Revolt of Owain Glyn Dŵr* (Oxford, 1995), esp. pp. 198–22.

[22] Griffiths, 'Patronage, politics and the Principality', p. 167.

[23] Griffiths, 'Patronage, politics and the Principality', p. 173.

[24] Carr, *Gentry of North Wales*, p. 39.

[25] W. R. B. Robinson, 'The Tudor revolution in Welsh government 1536–1543: Its effects on gentry participation', *EHR*, 103/406 (1988), 1–20.

ambitious, status-conscious gentry, devolved authority brought new opportunities to hold public offices, reaffirming the Welsh gentry's traditional role as leaders of their communities. This included the right to return representatives to the House of Commons and the office of Justice of the Peace, roles which had existed for the English gentry since the fourteenth century.[26] The gentry had acted as deputies to English officers since the Conquest and they were capable and experienced administrators.[27] Officeholding was intensely competitive for the gentry across England and Wales because it provided an opportunity to advance above other families.[28] In early modern Wales, however, it was a fundamental aspect of *uchelwriaeth* with important historical resonance that reflected the earlier period when Welshmen were restricted from access to high office.[29] However, participation in government also helped establish the Welsh gentry as part of a shared British realm, and Peter Roberts has suggested that the Welsh gentry embraced a 'British' identity. The accession of James VI of Scotland to the throne of England in 1603 only heightened the sense of a reunified British island, and Welshmen were instrumental in calls to recognise James as the leader of a British empire.[30] Humphrey Llwyd (1527–68), the Welsh cartographer and antiquarian, described himself as a 'Cambro-Briton', and this is a persuasive term for the enterprising Welsh gentry who embraced power and

---

[26] J. R. Maddicott, 'The county community and the making of public opinion in fourteenth-century England', *Transactions of the Royal Historical Society*, 5th series, 28 (1978), 27–43.

[27] For the competency of the gentry as local officers, see John Gwynfor Jones, *Law, Order and Government in Caernarfonshire, 1558–1640: Justices of the Peace and the gentry* (1996).

[28] Alison Wall, '"The greatest disgrace": The making and unmaking of JPs in Elizabethan and Jacobean England', *EHR*, 119/481 (2004), 312–32.

[29] Madeleine Gray, 'Power, Patronage and Politics: Office-holding and administration on the Crown estates in Wales', in R. W. Hoyle (ed.), *The Estates of the English Crown, 1558–1640* (Cambridge, 1992), p. 192. See also Jarrett, 'Officeholding and local politics in early modern Wales', 206–32.

[30] Peter Roberts, 'Tudor Wales, national identity and the British inheritance', in Brendan Bradshaw and Peter Roberts (eds), *British Consciousness and Identity: The making of Britain, 1533–1707* (Cambridge, 1998), pp. 8–42; Philip Jenkins, 'Seventeenth-century Wales: definition and identity', in Bradshaw and Roberts (eds), *British Consciousness and Identity: The making of Britain, 1533–1707*, pp. 213–35.

opportunity from the British Crown, while remaining part of their local, Welsh communities.[31] The Welsh gentry saw themselves as the lineal descendants of ancient Britons with legitimate claims to rule as part of a British realm. Although they embraced the idea of a shared British island, this was in a Welsh context which reflected historical ideas of Wales and the Welsh. As a social class, the early modern Welsh gentry were not anglicised after the Acts of Union and they did not, as Ceri W. Lewis has suggested, lose 'their native speech, their interest in the life and culture of Wales, and even, in some cases, their sense of national identity as well'.[32] As Shaun Evans and Robin Grove-White have demonstrated, the Welsh gentry navigated competing identities while retaining a strong engagement with Welsh culture and society.[33]

Fundamental aspects of the early modern Welsh gentry's conception of gentility were specific to Wales. They were the descendants and successors of their late medieval counterparts and they inherited the same conception of gentility, with its focus on lineage, officeholding and martial leadership. The Griffiths of Penrhyn, for example, were the descendants of Tudur ap Madog, who received land in the commote of Dindaethwy, Anglesey, from the Welsh princes.[34] The Maurices of Clenennau were the descendants of the thirteenth-century lord of Penyfed, Gruffudd Fychan ap Gruffudd ap Moreiddig Warwyn.[35] Even families which originated in England married into Welsh families and acquired Welsh ancestry: the Bulkeleys of Baron Hill were descended from William Bulkeley (b.1418) of Cheadle, Cheshire, who married Elen ferch Gwilym ap Gruffudd of Penrhyn.[36] Coupled with the Welsh gentry's loyalty to the Tudor and, later, Stuart regime,

---

[31] Philip Schwyzer, 'The age of the Cambro-Britons: hyphenated British identities in the seventeenth century', *The Seventeenth Century*, 33/4 (2018), 428–9.

[32] Ceri W. Lewis, 'The decline of professional poetry', in R. Geraint Gruffydd (ed.), *A Guide to Welsh Literature c.1550–1700*, vol. 3 (Cardiff, 1997) p. 52.

[33] Evans, '"To contynue in my bloud and name"'; Grove-White, *A Prism for His Times*.

[34] Carr, *Gentry of North Wales*, p. 87.

[35] T. Jones Pierce, 'The Clenennau estate', in J. Beverley Smith (ed.), *Medieval Welsh Society: Selected essays by T. Jones Pierce* (Cardiff, 1972), p. 233.

[36] Carr, *Gentry of North Wales*, p. 90.

the gentry maintained, in John Gwynfor Jones's words, 'a deep-seated pride in their lifestyle and their concepts of gentility'.[37] The concepts of gentility, as established by Jones himself, were based on a strong sense of honour and status, a continuous concern for individual and familial reputations.[38] However, there were also practical applications to gentility, and the Welsh gentry needed to be dutiful administrators, loyal Protestants and brave soldiers, as demanded of them by the state. As a social class, the Welsh gentry were fundamentally conservative and suspicious of change.[39] Nevertheless, conceptions of gentility in early modern Wales made slow adaptations. For example, the medieval focus on military prowess began to shift to an emphasis on public service, although an appreciation for martial values remained.[40] However, the emphasis on lineage remained a constant, reflected in the Welsh gentry's passion for genealogy and heraldic display.[41] It is less clear, however, to what extent the qualities of Welsh gentility applied to gentlewomen. Like their male equivalents, gentlewomen also obtained their status from ancestry and they were vital to the provision of hospitality. Clearly, though, gentlewomen did not fight in battles and they did not engage in officeholding. Welsh gentlewomen were also expected to be subordinate to the head of their household, which might be their brother or their son, though gentlewomen did not always recognise or accept their authority.[42] John Gwynfor Jones's work on praise poetry composed for the

---

[37] Jones, *Welsh Gentry*, p. xviii.

[38] See Jones, *Welsh Gentry*, for a comprehensive analysis of the principles of Welsh gentility.

[39] Clavier, *Royalism*, chapter ten.

[40] Jones, *Welsh Gentry*, chapter four; Rhys Morgan, *The Welsh and the Shaping of Modern Ireland, 1448–1641* (Woodbridge, 2014), p. 47.

[41] Francis Jones, 'An approach to Welsh genealogy', *Transactions of the Honourable Society of Cymmrodorion* (1948), 303–466; Michael Powell Siddons, 'Welsh Heraldry', *Transactions of the Honourable Society of Cymmrodorion* (1993), 27–46; Shaun Evans, 'Gruffudd Hiraethog, heraldic display and the "five courts" of Mostyn: Projecting status, honour and authority in sixteenth-century Wales', in Fiona Robertson and Peter N. Lindfield (eds), *The Display of Heraldry: The Heraldic Imagination in Arts and Culture* (London, 2019), pp. 116–33.

[42] Sadie Jarrett, '"By reason of her sex and widowhood": An early modern Welsh gentlewoman in the Court of Star Chamber', in K. J. Kesselring and N. Mears (eds), *Star Chamber Matters: The Court and its Records* (London, 2021), pp. 79–96.

Welsh gentry established that the cultural expectations of Welsh gentlewomen reflected the same expectations of gentlewomen in England: they should be charitable, meek, prudent and beautiful.[43] *Uchelwriaeth* comprises the qualities associated with the *uchelwyr*, the 'high men', and thus it is fundamentally masculine as a concept. Gentility, used throughout this book, is a more neutral word, rooted in the idea of shared ancestry and giving more scope to include gentlewomen.

Using the term 'gentility' invites comparisons with England. As the example of Welsh gentlewomen shows, there were significant similarities, but the Welsh gentry existed in a different historical and cultural environment from their English counterparts. Unlike in Wales, gentility was a slippery concept in early modern England. In Felicity Heal and Clive Holmes's study of the early modern gentry, English gentility represented 'land, lordship, and local acknowledgement'; in the socially mobile world of early modern England, professionals such as lawyers and clerics could also claim to be gentlemen, as well as those with wealth and landed estates.[44] In Wales, ancestry was the source of a family's gentility and it did not depend on land, external validation, profession or finance. However, the border between England and Wales was porous and the Welsh gentry were influenced by new ideas from England and further afield. For example, English gentility was associated with the right to bear arms and the Welsh gentry engaged enthusiastically, rather than accurately, in heraldry, which neatly depicted their various claims to noble ancestry. The gentry across England and Wales also felt the increasing influence of Renaissance humanism.[45] For example, the publication of works such as Thomas Elyot's *The Boke named the Governour* (London, 1531) and the 1561 translation by Thomas Hoby of Baldassare Castiglione's *The Book of the Courtier* (1528) stressed the importance of public office and scholarly activity.

[43] John Gwynfor Jones, 'Welsh gentlewomen: Piety and Christian conduct *c.*1560–1730', *Journal of Welsh Religious History*, 7 (1999), 1–39.
[44] Heal and Holmes, *Gentry in England and Wales*, pp. 7–10.
[45] W. P. Griffith, *Learning, Law and Religion: Higher education and Welsh society, c.1540–1640* (Cardiff, 1996).

Thus, in sixteenth-century England, some social commentators argued that service to the commonwealth was more important than lineage.[46] Leadership, however, was historically associated with the Welsh gentry and so they easily adapted to the focus on service in humanist thought without reducing the importance of ancestry. Certainly, a distinguished pedigree was also a key facet of English gentility; the gentry regularly claimed descent from families which came to England with the Norman Conquest.[47] Newly risen families were willing to invent genealogies to strengthen their claims to gentle status, while the culture of heraldic displays and funeral monuments demonstrates the importance of visibly displaying and promoting a family's lineage.[48] Unlike in Wales, however, there were competing standards of gentility, such as merit and honour, and gentility had an increasing focus on wealth from the mid-seventeenth century; in England, the routes to gentility were more diverse than in Wales.[49]

This book is an examination of Welsh gentility. It begins from the premise that the Welsh gentry saw themselves as Cambro-Britons who continued to maintain their engagement with Welsh culture and enhanced their Welsh identity through participation in the British state. It adopts Lloyd Bowen's position that the gentry were 'bilingual brokers', navigating between the localities in Wales and the centre in England.[50] The longevity of the Salesbury family, from c.1450 to 1719, allows us to see how Welsh gentility evolved over time and how the Welsh gentry adapted to significant

---

[46] Heal and Holmes, *Gentry in England and Wales*, pp. 9–10.

[47] See, for example, William Dugdale, *The Baronage of England; or, An Historical Account of the Lives and Most Memorable Actions of our English Nobility* (London, 1675–6).

[48] Nigel Llewellyn, 'Claims to status through visual codes: Heraldry on post-Reformation English funeral monuments', in Sydney Anglo (ed.), *Chivalry in the Renaissance* (Woodbridge, 1990), pp. 145–60; Jan Broadway, *'No historie so meete': Gentry culture and the development of local history in Elizabethan and early Stuart England* (Manchester, 2006), pp. 130–88; Richard Cust, 'The culture of dynasticism in early modern Cheshire', in Stéphane Jettot and Marie Lezowski (eds), *The Genealogical Enterprise: Social practices and collective imagination in Europe (15th–20th century)* (Brussels, 2016), pp. 209–33; Richard Cust and Peter Lake, *Gentry Culture and the Politics of Religion: Cheshire on the Eve of Civil War* (Manchester, 2020), pp. 24–44.

[49] Daniel Woolf, *The Social Circulation of the Past: English historical culture 1500–1730* (Oxford, 2003), pp. 81–2, 112.

[50] Bowen, 'Information, language and political culture', 127.

changes to life in early modern Britain. This includes not just the Reformation of the 1530s and the Civil Wars of the 1640s, but the rise of a more scholarly gentleman educated in universities and the Inns of Court, the economic difficulties of the sixteenth century, and Britain's nascent imperial ambitions. The Salesburys show that some aspects of Welsh gentility, particularly the defining focus on lineage, remained constant throughout the period. Equally, the Welsh gentry remained status-conscious and careful to protect their reputation and the future of their family. However, they were also adaptable and opportunistic, willing to improve their estates or make their fortunes as soldiers in overseas wars. Reflecting wider developments in society, the Salesburys in 1719 were much less likely to engage in armed disputes than their fifteenth- or sixteenth-century counterparts and they did not retain bands of followers. They no longer engaged in significant bardic patronage, but they kept hundreds of books in their study. Nevertheless, they still had a strong interest in their genealogy and their titles of Welsh nobility. This would have been recognisable to the earliest Salesbury patriarchs and they could still have spoken to each other in their shared Welsh language. My study of the Salesburys shows that Welsh gentility was not static between 1450 and 1719 and the Welsh gentry were not insular, responding to new ideas and opportunities from across the realm and internationally, while still retaining a strong cultural knowledge of their role in Welsh society as a lynchpin of local communities.

SOURCES

The estate papers of Wales are a vast and often underexplored collection of source material. The Salesbury family had two estates and, rather fittingly, they now have two separate collections of estate papers. These records form the bulk of the source material for this book. The nature of the collections reflects the division of the Salesbury patrimony between the two sons of William Salesbury (1580–1660). Owen Salesbury (1613–58) received the Rhug estate and Charles Salesbury (d.1666) received Bachymbyd. This, as discussed in chapters one and two, was a controversial decision and caused no little acrimony among the descendants of Owen Salesbury. The Rhug estate stayed in the Salesbury family until 1719 and it was eventually inherited by the Barons Newborough, who deposited the estate papers at Caernarfon Record Office, Gwynedd Archives. In 1670, the Bachymbyd estate passed through marriage to the Bagots of Blithfield Hall, Staffordshire, and they later deposited the estate papers at the National Library of Wales, Aberystwyth. As a result of the estates' division, the Rhug estate papers in Caernarfon primarily comprise material after Owen received the estate in 1640, with some earlier material relating to Rhug. However, William Salesbury evidently kept most of the Salesburys' historical papers and thus the Bachymbyd archive contains the majority of the pre-seventeenth-century material, including medieval documents predating the Salesburys' ownership of the estates. The Bachymbyd archive also includes much of the surviving Salesbury correspondence.[51] These letters mostly date from the seventeenth century, but there are fourteen letters from the sixteenth century, with the oldest letter written on 13 January 1565. Drawing on the richness of Wales's surviving estate papers, this book also uses material from the records of other Welsh gentry families, such as the Pryses of Gogerddan who inherited Salesbury records through marriage, the Barons Ellesmere, who were patrons of the Salesbury family, the Wynns of Wynnstay, and the Griffiths of Penrhyn.

Further light is shed on the family by legal records and early modern scholarship. Court records, particularly from the courts of Chancery and Star Chamber, but also Requests, Exchequer and Wards, provide important evidence of the Salesbury family's activities and their relationships with allies, rivals, tenants and

---

[51] For an invaluable guide to the Salesburys' letters, see Smith, *Salusbury Correspondence*, pp. 135–237.

servants. Probate records provide information on a variety of topics, including the organisation of the Salesbury estates, their relationships with kin, friends and servants, and, occasionally, religious beliefs. In addition, Welsh-language manuscripts are a key source for understanding the cultural world of the Salesburys, and *A Repertory of Welsh Manuscripts and Scribes,* c.*800*–c.*1800* (2022), by Daniel Huws, provides an invaluable access point.[52] The main focus of this book is the manuscripts written by William Salesbury (1580–1660): BL, Add. [Additional] MS 14974; BL, Add. MS 14973; NLW, Llanstephan 37B; and NLW, Llanstephan 170, but it also incorporates other manuscripts owned or annotated by the Salesbury family. The book also draws on praise poetry composed for the family, primarily using the transcriptions of the Salesbury poems produced by Arwyn Lloyd Hughes in his 1969 MA thesis, 'Noddwyr y beirdd yn Sir Feirionnydd' ('Patrons of the poets in Merioneth').[53]

Where possible, the book includes discussion of visual and material culture and built heritage. The Salesburys' houses have all been subject to major rebuilds and remodelling, though there are clues to their earlier forms within prints and paintings, including watercolours by Moses Griffith (1747–1819). There are few surviving portraits of the Salesbury family, although Blithfield Hall contains portraits of William Salesbury and his son Charles (d.1666), and the Tate has a portrait of Charles's wife, Elizabeth Thelwall (d.1693), with two of their grandchildren. Equally, there are virtually no surviving funeral monuments to the Salesbury family from the period, although a monument to Charles and Elizabeth's daughter Jane Salesbury (1651–95), wife of Sir Walter Bagot (1644–1704), survives in the church at Blithfield, Staffordshire. The notable exception to the absence of built heritage is Rûg Chapel in Corwen, Denbighshire, built by William Salesbury on his Rhug estate in 1637 and now in the care of Cadw.

---

[52] I am grateful to Daniel Huws and Gruffudd Antur for access to draft material during my research.
[53] For the Salesbury praise poems, see Hughes, 'Noddwyr y beirdd', 559–634.

The portrait of Elizabeth Thelwall and the funeral monument of Jane Salesbury are fleeting glimpses of Salesbury women because the surviving sources for the family rarely include them. This is partly due to the nature of the sources, which have a strong bias towards legal and government records. However, it is also a reflection of early modern society in England and Wales. The doctrine of coverture meant that married women had no separate legal identity from their husbands and so Salesbury women often only appear in the sources as widows. As a result, the perspective of the book skews towards men, but it endeavours to overcome the limitations of the sources and include the experiences of the Salesbury women wherever possible.

STRUCTURE

This book is organised thematically to highlight different aspects of gentility. In chapter one, we meet the Salesbury family and understand the importance of kinship to the Welsh gentry. It begins with the Salesburys' genealogy, both real and constructed, to examine how the Salesburys presented themselves as a gentry family and why noble ancestry was key to gentle status in early modern Wales. It then looks at the *pennau cenedl*, the heads of the Salesbury family. Each paterfamilias had an obligation to protect the family, its estates, and the security of future generations, but, as this chapter demonstrates, not every Salesbury gentleman had the skill or diligence to maintain the family's fortune or reputation. It highlights the precarious state of early modern gentry families and the ease with which a profligate paterfamilias or his heir could ruin them. From the *pennau cenedl*, the chapter moves on to consider the wives and daughters of the Salesbury family. In an ideal gentry marriage, husbands and wives were partners working together to run the family and secure its future, and there are tantalising examples which suggest a number of Salesbury marriages functioned in this way. At the same time, early modern

Wales, and Europe more generally, was a patriarchal society and wives were subordinate to their husbands, though the Salesburys show that wives were also fully aware of their privileges and entitlements and willing to enforce them.

Chapter two examines how the Salesburys established themselves as a landed gentry family with territorial influence across north Wales. Before the Acts of Union abolished Welsh land law, the Salesburys navigated a complicated dual legal system which required shrewdness and local knowledge to build up inheritable estates. There were myriad means by which gentry families could expand their holdings in late medieval Wales, but all had a shared aim to establish a patrimony for the future. At the same time, however, estates also conveyed historical legitimacy on a gentry family and associated them with previous owners. For example, the Salesburys valued the title of 'baron of Edeirnion' which came with their Rhug estate and which they claimed in the maternal line. They also purchased the neighbouring lordship of Glyndyfrdwy, the ancestral manor of Owain Glyndŵr, enhancing their claim to the barony of Edeirnion and capitalising on the changing reputation of Glyndŵr in sixteenth-century Wales. This came during a period of prosperity for the Salesburys, but the chapter also looks at the estates in crisis. The Salesburys were not immune to the wider early modern economic conditions and they attempted to improve their estates, though not without resistance from their tenants. The main danger, however, as suggested in the previous chapter, was a careless paterfamilias and the chapter looks in detail at how the estates were nearly lost. The chapter finishes with an exploration of the Salesburys' houses, particularly their importance as places of hospitality and a means of demonstrating the family's status.

Chapter three looks in more detail at the Salesburys' sphere of influence. It begins with the destabilising effects of noble patronage, which benefited individual gentry families, but also acted as a source of factionalism as families competed for power and influence. The Welsh gentry were intensely conscious of their status and reputation, which created significant tensions between families. The chapter examines the Salesburys' feuds with other gentry families and how they called upon a wide network of friends, tenants and servants to defend their reputation. It shows that the Salesburys continued to maintain a *plaid*, or retinue, into the early seventeenth century to engage in violence with the followers of rival gentry, but families also took their rivalries to the law courts, and legal records provide much of the evidence for the Salesburys' disputes. For the Salesburys, the law, rather than brawls or duels, became the main vehicle for maintaining their position in society, highlighting the decreasing levels of violence in early modern Wales. The chapter emphasises that the Salesburys were part of national and local networks of power and they retained a strong knowledge of Welsh culture and society.

Chapter four considers how the Salesburys engaged in Welsh culture. The Salesburys lived in a region known for its early modern scholarship and they were part of a vibrant community of gentlemen scholars. The influence of humanism on conceptions of gentility increased the value of learnedness and education and the Salesburys became enthusiastic scholars. This coincided with a general shift in Welsh gentry society away from bardic patronage, though the Salesburys continued to receive a small amount of praise poetry in the seventeenth century. The chapter starts with an exploration of how the Salesburys gained their education and notes the family's shift towards higher education from the mid-sixteenth century. By the seventeenth century, there is evidence that the Salesburys sent their children to boarding schools, indicating that the family valued education. Education in English institutions did not prevent the Salesburys from being keen scholars in the Welsh language. The chapter focuses in particular on the manuscripts of William Salesbury (1580–1660) who composed Welsh-language poetry and collected Welsh poems and antiquarian literature. William's manuscripts are also the most extensive sources for a Salesbury's religious beliefs and so this chapter also includes an assessment of the Salesburys' changing religious practices after the Reformation. The chapter demonstrates that the Salesburys engaged with new ideas and adapted their concept of gentility, while remaining conscious of how they were perceived by wider society.

Chapter five looks at the international connections of the Salesbury family. Wales's economic position encouraged the Welsh gentry, particularly their younger sons, to leave Wales and find employment as soldiers and traders. This coincided with Britain's growing expansionism from the late sixteenth century, increasing the opportunities for the gentry to engage in overseas activity. The chapter looks in particular at Sir Robert (1567–99), John (1575–1611) and William Salesbury (1580–1660), three brothers who all inherited the Salesbury patrimony and spent time abroad. The Nine Years' War, or Tyrone's Rebellion, in Ireland attracted large numbers of Welsh soldiers, including the three Salesbury brothers. Through their wider kindred, the Salesburys also had connections to Catholic dissidents on the continent, particularly in the Low Countries where British soldiers fought on both sides of the Dutch Revolt. This chapter expands on the influence of noble patronage explored in chapter three, demonstrating how noblemen enabled campaigning among their followers. Although the focus remains on the Salesburys, the chapter emphasises the importance of the Welsh diaspora and demonstrates how Welshmen tended to group together, maintaining connections forged in Wales as well as their shared language.

The book finishes with a discussion of how the Salesburys adapted to new conceptions of gentility in early modern Wales and how they reflected wider changes in British society.

1
THE SALESBURY FAMILY

The Painted Book of Erbistock is a beautifully decorated pedigree collection of the north Wales gentry. It describes the genealogy and heraldry of various distinguished families, and its name refers to the noted Welsh genealogist, John Salisbury of Erbistock (*fl. c.*1650). However, although John Salisbury completed the collection, it was started by his kinsman and friend, Owen Salesbury of Rhug (1613–58). The Salesburys of Rhug and Bachymbyd were, like their fellow Welsh gentry, enamoured with genealogy.[1] This was a distinguishing feature of the Welsh gentry: in 1791, a Welsh scholar complained that 'our good neighbours the English' were envious of the Welsh passion for genealogy because it enabled the Welsh to prove their claims to gentility.[2] Distinguished ancestry was important for gentry families on both sides of the Anglo-Welsh border, but the Welsh gentry placed an atypical, and noticeable, focus on their antecedents as the source of their gentle status. The early modern Welsh gentry had a greater focus on ancestry than the English gentry, and this continued into the eighteenth century. Even as English gentry families began to emphasise wealth as an indicator of gentility from the mid-seventeenth century, the Welsh gentry still prioritised ancestry.[3] A renowned pedigree conveyed authority and historical legitimacy on a Welsh gentry family; in the words of John Gwynfor Jones, the Welsh gentry used their genealogy 'to reinforce their pre-

---

[1] For the importance of genealogy in Welsh gentry society, see Francis Jones, 'An approach to Welsh genealogy', *Transactions of the Honourable Society of Cymmrodorion* (1948), 303–466; Ben Guy, *Medieval Welsh Genealogy: An introduction and textual study* (Woodbridge, 2020).

[2] NLW, Llanstephan 159, f. 6r.

[3] Daniel Woolf, *The Social Circulation of the Past: English historical culture 1500–1730* (Oxford, 2003), p. 81.

eminence in the present and to provide for its continuation'.[4] Wales was a kinship-focused society and the duties and responsibilities of the Welsh gentry went beyond the nuclear family.

In medieval Wales, only the gentry, or *uchelwyr*, held free status and this status was determined by ancestry. This was not unique to Wales: in France, for example, proof of *noblesse*, or nobility, relied on genealogy into the eighteenth century.[5] The gentry in England cultivated dynastic ambitions and expressed pride in their lineages. In Wales, however, any family with distinguished ancestry could claim gentility, regardless of their wealth or personal circumstances. The Painted Book of Erbistock contains various branches of the vast Salusbury kin, a number of whom possessed far less economic power than the Salesburys of Rhug and Bachymbyd. They were acknowledged, however, as gentry families, part of the Salusbury kindred with the same shared distinguished ancestry. This chapter begins by examining this ancestry and why it was central to the Salesburys' self-conception as a gentry family. However, the Salesburys also appreciated the need to safeguard their own interests as a nuclear family, and this chapter illustrates why protecting the patrimony was vital to the security of the Salesburys' interests. It explores the kinship relationships within the family and the role of women as conveyors of gentle status and important communication links with the wider kindred. It examines how the Salesburys positioned themselves as a gentry family and introduces the primary family members who form the foundation of this book.

ANCESTRY AND STATUS

The Salesburys' lineage survives in a number of pedigrees from the late sixteenth and seventeenth centuries. Some of these pedigrees may be later copies of earlier material, but the oldest

---

[4] Jones, *Welsh Gentry*, p. 72.
[5] Germain Butaud and Valerie Piétri, *Les Enjeux de la Généalogie (XIIe–XVIIIe siécles). Pouvoir et identité* (Paris, 2006), chapter three.

surviving pedigrees generally take John Salesbury (1533–80) as their main focus.[6] According to these pedigrees, the Salesbury surname originated with Abraham de Saltzburg, duke and prince of Bavaria. Abraham's son, Adam de Saltzburg, or Salusbury, came to England as part of the Norman forces under William I in 1066. The new king sent Adam to Denbigh, where he captained the garrison at the castle. The tale is patently false, because Denbigh Castle was built following Edward I's conquest of Wales in 1282–3, but it was repeated by nineteenth-century antiquarians.[7] Jacob Chaloner, the Chester-based genealogist, recorded in 1623–9 that the Salesburys were descended from one John Salisbury (d.1289), who arrived in Wales with Henry de Lacy, earl of Lincoln and first lord of Denbigh.[8] This is a far more plausible account and corresponds with the early history of the Salesbury family in Wales. Nevertheless, it still connects the Salesburys with England and English nobility, linking the family with the successful conquerors of Wales in the thirteenth century. The constructed descent from Adam de Saltzburg also firmly associated the Salesburys with the Norman Conquest, a popular fiction among early modern gentry families in England and Wales. Early modern families preferred victorious ancestors and they did not generally associate themselves with the defeated Saxons; David Powel wrote in his *Historie of Cambria* (1584) that 'it appeareth that all the ancient noblemen and gentlemen within this land, are descended either from the Normans and French or from the Brytaines'.[9] By the seventeenth century, there was a slight shift in English attitudes towards the 'Anglo-Saxons', a term which itself represents a constructed past. As Christopher Hill explored, radical thinkers mythologised pre-Conquest

[6] For examples of Salesbury pedigrees, see BL, Egerton MS 2586, f. 69; BL, Harley MS 1936, f. 15; BL, Harley MS 1971, f. 124; DRO, DD/WY/6674, ff. 13v–14r.

[7] John Williams, *Ancient and Modern Denbigh: A descriptive history of the castle, borough and liberties* (Denbigh, 1836), p. 163.

[8] BL, Harley MS 1971, f. 120r; Huws, *RWMS*, pp. 676–7.

[9] Jan Broadway, *'No historie so meete': Gentry culture and the development of local history in Elizabethan and early Stuart England* (Manchester, 2006), pp. 155–6; David Powel, *The Historie of Cambria, now called Wales* (London, 1584), p. 117.

England as a perfect society with no class division, destroyed by the so-called 'Norman Yoke'.[10] There was also growing scholarly interest in England's early history: for example, in the 1670s, William Nicolson gave a weekly Saxon lecture at The Queen's College, Oxford, and the college gained a reputation for Saxon studies.[11] Norman ancestry, however, still carried significant value for gentry families.

The Salesburys' Welsh ancestry, their descent 'from the Brytaines', conveyed longevity on the family. It emphasised the tacit claim that they had always been one of the distinguished families in England and Wales. In the Salesbury pedigree in his *Heraldic Visitations* (1586–1616), Lewis Dwnn included Englishmen, such as Sir William Damfret, and Welshmen, such as Cynwrig Sais ab Ithel Vaughan, so both strands of the Salesburys' ancestry were officially recognised by the College of Arms.[12] English-language patrilineal pedigrees did not incorporate the Salesburys' Welsh ancestry because the focus on direct paternal ancestry limited them to the origins of the Salesbury surname. However, there was a Welsh form of pedigree, *achau'r mamau* ('pedigrees of the mothers'), which focused on the Salesburys' Welsh ancestry. Unlike conventional patrilineal English pedigrees, *achau'r mamau* traced the agnatic lines of the subject's maternal ancestors.[13] They were written in Welsh, targeting a Welsh audience and demonstrating the Salesburys' position in Welsh society. There was a separate culture in Wales where the presentation of ancestry took an alternative form and valued different associations. Evidently, the Salesburys could move between the Welsh and English conceptions of lineage and there was no contradiction between

---

[10] Christopher Hill, *The Intellectual Origins of the English Revolution* (Oxford, 1997), chapter seventeen; see also Marjorie Chibnall, *The Debate on the Norman Conquest* (Manchester, 1999), pp. 35–8.

[11] Nicolas Barker, 'Editing the past: classical and historical scholarship', in John Barnard and D. F. McKenzie (eds), *The Cambridge History of the Book in Britain*, vol. 4: *1557–1695* (Cambridge, 2002), p. 220.

[12] Sir Samuel Rush Meyrick, *Heraldic Visitations of Wales and Part of the Marches*, vol. 2 (Llandovery, 1846), pp. 330–1.

[13] Guy, *Medieval Welsh Genealogy*, p. 24.

valuing Welsh ancestry in Welsh-language mediums, which were limited to a Welsh audience, and Norman or English ancestry in English-language mediums, which could be understood beyond Wales.

In Wales, and particularly in Welsh-language pedigrees, the Salesburys were presented almost exclusively as a high-status Welsh family. It is telling that their cousin, David Salusbury of Llanrhaeadr, who shared the same paternal ancestry, was described by William Cynwal in a *c.* 1570 pedigree roll as a 'Cymro glân o waed coch cyfan' ('A pure Welshman of whole red blood'), even though elsewhere the Salusbury kindred visibly celebrated their non-Welsh ancestry.[14] Salesbury *achau'r mamau* survive from the sixteenth and seventeenth centuries, including a mid-seventeenth-century copy of an Elizabethan original.[15] These pedigrees are descriptive Welsh-language texts, beginning with the subject of the pedigree and his patronymic, then describing mothers in each generation, as well as the patronymic of her father. For example, the paternal grandmother of John Salesbury (1533–80), Margaret, was the daughter of Ieuan ap Hywel ap Rhys, and Margaret's mother was Gwenhwyfar, daughter of Elis ap Gruffudd ab Einion. In this way, the number of branches multiplies with each generation and the subject of the pedigree establishes connections with considerably more ancestors than a patrilineal pedigree, even one which includes wives and their fathers. Although *achau'r mamau* focus on maternal lines, the function of the pedigree is to emphasise descent from great men, thereby demonstrating the status of the pedigree's subject and his family. These are still masculine documents which prioritise the status of men, but women act as conduits for this status. After all, in a society which prioritised ancestry and kinship, excluding women from the transmission of status would limit a family to its patrilineal line. In such a scenario, the Salesburys'

---

[14] BUASC, BMSS/119.
[15] For examples of Salesbury *achau'r mamau*, see BL, Add. MS 14918, ff. 154v–155r; BL, Add. MS 14919, f. 36r; BL, Stowe MS 669, ff. 98v–99v.

status would rest on their fictional noble ancestor, Abraham de Saltzburg, the duke and prince of Bavaria, and his son Adam Salesbury of Denbigh Castle. The focus on matrilineal lines, however, significantly expanded the amount of status that could be claimed by a Welsh gentry family. Thomas Charles Edwards has noted that free or noble status in medieval Wales depended on a man's descent in both his paternal and maternal lines, thus there was a cultural understanding that maternal ancestry contributed to a person's status.[16]

The Salesburys claimed to be part of four of the Fifteen Noble Tribes of Gwynedd, the collective genealogical name for the descendants of a group of early medieval Welsh noblemen. Although the noblemen in question existed and the Salesbury pedigrees were plausible in term of generation gaps, the idea of the Fifteen Noble Tribes is now known to be a fifteenth-century fiction which seems to have been devised by Welsh poet-genealogists purely to increase the status of the north Wales gentry, but it was a recognised and important claim to gentility in early modern Wales.[17] Through their maternal ancestry, the Salesburys claimed descent from Llywarch ap Bran (*fl. c.*1137), Marchudd ap Cynan (b.*c.*849), Hedd Molwynog and Marchweithian, Lord of Is Aled.[18] This included two lines of descent from Llywarch ap Bran, further emphasising their connection to him. Beyond the Tribes, the Salesburys also claimed descent from various other figures of Welsh history, including some of the Five Royal Tribes of Wales, another late medieval invention of the poet-genealogists. For example, the Salesburys' pedigree includes Bleddyn ap Cynfyn (d.1075), king of Gwynedd and Powys, and Gruffydd ap Cynan (*c.*1055–1137), king of Gwynedd, who was captured by the earl of Chester at Rhug, connecting one of the Salesburys' ancestors

---

[16] T. M. Charles-Edwards, *Early Irish and Welsh Kinship* (Oxford, 1993), p. 409.

[17] Francis Jones, 'Arms of the XV Noble Tribes of North Wales', *The Coat of Arms*, 5/34 (1958), 89–94.

[18] These dates are later attributions.

with their estate in Merioneth.[19] They also claimed a lineage from Gruffydd ap Cynan's son, Owain Gwynedd, king of Gwynedd and first prince of Wales (*c.*1100–70). The Salesburys twice claimed descent from Ednyfed Fychan (*c.*1170–1246), steward to the kingdom of Gwynedd and the ancestor of the Tudor dynasty, and this was no doubt an especially pleasing coincidence during the reign of Elizabeth I, when the surviving Salesbury *achau'r mamau* were first composed. The Salesburys did not ignore English royalty, and their *achau'r mamau* includes John (1166–1216), king of England, because they claimed descent from Llywelyn Fawr (the Great), prince of Gwynedd (1173–1240), who married John's daughter, Joan.[20] Here, the genealogist prioritised status over accuracy, because the pedigree states that Llywelyn married King John's granddaughter, Margaret, and claims that Llywelyn was descended from Beli Mawr, the legendary king of the Britons, allegedly descended himself from Brutus of Troy. This lineage ultimately draws on the medieval pedigrees of Llywelyn ab Iorwerth, with an eventual link back to Adam and Eve.[21]

The accuracy of these pedigrees was not important. These documents were not intended as records of a family's history in the same way as a modern family tree. They existed as a demonstration of a family's status and to legitimise their claims to gentility. The Salesburys' pedigree included kings and noblemen and they shared ancestry with the reigning monarch; this pedigree, more than wealth or honour, manifested their position as a gentry family in early modern Wales. This was not new and it reflected a cultural peculiarity which had its roots in medieval Wales. For example, in the eleventh-century Arthurian tale of Culhwch ac Olwen, Culhwch was the son of King Arthur's

---

[19] Paul Russell (ed.), *Vita Griffini Filii Conani: The Medieval Latin Life of Gruffudd Ap Cynan* (Cardiff, 2012), pp. 70–3; A. D. Carr, 'Appendix 2: Parishes and townships in medieval Merioneth: Edeirnion', in J. Beverley Smith and L. Beverley Smith (eds), *A History of Merioneth: Middle Ages*, vol. 2 (Cardiff, 2001), pp. 138–9.

[20] BL, Stowe MS 669, ff. 98v–99v.

[21] Guy, *Medieval Welsh Genealogy*, pp. 234–5.

mother's sister, a maternal connection which transmitted status to Culhwch. Equally, a twelfth-century biographer of Gruffydd ap Cynan established Gruffydd's status by connecting him through multiple maternal lines to numerous royal dynasties.[22] However, there were also more practical concerns around maintaining knowledge of maternal kinship. For instance, Robert Salesbury (d.1550) inherited land in *c.*1530 from Hywel ap Rhys ap Dafydd, his maternal great-grandfather; Robert was his 'kinsman and next heir'.[23] This was unusual because Welsh property law restricted the ability of women to inherit land, and inheritance under Welsh law focused on degrees of male kindred. Historically, there was no requirement to retain knowledge of a mother's pedigree and, although the 1284 Statute of Rhuddlan relaxed the laws on female landownership, Welsh law survived longer in the marcher lordships and it was particularly strong in north-east Wales, where the Salesburys lived. Although Rhug was part of the Principality of North Wales, their Bachymbyd estate fell in the marcher lordships of Denbigh and Ruthin, and the latter retained a strict ban on female inheritance into the fifteenth century.[24] Culturally, women were not valued as transmitters of land, but the *achau'r mamau* show that they were important transmitters of status instead.[25]

For example, in a praise poem written for John Salesbury (d.1580), Edward ap Raff said that John's marriage to his wife, Elizabeth Salusbury of Lleweni, built the family 'ar ddwybleth ddyblig' ('on two interwoven plaits').[26] When Simwnt Fychan praised their eldest son, Sir Robert Salesbury, he described Sir Robert's marriage to Elinor Bagnall (d.1656) as the joining of two

---

[22] Charles-Edwards, *Early Irish and Welsh Kinship*, pp. 174, 222.

[23] NLW, Bachymbyd 96.

[24] R. R. Davies, 'The status of women and the practice of marriage in late-medieval Wales', in Dafydd Jenkins and Morfydd E. Owen (eds), *The Welsh Law of Women* (Cardiff, 1980), pp. 98–103.

[25] Notably, customary widowhood provision in Wales entitled a woman to a share of her deceased husband's moveable goods, rather than his land. Although the Acts of Union abolished Welsh law in the 1530s, widowhood provision survived until 1695. See below, pp. 24–7.

[26] Hughes, 'Noddwyr y beirdd', 580.

fair houses of famous ancestors.[27] The marriages were unions of equal status and women brought the wealth of their distinguished pedigree to enhance the status of their children. In a society where ancestry, rather than land, established gentility, women made a vital and priceless contribution to the family. This was particularly useful for the Salesbury family who, as their patrilineal pedigrees demonstrate, originated outside Wales and arrived as English settlers. Marriage to the daughters of Welsh families, however, established the Salesburys as *Cymry glân* (pure Welshmen) and enabled them to demonstrate their descent not just from the dukes of Bavaria and the Norman Conquest, but also from Llywelyn the Great and Beli Mawr. Other English settlers, such as the Pulestons of Emral, also married the daughters of local families and established themselves as Welsh gentry.[28] With their ancestry, the Salesburys created their identity as a gentry family and emphasised that they were an ancient British family.

THE PATERFAMILIAS

Until the 1536 Act of Union abolished the remaining Welsh legal system, knowledge of one's ancestry also affected inheritance. It is thus not surprising that early modern Wales placed great emphasis on kinship relations. The kindred shared ancestry and status, but it was also historically the owner of land, parcelled out between brothers and cousins. The Welsh gentry had a duty to their kindred, the people with whom they shared their blood and name. Under Welsh law, the *pencenedl*, or paterfamilias, the head of the family, was a term for the head of the kindred, and a dutiful gentleman did not forget his obligations to others who shared his surname. The ultimate duty, however, was to the nuclear family. The gentry had a responsibility to protect future generations and ensure the continued existence of the family name and fortune. To

---

[27] Hughes, 'Noddwyr y beirdd', 597.
[28] A. D. Carr, *Gentry of North Wales*, pp. 158–9.

a large extent, as the history of the Salesburys will demonstrate, this depended on the skill and interest of the paterfamilias. The Salesburys were not always fortunate in this regard and, in times of difficulty, their continued survival depended on the support of the household and the wider kindred.

John Salesbury (b.*c.*1450), the first Salesbury to own the Bachymbyd estate, was one of ten children, five sons and five daughters, produced by Thomas Salusbury (d.1491) of Lleweni and his wife, Elizabeth Donne, the daughter of Sir John Donne of Utkinton, Cheshire. John was the third or fourth son, and thus far from inheriting the Salusburys' Lleweni estate, which had always been held by English tenure and descended according to the rules of primogeniture to the eldest legitimate son. Thus, Lleweni went to Thomas Salusbury's heir, Sir Thomas Salusbury. The second son, Foulk, joined the Church and became dean of St Asaph. The remaining three sons, Henry, John and Robert, all founded successful cadet branches of the family at Llanrhaeadr, Bachymbyd and Llanrwst, respectively. This may reflect the continued cultural influence of Welsh inheritance practices. These were still prevalent in Wales at this time and required certain lands to be divided between all sons, legitimate or not.[29] The Salusburys' five daughters married into respectable Welsh gentry families. This indicates that Thomas and Elizabeth Salusbury strove to ensure that all their children could enjoy comfortable lives according to their status and it was an impressive achievement that they succeeded with all ten children. It indicates their position in the community that they could organise good marriages for their daughters, while their sons also married into elite north Wales families. As a result, the marriages established numerous kinship relationships across the region. John Salesbury, for example, married Lowri, daughter of Robert ap Maredudd ap Tudur, part of the powerful Marchweithion kindred. Lowri's uncle, Rhys Fawr ap Maredudd, fought at the Battle of Bosworth Field in 1485 for Henry Tudor and reputedly carried Henry's standard

---

[29] For further discussion of Welsh inheritance practices, see chapter two.

when his original standard-bearer was killed.[30] The Salusburys of Lleweni were also wealthy enough to ensure three of their younger sons could develop their own estates, further increasing the family's power base in north Wales. Thomas Salusbury was a responsible gentleman who ensured the future of his family name and prosperity for his children.

As head of his own family, John Salesbury of Bachymbyd drew on the model of his father. John established his family's sphere of influence in the lordships of Denbigh and Ruthin by initiating the purchase of Bachymbyd in 1476. This may have been connected to his marriage to Lowri; John would have been in his mid-twenties at this time. Given the success of John's brothers, it is likely that his father helped in some way with the purchase, although Lowri's family would also have been useful contacts because Bachymbyd was held under Welsh law and required special legal devices to circumvent restrictions on its sale. With his wife Lowri, John had five sons, Piers, Foulk, Robert, John and Thomas, and a daughter, Katherine. The children are less well-documented than in the previous generation, but the fifth son, Thomas, held land at Llanfwrog and married into an English family, suggesting that John and Lowri took care over the fortunes of their younger children.[31] The eldest son and heir, Piers, had an excellent match with Margaret Wen, the wealthy heiress of Ieuan ap Hywel ap Rhys, and Margaret brought the Rhug estate into the control of the Salesbury family. In 1503, Piers and Margaret entailed the Bachymbyd estate in the male line and jointly held Bachymbyd for the term of their lives.[32]

It is likely that Piers and Margaret married around this time and thus, by the start of the sixteenth century, the Salesbury family had two estates at Bachymbyd and Rhug, creating their sphere of influence in the two marcher lordships of Denbigh and Ruthin, as well as the commote of Edeirnion in the Principality of

---

[30] Enid Roberts, 'Teulu Plas Iolyn', *Transactions of the Denbighshire Historical Society*, 13 (1964), 42–4.
[31] DRO, DD/DM/1647, f. 24r.
[32] NLW, Bachymbyd 281.

North Wales. This was a strong foundation for the family's future economic security, highlighting the advantages of providing for a younger son and arranging judicious marriages. The early history of the Salesbury family is relatively murky, but there is a clear sense that they were establishing themselves as local gentry and ensuring that their branch of the kindred could support itself. They were evidently regarded well enough in their community that the heiress of Rhug, an estate with cultural significance in the local area, married into the family. Indeed, although the paterfamilias was the head of the family, it is always worth remembering that the ideal household in this period was a partnership between husband and wife.[33] The 1503 entail gave Margaret shared ownership of Bachymbyd and protected her children's interest in the estate; the decisions of the paterfamilias appear in the surviving documents, but wives could still be involved in the decision-making process. After Margaret's death, Piers remarried, to Marsli ferch Robert, and they had three sons together, but the entail continued to protect the rights of Margaret's children to inherit the Salesbury lands.[34]

Piers and Margaret Salesbury had ten children: six sons and four daughters. Again, the daughters, Katherine, Ellen, Alys and Elizabeth, married into other respectable Welsh gentry families and the younger sons, Henry, Foulk, Thomas Fychan, Edward and John Wyn, had lands of their own. The eldest son and heir, Robert, married Katherine, daughter of John ap Madog of Bodfel, part of another local gentry family. Between Piers and his son Robert, there is a glimpse of a sound working relationship between the head of the family and his heir. Piers did not die until 1548, and thus their father-son relationship survived well into Robert's adulthood and nearly two decades after Robert began a family of his own in 1533, with the birth of his son, John. Piers and Robert's lives encompassed a period of significant change, namely

[33] Ralph A. Houlbrooke, *The English Family 1450–1700* (London, 1984), p. 19.
[34] DRO, DD/WY/6674, f. 25r. W. J. Smith in his *Salusbury Correspondence* believes Marsli was a mistress and Piers's second wife was Ermin, daughter of Roger Puleston of Emral (Pedigree Table IIA). Smith gives no evidence for his claim.

the Reformation from 1534 and the Acts of Union in 1536–43. This also coincided with Piers's advancing age and Robert's early married life. As a result, the 1530s saw Robert increasingly involved with the administration of his father's estates and the other activities required of a gentleman. For example, in 1537, acting on Piers's behalf, Robert personally took a traitorous priest to a trial before the Council in the Marches.[35] In 1544, Robert was steward of the lordship of Ruthin, an office previously held by his father. Piers and Robert also leased land jointly, such as their lease of the demesne of Ruthin in 1539.[36] However, from the mid-1530s, Robert began to appear on his own in deeds connected to the Salesbury estates, suggesting that Piers had retired from the administration of the family affairs. Piers could retire satisfied that he had provided a model for his son to understand how to be the head of a Welsh gentry family.[37] Their partnership was the ideal father–son relationship, stewarding the Salesbury fortunes together and passing on knowledge to the next generation.[38]

However, after Piers's death, the Salesbury paterfamilias never achieved the same closeness with his eldest son and heir, primarily because only one more head of the Salesbury family lived long enough to see his son reach the age of majority at twenty-one. Robert died when his son, John, was seventeen. John died when his own son, the future Sir Robert, was thirteen. Sir Robert died when his son, yet another John, was just a baby, and, after a period of difficulty, the estates eventually passed to the baby's uncle, William. William lived to be nearly eighty years old, but he had a tumultuous relationship with his heir, Owen, who died two years before his father. At Owen's death, his son, William, was a minor of around nineteen years old. William died himself when his own son and heir, Owen, was around fourteen years old. Owen had no

[35] TNA, SP 1/120, f. 87.
[36] *LP*, vol. 14, part 1, p. 164.
[37] Jennifer Jordan, '"To Make a Man Without Reason": Examining manhood and manliness in early modern England', in John H. Arnold and Shaun Brady (eds), *What is Masculinity? Historical dynamics from antiquity to the contemporary world* (Basingstoke, 2010), pp. 245–62.
[38] Houlbrooke, *The English Family*, p. 179.

sons and the estates passed to his younger brother, Roger, before they were eventually inherited by Owen's daughters, Elizabeth and Margaret. The Salesburys were unfortunate that the head of the family rarely lived beyond middle age and often died young. There were also, as shall be seen, implications for the estate, which needed to support the gentleman's widow.

John Salesbury (1533–80)

Death at a young age was not, of course, the fault of the paterfamilias. However, the Salesburys show that a competent gentleman could prepare for that eventuality and limit the impact on his family. For example, on 14 May 1548, Robert Salesbury (d.1550) granted the manors of Rhug, Glyndyfrdwy and Dinmael, all in Merioneth, to his eldest son and heir, John (1533–80).[39] This meant that John had control of a significant portion of the Salesbury estates. Thus, when Robert died in 1550, he had taken measures to ensure the security of his heir's inheritance and the family's future; his prudent decision limited the impact of his death on the family. Although a minor, John functioned as a landowner in his own right, and his control of the Merioneth lands caused confusion during his wardship as an underage heir because John did not realise that he needed to sue out his livery in the court of Wards.[40] In his will, Robert appointed his friends and kinsmen, Sir John Salusbury of Lleweni, John Conwy, and John Wyn ap Hugh, to discharge his debts of £400, using a third of his lands to raise the money. Although Robert was only middle-aged, his affairs were in order and the succession of his son proceeded relatively smoothly, with the exception of minor administrative matters in the court of Wards. John's confusion about the court was possibly the result of ignorance, as the court, established in 1540, was still relatively new in 1550.

[39] NLW, Bachymbyd 113; *CPR: 1547–1548*, p. 374.
[40] For more on wardship, see below, pp. 35–7.

John, however, experienced a valuable lesson. He was an exemplary paterfamilias, who significantly expanded the Salesbury estates and explored new income streams, such as mining licences. Seventeen years old when his father died, John had learnt how to administer the Salesbury estates, and he understood his responsibilities to the Salesbury family. Like his father before him, John died relatively young, at the age of forty-seven on 17 November 1580. John was very careful to provide for all his surviving children in his will and he gave detailed instructions on the wardship arrangements for his eldest son. His heir, the future Sir Robert, was thirteen years old and John also had a younger son, John (1575–1611), as well as a daughter, his eldest living child, Margaret (1565–1650). John's wife, Elizabeth Salusbury (d.c.1584), daughter of Sir John Salusbury of Lleweni, was also heavily pregnant with their youngest child, William (1580–1660), who was born after his father's death. Nevertheless, John included his unborn child in his will, bequeathing an annuity of twenty marks 'in case Elizabeth Salisburye my wieff beinge now with Childe doe beare a Sonne'.[41] If the baby was a daughter, John bequeathed £200 for her preferment in marriage. Sir Robert, as the heir, inherited his father's estates, but his younger brother received the park and township of Segrwyd, Denbighshire. To safeguard his children's inheritance, John bequeathed the Bachymbyd estate to his nephews, John Conwy of Bodrhyddan and Edward Thelwall of Plas y Ward, and his wife's brother, Thomas Salusbury of Denbigh Castle. They were the children's closest relatives outside the nuclear family and represented both John and Elizabeth's sides of the family. They received the estate for a term of eight years, the length of time until Sir Robert reached his majority. John asked them to use the profits of the estate to repay his debts, raise the marriage portion for his daughter Margaret, and to ensure 'the prefermente and avancement of all the rest of my Children', which excluded the eldest son, Sir Robert, who was more secure than his younger siblings as his father's heir. Margaret received

[41] TNA, PROB 11/63/70.

a marriage portion of £800, although, according to William Salesbury's later testimony, the money came from her mother's estate, rather than Bachymbyd.[42]

For his heir, John asked his patron, Ambrose Dudley, earl of Warwick, and his wife, Anne, to request the wardship. The reply, on 5 October 1580, became a highly prized letter in the Salesbury family; William Salesbury endorsed it as 'from the L. and lady Warwik to my Father upon his Death bedd'. Anne wrote to John and told him that she and her husband hoped he would survive 'the daunger of your sicknesse . . . so as we maie have your Service which heretofore wee have founde to be faythfull and honest'.[43] She confirmed that the Lord Treasurer, William Cecil, had granted the wardship to her husband, not to Anne herself, because the Lord Treasurer refused to grant wardships to women, who, in his opinion, 'prove so careless of there chyldrens well being if they [re]marry'. However, Anne asked John to tell them how he had planned to raise his son and how he wanted Warwick to bring him up: 'my Lord will have greate care thereof'. John was steward of Warwick's lordship of Ruthin and the earl and countess valued John's faithful service to them. John used this relationship to secure his son's future and ensure he had a more straightforward wardship than John himself experienced. In his will, John bequeathed his 'Amblinge stone horsse' to the earl and countess of Warwick and asked that 'theie doe vouchesafe to have care and regarde that myne eldest sonne be well broughte uppe in vertue and learninge'.[44] He hoped that Robert would marry the daughter of Sir George Bromley, justice of Chester, and that he 'shoulde be putte to learninge in Mr Bromleye's howsse'. Dutifully following John's wishes, Warwick sold the wardship to Sir George on 3 June 1583, although Sir Robert married Elinor Bagnall (d.1656), daughter of Sir Henry Bagnall, rather than a Bromley daughter.[45] When Anne, countess of Warwick, replied

[42] NLW, Bachymbyd Letters 48.
[43] NLW, Bachymbyd Letters 3.
[44] TNA, PROB 11/63/70.
[45] NLW, Bachymbyd 983.

to John's wardship request, she said, 'I hope yow shall live to see your . . . son growe a man'.[46] John did not live to see Sir Robert reach his majority and he did not ever meet his youngest child, William, who would eventually inherit the Salesbury estates and prove in many ways to be as exemplary a paterfamilias as John. However, John understood the importance of securing the future of his family's estates and he provided for all his children, echoing the model from previous generations of the Salesbury family.

The Salesbury family in crisis

This model began to fracture in the next generation. In 1585, Sir Robert Salesbury purchased his wardship from Sir George Bromley, raising £140 by selling land which had been bequeathed to his younger brothers by their father.[47] This was the first indication that Sir Robert did not necessarily act to protect his family and it became a source of difficulty for John and William, who struggled financially. Sir Robert finally sued out his livery on 12 May 1592, nearly four years after he turned twenty-one on 25 June 1588; he was possibly in no hurry because he owned his own wardship and did not want to pay a fine in the court of Wards.[48] After Sir Robert's death on 14 July 1599, John and William petitioned the overseer of Sir Robert's will, Thomas Egerton. They asked him 'to help us as you have alwayes relieved all men . . . and that it will pleas your honore to remember our brothers wille for our maintenance'.[49] In his will, showing some sense of fraternal responsibility, Sir Robert had left John and William 'so much money yerely towardes their maytenance and better stay of livinge as the said Right honorable the Lord Keeper [Thomas Egerton] shall appoynte, limitt or set downe' and several annuities or rents, as well as the remainder

---

[46] NLW, Bachymbyd Letters 3.
[47] SA, 212/364/1. I am grateful to Melvin Humphreys for this reference.
[48] TNA, WARD 9/66, ff. 433v–435r.
[49] SA, 212/364/1.

of his estates.⁵⁰ However, John and William told Egerton that Sir Robert had not fulfilled his financial obligations to them in his lifetime and that they were owed money from his estate, in addition to Sir Robert's bequests. This included the money that their father, John Salesbury, left to them in his own will, which they had never received. Even though John Salesbury had bequeathed part of the Bachymbyd demesne for the advancement of his younger children, Sir Robert took the annual profit of £80 for his own use for three years, a total of £240, before he reached his majority. In addition, part of the demesne had been occupied by their uncle, Piers Salesbury, and John and William were owed the profit of £45. John and William had also not received any money from their mother's estate, which she bequeathed to them 'uppon her death bedd'; their share amounted to £300 each. William said that he had never received any of the annuity of twenty marks granted to him in his father's will. Sir Robert had allowed him 'some small exhibition for [a] fewe yeares in the Countrey Schooles' and £30 for the year William spent at Oriel College, Oxford, in 1599–1600. William claimed a total debt from Sir Robert's estate of £186 13s. 4d, a substantial sum of money. In total, John and William claimed £1,211 13s. 4d from Sir Robert's estate. All the brothers' claims were co-signed or otherwise supported by witnesses, usually Richard Worrall, the Salesbury steward, who had been a trusted servant of their father, John, and who remained an important figure in the lives of John's sons.⁵¹

Being the head of a gentry family came with responsibilities. Sir Robert Salesbury's younger brothers were part of his immediate family and shared his blood and name. However, Sir Robert showed a flagrant disregard for their financial security: John and William wanted money which had been bequeathed to them by their parents and which Sir Robert had used for his own purposes. This was problematic on two counts because not only did Sir Robert fail to support his younger brothers, he also left a

---

⁵⁰ TNA, PROB 11/96/125.
⁵¹ For more on Worrall, see below, pp. 142–9.

significantly indebted estate to his heir, John, a baby of around one year. William later said that Sir Robert died with £1,000 in debt, a sum which did not include John and William's claims on his estate.[52] Their father had endeavoured to provide for his whole family, but Sir Robert jeopardised the security of John's younger children and then died with considerable debt charged upon his estate, risking the security of the Salesbury landholdings. Early modern literature recognised the difficulties of being a younger son, characterising them as embittered and impoverished, an image familiar enough for contemporary commentators to question the value of primogeniture and the need to establish younger sons in suitable careers to avoid their dependence on the eldest son.[53] John Salesbury could only provide money for his younger sons: John was five years old at his father's death and William was not even born. John's plan for his children depended on the moral virtue of his heir, who chose to keep his younger brothers' money for himself.

Sir Robert's behaviour had a major impact on the Salesbury family which reverberated into future generations. William Salesbury had a particularly difficult relationship with his eldest brother. When William became head of the Salesbury family and a father himself, he resolved that his younger sons would never be dependent on their older brother, to the extent that he divided the Salesbury estates in two.[54] In the 1670s, in a Chancery case to decide the future of the two estates, Eubule Thelwall, the son of William's closest friend, described William's unhappy childhood.[55] William's mother, Elizabeth, married Sir Henry Jones (*c.* 1532–86) of Abermarlais, Carmarthenshire, on 31 August 1584, nearly four years after her first husband's death.[56] For the earliest years of his life, William lived with his mother, but she died soon after

---

[52] NLW, Bachymbyd Letters 48.
[53] Joan Thirsk, 'Younger sons in the seventeenth century', *History*, 54/182 (1969), 360–72.
[54] See below, pp. 44–6, 91–3.
[55] CRO, XD2/463.
[56] P. S. Edwards, *HPO (1509–1558)*: 'Jones, Henry I (?1532–86)'.

her remarriage. Thelwall said that, after his mother's death, William 'was not looked after but left with his nurse [for] 5 yeares'. Once Sir Robert reached his majority, he sent William to school, information corroborated by William's acknowledgement that Sir Robert spent a small sum of money on his education. William attended Ruthin School with Godfrey Goodman, the future bishop of Gloucester, and William was part of the school's target demographic: it educated the sons of local gentry families.[57] However, William was 'taken from school and forced to waite at his brother's table with a trencher'.

Instead of receiving a gentleman's education, William was now a servant in his eldest brother's home, his own family house. Thelwall said that William was so disgusted by the situation that he left the house to become a soldier in Ireland, where he refused to serve under his brother, Captain John, and joined the company of his cousin, Owen Salusbury, instead. After fighting in Ireland, William became a sailor and then 'lived on that fortune he had by his owne industry without any addicion or help from his brothers'. The problem was financial: Sir Robert was reluctant to spend money on his youngest brother, even though their father had provided for his maintenance. Sir Robert incurred debts as a soldier in Ireland and it is likely that he believed the estate could not afford to keep William at school. The relationship did not entirely break down because, at an unknown date in the 1590s, William was included on a list of tenants on the Salesbury estates and he held Pool Park, a farmhouse with around 1,000 acres for which he paid no rent.[58] However, William's experience of being a younger son made him determined not to allow the same mistakes to be repeated in the next generation.

William's early life demonstrates that a gentleman's efforts to secure his children's future could be fruitless if his intentions were not enacted. Sir Robert used the money and lands left to his younger brothers to further his own interests and his own infant

---

[57] NLW, Bachymbyd Letters 43.
[58] BL, Add. MS 14974, ff. 88r–99v.

son inherited an indebted estate. Unlike his father, there is no evidence that Sir Robert attempted to find a guardian for his son, although Sir Robert was ill for five months before his death on 14 July 1599.[59] One month before his death, Sir Robert sold his estate in trust to Humphrey Middleton of Garthgynan, Denbighshire, and Hugh Salesbury of Ruthin, Denbighshire. In his will, Sir Robert appointed his cousins, Edward Puleston of Llwynycnotiau, Denbighshire, and Edward Thelwall of Plas y Ward, Denbighshire, as his executors.[60] However, they refused the leases to discharge the £1,000 debt on the estate and Sir Robert's middle brother, John, dealt with the moneylender, Sir Thomas Myddelton, instead.[61] Sir Robert's will was complicated; it contained multiple small bequests to his servants and cousins, and his heir was only a baby, thus the executors would have been responsible for the profits of the estates for twenty years. Possibly, Thelwall and Puleston refused the extended responsibility or perhaps they did not want to be involved with the significant debt on the estate. In any event, the middle brother, John, took over the administration of the Salesbury holdings, although there is no evidence that this was in accordance with Sir Robert's wishes. The wardship of Sir Robert's heir was granted to one Thomas Marbury on 30 November 1600 and it was confirmed by letters patent on 21 January 1601.[62] Thomas Marbury was presumably part of the prominent, eponymous gentry family of Marbury, Cheshire, but he had little involvement with his ward. In fact, John Salesbury, not Thomas Marbury, stood bound for three deeds of obligations for the wardship on 30 May 1600 and agreed to pay £510 in three instalments between September 1600 and March 1601.[63]

When an heir was under age, a third of the freehold land came under the control of the Crown, and the Crown leased

[59] R. A. Roberts (ed.), *Calendar of the Cecil Papers in Hatfield House*, vol. 9 (London, 1902), p. 181.
[60] TNA, PROB 11/96/125.
[61] NLW, Chirk F12540, p. 252.
[62] THL, Ellesmere MS 669; TNA, WARD 9/108, ff. 510v–511r.
[63] TNA, WARD 9/159, f. 92v.

it out. In June 1601, John leased the Crown's third part of the Salesbury estate, then he surrendered it before March 1602 and was replaced as the lessee by his old friend, Sir John Townshend.[64] On 16 May 1602, Sir John Townshend wrote to his 'Deare and worthy friend . . . Jacke' that 'I have the lease oute of the courte of Wardes'.[65] They were evidently working together to keep John's control of the Salesbury estates. The sheriff's book for Merioneth confirms that John still occupied a third part of the manors of Glyndyfrdwy and Rhug.[66] However, on 2 August 1603, Sir John died intestate, after a duel on Hounslow Heath, and his administrators resigned the lease.[67] The court of Wards granted the lease again to John Salesbury on 30 March 1604, on the condition that he pay the outstanding sum required on the £165 fine owed when Sir John entered the lease, as well as the rents and charges due at Michaelmas 1603.[68] Retaining control of the Salesbury patrimony was an expensive endeavour. However, it was also a successful one because John held significant influence over his family estates during his nephew's minority. For example, on 11 December 1601, John renegotiated the jointure land of his sister-in-law, Elinor, exchanging her estate at Pool Park for the Rhug estate for a term of seventeen years, almost certainly prompted by Elinor's remarriage to Thomas Needham.[69]

It is plausible that John retained control of Elinor's young son and that the baby continued to live at Bachymbyd. In an inventory of 15 June 1601, Bachymbyd was the only Salesbury house with a nursery, and both John and William Salesbury were invariably described as 'of Bachymbyd' in deeds dating to the time of their nephew's wardship.[70] By late 1603, William Salesbury had returned

---

[64] TNA, WARD 9/120, ff. 177v–180r.
[65] NLW, Bachymbyd Letters 6.
[66] TNA, WARD 9/634.
[67] Cecil H. Clough, 'Townshend, Sir John', *ODNB* (2005).
[68] TNA, WARD 9/120, ff. 177v–180r.
[69] CRO, XD2/494.
[70] THL, Ellesmere MS 1782g. For John's and William's primary residence, see, for example, NLW, Bachymbyd 693 (16 August 1602); Bachymbyd 804 (9 June 1604); Bachymbyd 166 (15 May 1605).

from sea, and he too became involved in the administration of the Salesbury patrimony. On 1 January 1604, Sir Robert's executors, Edward Thelwall and Edward Puleston, conveyed Sir Robert's estates to John and William, 'upon [John and William's] speciall entreatie and request' for the fifteen years remaining on the original twenty-one-year lease.[71] Puleston and Thelwall had not wanted to be executors of Sir Robert's will and accept responsibility for his debts; doubtless they were pleased to relinquish Sir Robert's lease to his younger brothers. The brothers were also diligent in their stewardship of the Salesbury estates; for example, in a bid to settle some of his debts, Sir Robert had sold at least 6,500 acres of his land in Merioneth to Sir Thomas Myddelton, and John challenged Sir Thomas in court to reclaim it.[72] It was a level of financial responsibility which proved uncharacteristic for John when he had full control of the Salesbury estates.

Sir Robert's heir died aged ten years old on 1 January 1608.[73] As the new head of the Salesbury family, John Salesbury proved to be irresponsible and wasteful. Despite the suggestion that John was a responsible custodian during his nephew's life, he was the most dangerous and incompetent paterfamilias in the family's history, bringing the Salesbury estates close to ruin. John's primary weakness was financial mismanagement and perhaps he was only competent during his nephew's lifetime because the estates were ultimately overseen by Thomas Egerton, Lord Keeper and later Baron Ellesmere and Lord Chancellor. John, known to contemporaries as Captain John, was a former soldier prone to engaging in hot-headed brawls and he had spent time in the Marshalsea after participating in the 1601 Essex Revolt.[74] He was also prone to incurring substantial debts, and his desperate bid to repay them threatened the security of the Salesbury patrimony. In his four years as head of the family, John sold the Bachymbyd estate to a London moneylender and goldsmith called John Williams

[71] DRO, DD/WY/4194.
[72] CRO, XD2/1265.
[73] NLW, Bachymbyd 490.
[74] See below, pp. 123–7.

and leased significant portions of the Salesbury patrimony for long periods to his friends.[75] When William Salesbury inherited the patrimony from his brother in 1611, he had a yearly income of less than £30 from an estate worth over £707 a year in 1601.[76]

William Salesbury (1580–1660)

Fortunately, William understood his duty to the Salesbury patrimony. When William sued John Williams for the ownership of Bachymbyd, William said that Bachymbyd was his 'father's principall house', continuing 'the name and blood of the Salisburyes'.[77] William recognised that he had a responsibility to his family to protect their patrimony, both his ancestors and future generations. His older brothers were much more careless, especially John, whose debts nearly ruined the family. William understood that his estates were founded by his ancestors and thus they were tied to his status as a gentleman, as well as providing an income for the family to maintain their lifestyle. In the next generation, William ensured that none of his children needed to depend on their oldest brother for support or maintenance. His daughter, Margaret, married Thomas Ravenscroft of Bretton, Flintshire. William apprenticed his second son, John, to a London merchant, thereby setting him up in a career, and his third son, Robert, also spent time in London. Owen, the eldest son, and Charles, the youngest, were both students at Gray's Inn and therefore obtained a legal education. However, although Owen as the eldest son inherited Rhug, which was entailed in the male line upon William's marriage to Dorothy Vaughan in 1611, William intended to divide his remaining estates between his three younger sons.[78] Unfortunately for William, John died in 1639 in his late teens and Robert in 1646 in his twenties. As a result, William settled his Denbighshire lands, including the Bachymbyd and Pool

---
[75] See below, pp. 85–9.
[76] NLW, Bachymbyd Letters 48; THL, Ellesmere MS 1782e.
[77] NLW, Bachymbyd 720.
[78] CRO, XD2/463.

Park estates, on his youngest son, Charles. Although William valued the integrity of the Salesbury patrimony, it was more important to him that he provided for the future of his children. According to a witness many years later, William made it clear that he would not 'leave them destitute of mainteynance as he had bin or to the mercy of the elder brother'.[79] This statement reflects William's tribulations as a young man and the necessity of making his own way in the world before inheriting a decimated estate from his neglectful older brother.

However, although William was only the second and last Salesbury paterfamilias to see his eldest son reach adulthood, William and Owen had a difficult relationship. William was a dutiful father who provided Owen with the necessary education for his status as a gentleman.[80] Their early letters were full of affection for each other, with Owen reporting on his activities and William updating Owen on family life and business.[81] As a pupil at Winchester College, Owen said that his father was 'allwaies readier to make faultes noe faultes . . . and beinge faultes is allwaies reddier to forgive then to punnish or correct beinge confessed'.[82] The letters are the easy communication between a father and son, with the occasional remonstrance from William that Owen did not write often enough. Later, while living in London as a student at Gray's Inn, Owen told his father that 'I will by the grace of god spende my time as well as I can to your likinge and my future good'.[83] Unfortunately, a few weeks after that letter from London, Owen acted contrary to William's liking and William was not quick to forgive him. They did not write to each other again, or at least none of the letters were kept among the family's papers. On 28 October 1635, Owen married Mary Goodman, daughter of Gabriel Goodman of Abenbury, without his father's consent.[84] He

[79] CRO, XD2/463.
[80] See below, pp. 158–61.
[81] NLW, Bachymbyd Letters 18–28; 33. The letters are calendared in Smith, *Salusbury Correspondence*, pp. 149–57.
[82] NLW, Bachymbyd Letters 20.
[83] NLW, Bachymbyd Letters 28.
[84] DRO, DD/WY/674, f. 13v.

directly disobeyed William's order, and his oath before witnesses, not to marry Mary until William had reached a financial agreement with her family.[85] Thus, not only did Owen disobey his father, he also failed to secure his wife's portion, which William needed as a portion for his own daughter's marriage. Owen's illicit marriage threatened his family; it particularly affected his sister, Margaret, who did not marry until 1638, but raising marriage portions could also affect the maintenance of younger sons or require mortgaging part of the estate, endangering the patrimony.[86] William had carefully repaired the damage caused to the Salesbury estates by his brothers and now his own son failed to safeguard the family finances. William felt betrayed by Owen and believed he colluded with the Goodman family to secure his wife's fortune without owing any money to William.[87] Afterwards, William refused to pay his son an allowance and Owen relied on the Goodman family for financial support.[88]

The battle for Bachymbyd

After William's death, the head of the Salesbury family never again owned both the Rhug and Bachymbyd estates. Charles Salesbury died in 1666, after suffering the loss of three of his children including his son, and Bachymbyd and the Denbighshire lands were inherited by his only surviving child, Jane. Owen Salesbury, who received Rhug and the Merioneth lands, died before his father in 1658 and his share of the patrimony passed to his eldest son, William (1639–77). Wales had experienced considerable change since the Rhug and Bachymbyd estates were first occupied by the Salesburys in the late fifteenth and early sixteenth centuries. When Owen Salesbury died, the country had recently suffered a brutal civil war, in which Owen did not take the same side as his ardently Royalist father and

---

[85] NLW, Bachymbyd Letters 29.
[86] Heal and Holmes, *Gentry in England and Wales*, p. 67.
[87] NLW, Bachymbyd Letters 44.
[88] NLW, Bachymbyd Letters 43.

younger brother, Charles, or at least he did not actively fight for the king.[89] The bonds of familial loyalty were not what they once were, even among the traditionally kinship-focused Welsh gentry. Owen's son, William, inherited vast estates even without Bachymbyd. William's mother, Mary Goodman, had been an extremely wealthy heiress who inherited both her father's and uncle's estates. William, however, wanted Bachymbyd. This might be an echo of the same pride that compelled his namesake grandfather to reclaim Bachymbyd from the moneylender John Williams, but there was no suggestion of this argument when William took his dispute to the court of Chancery and sued his cousin Jane for the ownership of the estate in a case which lasted from 1671 to 1677. Instead, William's suit emphasised that he was the eldest son of the eldest son and therefore Bachymbyd belonged to him by right. Culturally, this was a long way from the old Welsh laws of inheritance which provided for every son.

William's suit did not succeed, but he came very close.[90] He accused his cousin Jane and her mother, Elizabeth Thelwall, of forging documents which supported Jane's lawful inheritance from her father, Charles. The suit lasted six years and it included various countersuits brought by the Bagot defendants.[91] In essence, William alleged that the Bachymbyd estate had been entailed in the male line upon the marriage of his grandparents, William Salesbury the Elder and Dorothy Vaughan in December 1612. Establishing the truth of the case was made more difficult by the death of Edward Vaughan, Dorothy's brother, and thus the Vaughans' copy of the marriage articles passed in trust to Charles Salesbury. Charles's widow, Elizabeth Thelwall, gained control of Charles's documents as executrix of Charles's will. William accused Elizabeth of destroying the marriage articles to ensure her daughter, Jane, could inherit Bachymbyd. However,

---

[89] See below, pp. 215–18.
[90] For a detailed examination of his suit, see Sadie Jarrett, 'Credibility in the Court of Chancery: Salesbury v. Bagot, 1671–1677', *The Seventeenth Century*, 36/1 (2021), 55–79.
[91] TNA, C 5/447/83; C 5/446/5; C 10/173/11; C 5/550/32; C 5/446/195; C 8/202/58.

this was a falsity because Charles bequeathed the Vaughan trust to his nephews: William himself and his younger brother, Gabriel Salesbury. William and Gabriel released the Vaughans' estate at Llwydiarth to Edward Vaughan on 2 September 1671, thus they did gain control of the trust.[92] The focus on the Vaughans' copy of the marriage articles in William's suit is peculiar because he produced the Salesburys' copy to support his case and argued that his grandfather William the Elder broke his own marriage settlement when he granted Bachymbyd to Charles, the younger son. However, Jane and Elizabeth's defence was not helped by Owen's death in middle age when William the Younger was a minor; William claimed that he could not properly secure his inheritance until he came of age, although he was in his thirties by the time of the Chancery suit in 1671–7.

In William's suit, there were successive miscarriages of justice in each generation. In fact, William's suit was based on fiction. He claimed that his father Owen did not sue his grandfather, William the Elder, because Owen had too much respect for him. This is a picture of a filial relationship not supported by William the Elder's own correspondence during his lifetime or by deponents questioned during the suit, because William never forgave Owen for marrying without his consent and cheating the Salesbury family out of Owen's wife's portion. Equally, the marriage articles produced in the case were a forgery: William the Elder could not have entailed Bachymbyd in the male line upon his marriage to Dorothy Vaughan because his brother John Salesbury had sold the estate to John Williams the moneylender nearly a year previously in January 1611. William did not successfully buy back the estate until 1615. William settled a jointure on Dorothy in April 1615, but gave her Rhug, which was duly entailed in the male line and thus passed to Owen, rather than mortgage-encumbered Bachymbyd.[93] After repurchasing much of his ancestral estate and reclaiming ownership of controversial leases, William said that he

---
[92] DRO, DD/WY/4077.
[93] NLW, Bachymbyd 729.

was 'left at libertie to convey all, or as much as he pleased to any . . . son'.[94] The marriage articles were also not the only forged documents in the suit: William the Younger's brother, Gabriel, was forced to flee to France after a 1675 trial at the Denbighshire Great Sessions found that a deed he and William used to support their version of Dorothy's jointure was actually a forgery. The forgery was uncovered because Gabriel used a middleman, Lawrence Clarke, to recruit a forger called Ralph Holborne, but Clarke paid Holborne only £10 of the £35 fee and, in retaliation, Holborne told Jane's husband, Sir Walter Bagot, about the forged deed.[95]

However, the Lord Chancellor found that William the Younger presented a more credible suit than the defendants. William was the eldest son of the eldest son and his grandfather had acted against the conventions of primogeniture by granting Bachymbyd to a younger son.[96] It is notable that William the Younger never sued his uncle Charles for the ownership of Bachymbyd, waiting instead until Bachymbyd passed to Charles's daughter, Jane. Despite knowledge that the plaintiff was willing to use forged documents to support his case, the Lord Chancellor found in William's favour on almost every point. William only failed in his ambition to take Bachymbyd from its rightful owner because of a legal technicality: in 1657, William the Elder used a final concord to transfer Pool Park, the jointure of his sister-in-law, Elinor Bagnall, to Charles so that Charles could settle the estate on his wife for her jointure. Pool Park was part of the alleged entail on Bachymbyd, but Owen Salesbury, who did not die until 1658, did not challenge his father for the land. Consequently, the Lord Chancellor ruled that Owen's inaction broke the entail on Bachymbyd, an entail which never actually existed.[97]

---

[94] NLW, Bachymbyd Letters 44.
[95] NLW, Bachymbyd Letters 122; 228.
[96] Joan Thirsk, 'The European Debate on Customs of Inheritance, 1500–1700', in Jack Goody, Joan Thirsk and E. P. Thompson (eds), *Family and Inheritance: Rural Society in Western Europe, 1200–1800* (Cambridge, 1976), pp. 178–80.
[97] CRO, XD2/470.

On 2 November 1672, Eubule Thelwall, Jane Salesbury's uncle through her mother, Elizabeth Thelwall, updated Sir Walter Bagot about the progress of their dispute with William Salesbury. By this point, Gabriel Salesbury had fled to France after his forgery was exposed and William's wife, Mary Mostyn, was gravely ill with a disease that would kill her, almost certainly the same disease that also killed three of William and Mary's children in 1672. Thelwall said, however, that William himself

> was never merrier. But his passions were never squared to reason. The burial of three children, the doubtful condicion of his wife, the defeat of his confidence and the stain upon his family all in one year would not have been things indifferent to others.

Thelwall gives the impression of a cold and unreasonable man, unbothered by the deaths of his close family or his reputation, concerned only to reclaim what he saw as rightfully his and uncaring if it damaged his relationship with his cousin. Thelwall also suggests that William was acting counterculturally, that society expected him to grieve his wife and children and feel shame about his brother's dishonourable behaviour.[98]

William did not succeed in taking Bachymbyd from his cousin and her husband and thereby reuniting the two Salesbury estates. William, and his father Owen, were Salesburys of Rhug, unlike their forefathers who had been Salesburys of Rhug and Bachymbyd. The Bagot family valued their Bachymbyd estate immensely and it was of far more economic importance to them than to William Salesbury, who still had Rhug and his mother's vast Goodman estates around Wrexham. Bachymbyd also supported Jane's widowed mother, Elizabeth Thelwall, and provided for younger sons of the Bagot family. However, the marriage of Jane Salesbury and Sir Walter Bagot was not merely economic: Jane and Walter's descendants valued their Salesbury ancestry, and

---

[98] Anne Lawrence, 'Godly grief: individual responses to death in seventeenth-century Britain', in R. A. Houlbrooke (ed.), *Death, Ritual and Bereavement* (London, 1989), pp. 65–71.

the Bagots' house at Blithfield Hall, Staffordshire, still contains important Salesbury artefacts, including portraits of William Salesbury the Elder and his son Charles, letters from Charles I praising William for his service in the Civil War, and a replica of a cap given to the Salesbury family by Charles II.[99]

The end of the male line

When William died in 1677, his remaining four children were still alive: his eldest son and heir Owen, John, Roger and one daughter, Lumley. In their father's will, John and Roger received £800 each and Lumley received a portion of £1,000. William said that if his executors were not able to raise the money, Owen was responsible for providing the legacies to his younger siblings. William said

> as that I of late have been att very great trouble and expence both att law and in equity about the Recovery and Regaineing of my Ancestors estate . . . though I am fully convinced in my mind and conscience that I have a good right and title thereunto.

William added, unsurprisingly, that he had always intended to settle his entire estate on his eldest son and heir, subject to the payments for his other children, and so he did not leave any land for John, Roger or Lumley, but left them dependent on their eldest brother.[100] According to the terms of William's marriage to Mary Mostyn, Rhug was entailed in the male line and the entail was repeated by William's son, Owen, in a fine and recovery of 1686, limiting the inheritance of Rhug to Owen Salesbury's male heirs, then Roger Salesbury's male heirs, then the male heirs of their uncle, Gabriel Salesbury, then Owen Salesbury's right heirs.[101] John Salesbury, the

---

[99] I am grateful to Charles and Cosy Bagot-Jewitt for generously allowing me to visit their home at Blithfield. The original cap is now kept at Staffordshire County Museum, 67.087.0001.
[100] CRO, XD2/38.
[101] NLW, Gogerddan LB1/1; CRO, XD2/521.

other surviving younger son, of William, had died by the time of the fine, because he was not included as a potential heir.

In many respects, this was sensible planning. It secured the future of the estate in the male line, keeping it in the Salesbury family. A shared name was an increasingly important concept in seventeenth-century English inheritance practices.[102] The flaw, however, was that it depended on the paterfamilias and his closest male relatives producing sons. Owen Salesbury married Elizabeth Bateman and they had two daughters, Elizabeth and Margaret, and no sons. Roger Salesbury, meanwhile, married Jane Vaughan of Glanllyn and they did not have any children. Gabriel Salesbury, Owen and Roger's uncle, never married and thus he could not produce any legitimate heirs. When Owen Salesbury died in 1694, the estate passed to Roger Salesbury as Owen's male heir, rather than Owen's daughters. Gabriel Salesbury died in early 1711, leaving his own estate to Roger, as well as £100 to his great-nieces, Elizabeth and Margaret Salesbury. Roger Salesbury died in 1719 and he left the Salesbury estate to Elizabeth and Margaret. This complied with the entail as they were Owen's right heirs after the death of his uncle and brother, and in the absence of sons.

This narrative, however, disguises a considerable and expensive legal battle between Roger Salesbury on the one hand and his nieces, Elizabeth and Margaret, and their mother, Elizabeth Bateman, on the other. The dispute centred on Elizabeth and Margaret's portions of £1,500 each and their mother's dower. Even Gabriel Salesbury was caught up in it because he had an annuity of £60 charged upon the estate. Once again, the incident highlights the importance of a paterfamilias making adequate preparations for the next generation and the necessity of choosing reliable and trustworthy people to protect his children's interests. Gabriel Salesbury, for example, said that he was retired from business concerns and lived far from Rhug in London, so asked if

---

[102] Deborah J. Anthony, 'To Have, to Hold, and to Vanquish: Property and inheritance in the history of marriage and surnames', *British Journal of American Legal Studies*, 5 (2016), 233–8.

he could be removed as a trustee of the estate. All the remaining trustees were willing to act, but said they had not yet undertaken any activity as trustees. The main problem, however, was that the profits of the estate were insufficient to raise the amount of money for everybody with a claim on the estate, a total of £3,000 or £4,000. The Rhug demesne, for example, formed part of Elizabeth Bateman's dower, but the land was also needed to pay Gabriel's annuity and raise the portions for Elizabeth and Margaret. Roger Salesbury said that he wanted to pay his nieces' portions, but he did not have enough money. There were also debts on the estate at Owen's death in 1694, including £460 owed to Gabriel Salesbury for his annuity, a large proportion of which was still unpaid at the time of the Chancery suit.

In total, Roger said in his Chancery deposition that the annual rent raised £223 13s. 1d.[103] Roger rented Elizabeth Bateman's third of the Rhug demesne, paying his sister-in-law £40 a year, and the arrangement meant that Roger could maintain the repair of the house and improve the land. Roger claimed that he overpaid Elizabeth for her third; it would be too expensive, he said, for a tenant to pay such a sum for the demesne and still make a profit after repairs and other expenses. However, the house and demesne had always been occupied by the Salesbury family and thus it had never been assessed for its rental value. The lands in question were liable for taxes, and the commissioners undertaking the Chancery depositions saw and endorsed the account books which recorded the sums. All the deponents agreed that the tenants' rents had not been increased during Roger's time as head of the family.[104] Essentially, Roger and Elizabeth disputed Rhug's annual income: Elizabeth believed that Roger could pay her dower and her daughters' maintenance, as well as Gabriel's annuity. Roger said that the estate's outgoings were too high and there were too many charges on the land.

[103] TNA, C 22/185/17.
[104] TNA, C 22/185/17; C 22/1005/53.

On 8 July 1698, the Lord Chancellor decreed that the trust estate should be administered by a receiver who would report the rents and profits to one of the Masters of the Court, Sir John Hoskyns, until £6,000 was raised for the girls' portions. The Master of the Court was to decide a suitable amount for their yearly maintenance.[105] This was originally set at £30 each per annum and it was increased on 15 July 1711 to £80 each per annum.[106] In about 1700, Sir John Hoskyns judged that the yearly value of the trust was £707 17s. From the time of Owen Salesbury's death, Roger had received rents and profits totalling £2,029 13s. from the lands charged with providing for Owen's family. Sir John allowed £1,099 1s. 10d for Roger's expenses, which included taxes for the mills and demesne, then he ordered Roger to pay £930 12s. towards his nieces' portions. However, the dispute was not so easily resolved and it rumbled on in Chancery for well over a decade. Problematically, Elizabeth Bateman remarried after the 1700 ruling and there was now no one to enforce the girls' interests, because they were still underage. As a result, Roger did not give an account of his yearly rents and profits to Sir John Hoskyns, although receivers were appointed to record the money. The profits should have been put out at interest to raise money for the girls, but, according to the Lord Chancellor's order of 13 July 1715, this was 'notoriously neglected by the said Defendant [Roger Salesbury]'.[107] The Lord Chancellor compelled everyone involved in the suit to appear at a hearing to account for all the money received, including representatives of two receivers who had died since their tenure. By this point, Elizabeth Salesbury had already been married and widowed, and she was named as Elizabeth Barnston in her deposition.

Evidently, Elizabeth and Margaret Salesbury struggled to obtain the money owed to them under the terms of their father's will. In the end, the dispute became obsolete because

[105] NLW, Gogerddan LB5/1.
[106] NLW, Gogerddan LB5/1.
[107] NLW, Gogerddan LB5/1.

Roger Salesbury died in the summer of 1719 and left all his manors, lordships, tenements and hereditaments in Merioneth, Caernarfonshire, Denbighshire and Flintshire in two equal shares to his nieces, Elizabeth and Margaret, then to their male heirs. He also stipulated that each share should be charged with £2,000 to provide for younger children. If either of them did not produce a male heir, then their respective share went, not to the other sister, but to their aunt, Roger's sister, Lumley, who would also inherit the whole estate if neither Elizabeth nor Margaret had sons. If Lumley did not have a son, Roger wanted his estate to go to Thomas Salusbury of Erbistock, Flintshire. Roger also asked that any male heirs take the Salesbury surname. As for the money owed to Elizabeth and Margaret in Chancery, Roger bequeathed the remainder to Lumley Salesbury, as well as £2,000 charged upon the estate. Lumley was the sole executrix of her brother's will. Lumley Salesbury lived until 1741, residing in Holborn, London, and she never married. She left her own estate to Maria Charlotta Pugh, the daughter of her niece Elizabeth Salesbury and Elizabeth's second husband, Rowland Pugh.[108] As a result, there is little suggestion that the Chancery suit caused any long-lasting disagreement in the family. Roger left the Salesbury estate to his two nieces and Elizabeth Salesbury remained close to her aunt, enough that Lumley made Elizabeth's daughter her heir. Maria Charlotta Pugh eventually inherited Rhug and, when she died in 1780, she left it by will to her cousin, Colonel Edward Williames Vaughan (d.1807), the second son of Sir Robert Howell Vaughan (1723–92) of Nannau.[109] Roger Salesbury's intention that a male heir should take his surname was not followed.

A Salesbury gentleman owned the family estates from 1482 to 1719. This was an impressively long period, spanning nearly two and a half centuries. This continuity depended on a father producing a male heir, which the Salesburys achieved until Owen Salesbury, who was survived by two daughters in 1694, and his brother, Roger

[108] TNA, PROB 11/713/89.
[109] TNA, PROB 11/1069/80.

Salesbury, who died childless in 1719. Wales in 1719 was a very different place from when John Salesbury, a younger son of Thomas Salusbury of Lleweni, first began purchasing a landholding at Bachymbyd in the marcher lordship of Denbigh in the mid-1470s. At that time, Bachymbyd was subject to Welsh land law, which was swept away by the legal reforms of the 1536–43 Acts of Union. The Reformation brought opportunities to expand the Salesbury estates by purchasing ex-monastic land, a project begun by Robert Salesbury and completed by his son, John. The Elizabethan wars in Ireland enabled John's younger sons to forge careers as soldiers, useful experience when the youngest, William, fought for the king in the 1642–51 Civil Wars. From the mid-seventeenth century, the Salesbury estates were divided and a Salesbury gentleman owned only Rhug, not the original ancestral home of Bachymbyd, but the family continued to be wealthy and influential in north Wales.

At the start of the Salesburys' tenure at Rhug and Bachymbyd, Welsh society was intensely kinship-focused. There is some suggestion that these bonds had weakened somewhat by the early eighteenth century, but the Welsh gentry still had an obligation to preserve their wealth and status for future generations of their family. The Salesbury paterfamilias was not always successful. The first head of the family, John, and his heir, Piers, established a strong foundation on which the Salesburys could build, and Piers lived long enough to see his son and heir became a competent successor. After Piers, no future Salesbury paterfamilias lived to see his son and heir reach his majority, with the exception of William Salesbury (d.1660), who never forgave Owen for marrying without his consent. This absence of working relationships between the head of the family and his adult heir highlights that there were other influences which helped the family through times of adversity. For example, mothers could be strong advocates for their children, but it could be more difficult if they remarried after their husband's death, as in the case of Elizabeth Bateman and her Chancery suit against Roger Salesbury. This echoed the problem that Anne, countess of Warwick, encountered over a hundred years earlier in 1580 when her husband, Ambrose Dudley, earl of Warwick, was awarded the guardianship of John Salesbury's son and heir by the court of Wards because the Lord Treasurer said that women became careless of their children's interests if they remarried. This reflects the position of women in early modern society, one which was deferential towards their husband. As the Salesbury women show, however, they also understood how to navigate the strictures of a patriarchal world and they had a keen understanding of their role and entitlements within the family.

WOMEN IN THE SALESBURY FAMILY

As the doctrine of coverture subsumed a woman's legal identity into her husband's, wives are largely absent from the Salesbury archives.[110] Only a fraction of letters in the surviving Salesbury correspondence, for example, are from women. This is not the case for other gentry families; for example, the correspondence of the fifteenth-century Paston family of Norfolk includes a high number of letters written by women.[111] Although early modern Welsh society acknowledged maternal ancestry as a source of status, it was still intensely patriarchal. Traditionally, medieval Welsh law prioritised the inheritance of sons over daughters, a practice reinforced by the adoption of primogeniture from the sixteenth century. Women were subordinate to men of the same status and under the authority of the head of the household, even if he were a son or younger brother.[112] The status of women changed throughout their life. For example, Salesbury widows are far more visible in the archives than Salesbury wives or daughters; widows had control of their finances and their own legal identity.

[110] Amy Louise Erickson, *Women and Property in Early Modern England* (London, 1993; 2002 edn), pp. 24–5.
[111] Diane Watt, *The Paston Women: Selected Letters* (Woodbridge, 2004).
[112] Jarrett, "'By reason of her sex and widowhood'", pp. 79–96.

Within a gentry family, however, wives were powerful figures, second only to their husband as head of the household. They were mothers of the next generation and worked with their husband to protect the family and its future.

The partnership between a husband and wife was foundational to the nuclear family and their roles and responsibilities complemented each other. Even though a wife was considered subordinate to her husband, contemporary advice books cautioned men to rule with love and to respect the companionship provided by their wives.[113] However, this was advice only, and there were also unhappy marriages: Sir William Andrewes, for example, was accused of abusing his wife, Anne Temple (b.1601).[114] There is little surviving information about the quality of the Salesbury marriages. Welsh-language praise poetry is one of the few sources which include a fairly significant focus on wives in Welsh gentry families. The poems were performed aloud in the hall of a gentry house, or *plasty*, and they praised a gentleman's accomplishments, such as his ancestry, his courage and the excellence of his wife. In praise poetry, gentlemen were rich, noble and brave, and their wives were meek, beautiful, and provided generous hospitality to guests.[115] The stereotypes in praise poetry provide little insight into the lives of the Salesbury wives. For example, the poet Lewis Morgannwg wrote an elegy upon the death of Robert Salesbury in 1550 and said of his wife, Katherine ferch Ieuan:

> A Chatrin ferch teurn fu
> Merch Sion eurferch synhwyrfawr
> a wisg aur merch ysgwier mawr.[116]

---

[113] Alexandra Shepard, *Meanings of Manhood in Early Modern England* (Oxford, 2006), pp. 80–2.

[114] Rosemary O'Day, *An Elite Family in Early Modern England: The Temples of Stowe and Burton Dassett, 1570–1656* (Woodbridge, 2018), pp. 340–3.

[115] Dafydd Johnston, 'Lewys Glyn Cothi: Bardd y gwragedd', *Taliesin*, 74 (1991), 68–9. For a discussion of how medieval sources portrayed Welsh women, see Sioned Davies, 'Y ferch yng Nghymru yn yr Oesoedd Canol', *Cof Cenedl*, 9 (1994), 3–32.

[116] Hughes, 'Noddwyr y beirdd', 559.

[And Katherine, the daughter of a sovereign, the daughter of John, a splendid woman of great wisdom who wears gold, the daughter of a great squire.]

Meanwhile, in the next generation, Siôn Tudur praised the fine eyebrows ('meinael') of Elizabeth Salusbury of Lleweni, the wife of John Salesbury (d.1580). The praise poetry shows what Welsh society valued in a wife and rarely anything about the wives themselves.

Gentlewomen needed to cultivate two opposing personalities: deference to their husband and assertiveness to run the household and provide education for daughters and younger sons.[117] This did not mean, however, that women were restricted to the household, and they could also be active in land management and administration: Lady Hester Sandys (1570–1656), the wife of Sir Thomas Temple (c.1567–1637) managed her own jointure land while her husband was still alive, for example.[118] However, women were closely associated with the house and the household. In Wales, the gentry's *plastai*, or country houses, were the centre of their sphere of influence. As in England, it was a political commonwealth in miniature, overseen by the head of the family.[119] There was a contemporary understanding that a gentleman's house reflected his character and social status; houses were at the heart of the gentry's domestic and public life.[120]

Houses were also places of hospitality, a crucial pillar of Welsh gentility.[121] Wives had an important role to play in the provision of hospitality and, if Felicity Heal's research on England is also applicable to Wales, they received hospitality with their husbands at the homes of other gentry families from the mid-sixteenth century onwards.[122] Lewys Morgannwg said that Katherine ferch

---

[117] See Linda Pollock, '"Teach her to live under obedience": The making of women in the upper ranks of early modern England', *Continuity and Change*, 4/2 (1989), 231–58.
[118] O'Day, *An Elite Family*, pp. 97–104.
[119] Jones, *Welsh Gentry*, pp. 206–9.
[120] Heal and Holmes, *Gentry in England and Wales*, pp. 297–8.
[121] Jones, *Welsh Gentry*, pp. 210–13.
[122] Felicity Heal, *Hospitality in Early Modern England* (Oxford, 1990), p. 57.

Ieuan kept 'dribwrdd / i roi i bawb bwyd ar bob bwrdd' ('three tables / to provide food for everyone on every table').[123] The poem praised the Salesburys for having the wealth and space to give generously, but Lewys Morgannwg explicitly identifies Katherine as the coordinator of the family's hospitality. Welsh gentlewomen were expected to be charitable and generous, central figures in the family's relationships with others. For example, the poet William Cynwal described Elin Llwyd, wife of John Wyn ap Maredudd, as 'A giver of fire-coloured apparel to the wretched and naked; she prospered her shire and was a prudent lady who was exceptionally merciful'.[124] A gentleman's wife thus played a vitally important role in maintaining the family's power and status in the local community. Hospitality was coded and ritualised, reinforcing the social hierarchy.[125] It strengthened a gentleman's bonds with his tenants, servants and kindred, and emphasised the central position of his house in their own particular world. Writing about John Salesbury (d.1580), Simwnt Fychan said that the Salesburys' house at Bachymbyd was 'lle i ynnill iechyd lle in llechir . . . / lle iawn i dyvod' ('a place to achieve well-being, a place where we are sheltered . . . a fine place to frequent').[126] The house was welcoming and hospitable, an atmosphere achieved through the activities of women, particularly John Salesbury's wife, Elizabeth Salusbury. There was also a Christian element to a gentry family's hospitality, displaying piety by providing for guests.[127] This connected to another aspect of a wife's role in the household: responsibility for religion and religious education, expressed in the repeated association between gentlewomen and *duwiolaeth*, piety or godliness, in praise poetry.[128]

With limited information on the Salesbury wives, it is impossible to know if they had happy marriages, if their husbands

---

[123] Hughes, 'Noddwyr y Beirdd', 559.
[124] Jones, 'Welsh gentlewomen', 12.
[125] Heal, *Hospitality*, p. 7.
[126] Hughes, 'Noddwyr y Beirdd', 570.
[127] Jones, *Welsh Gentry*, pp. 210–12.
[128] Heal and Holmes, *Gentry in England and Wales*, p. 76; Jones, 'Welsh gentlewomen', 15–22.

failed to rule with love or respect their companionship, or if they were kind, generous and pious women beyond the stereotypical phrases of the praise poems. However, there are indications that Salesbury patriarchs acted in a partnership with their wives, fulfilling their duty to be a good leader in the household, as well as in wider society.[129] For example, Robert Salesbury (d.1550) and Katherine ferch Ieuan bought substantial amounts of land together, including the Pool Park estate which eventually became the primary jointure land for Salesbury wives, and the former monastic land of Valle Crucis Abbey in Denbighshire.[130] Equally, Robert and Katherine's son, John (d.1580), named his wife, Elizabeth Salusbury of Lleweni, and their daughter, Margaret, as joint executrices of his will, suggesting that women understood the administration of the family estates and husbands trusted them to execute their wills properly.[131] This practice was not repeated by all the Salesbury patriarchs, but the difficulty of establishing when their wives died makes it problematic to draw conclusions from their wills about their relationships. However, one Salesbury gentleman, Charles Salesbury of Bachymbyd (d.1666), had a strong partnership with his wife, Elizabeth Thelwall, daughter of John Thelwall of Plas Coch. John Thelwall and Charles's father, William Salesbury (d.1660), were close friends: William's son-in-law, Thomas Ravenscroft, said that John Thelwall 'was more privy to the Affaires of William Salesbury then any man'.[132]

Charles and Elizabeth's marriage in 1646 was thus an excellent match between the children of two good friends and the marriage arrangements were extremely amicable. Elizabeth brought a portion of £800 to the marriage and she received a jointure worth £197 a year, including the Pool Park estate. A further £20 was added after the death of Elinor Bagnall (d.1656), William Salesbury's widowed sister-in-law. William also granted the use of Bachymbyd, Clocaenog Park, and several other lands

---

[129] Jones, *Welsh Gentry*, pp. 96–7.
[130] NLW, Bachymbyd 527.
[131] TNA, PROB 11/63/70.
[132] CRO, XD2/463.

to Charles and 'his heirs of Elizabeth', settling the estate in tail general, which permitted the inheritance of both sons and daughters. William, despite the claims of his grandson in the 1670s Chancery case, certainly did not object to daughters inheriting the Salesbury estates. Charles and Elizabeth had four children, although three of them, Margaret, John and Dorothy, died young and predeceased their parents.[133] Only Jane, the middle daughter, survived to adulthood. Charles and Elizabeth grieved the loss of their children.[134] On 22 October 1663, Charles's cousin, Howell Vaughan, wrote to Charles after Margaret's death and said, 'I beseech you comfort your bedfellow [Elizabeth] . . . you are the stronger vessel and gently present my service to my cosin your bedfellow, for women are tender naturd'.[135] This was the ideal partnership between a husband and wife: Charles was the 'stronger vessel' providing support and comfort to his 'tender naturd' wife, and together they coped with the death of their young children. Highlighting the strength of their union, they built a new house at Bachymbyd, which still survives today. Above the door, there is an inscription with the year of completion in 1666 and the initials C. E. S. for Charles and Elizabeth Salesbury, with an impaled Salesbury and Thelwall coat of arms.[136]

Sadly, Charles died in the same year that they completed their house, and Elizabeth was the executrix of his will. As a widow, Elizabeth acquires visibility in the sources, no longer subsumed into her husband's legal identity, and she was a determined and strong-willed woman. In 1669, she began to arrange the marriage of her only surviving child, Jane, to the future Sir Walter Bagot. Elizabeth was heavily involved in the negotiations, although her brother, Eubule Thelwall, undertook the correspondence with Walter's father, Sir Edward Bagot. At Christmas 1669, the marriage arrangements nearly collapsed because Sir Edward

[133] DRO, DD/WY/6674, f. 74r.
[134] Lawrence, 'Godly grief', pp. 66–9.
[135] DRO, DD/WY/6548.
[136] I am grateful to the owners of Bachymbyd Fawr for generously allowing me to visit their home during my doctoral research.

wanted a charge of £1,000 on the Bachymbyd estate to provide for his younger sons. Thelwall told Sir Edward that he could not expect Elizabeth's 'absolute condescension at the first proposal . . . . she will give her resolution at the end of the holidays'.[137] Giving an indication of the relative autonomy of the Salesbury women, Jane was part of the negotiations too: one of Thelwall's letters rebuked Sir Edward for excluding Jane, 'which how my neece resented . . . she is no stranger to her business'.[138] It is significant, however, that men corresponded over the match, even if Elizabeth and Jane had the power to veto any arrangements. Elizabeth was a capable administrator who understood how to navigate the world of the early modern gentry, but her daughter would lose control of the Salesburys' substantial fortune to her husband once she married. After the Christmas negotiations faltered, Thelwall told Sir Edward, 'I never meant when I wrote that my Sister was distrustfull, that she was soe particularly as to you, but perhaps of me also and every man'.[139] It is unsurprising that Elizabeth was reluctant to agree to any terms which were detrimental to Jane or her fortune. Care for the future of the family and its estate was not limited to the paterfamilias, but encompassed his wife too.

However, Elizabeth also had particular concerns about the security of women. When Elizabeth died an elderly lady in 1693, she had suffered the loss of her husband and three of her four children, but she had also arranged an excellent marriage for her daughter and had ten grandchildren. She was also a very wealthy woman, supported by the generous jointure arranged during her marriage to Charles. Although the jointure reverted back into the estate, Elizabeth left most of her own money to her granddaughters: £1,000 each to the two eldest, Mary and Elizabeth, and £500 each to the two youngest, Jane and Ann. She bequeathed only £100 on the day of his marriage to the Bagot heir, Edward, and smaller sums to his brothers. Elizabeth

---

[137] NLW, Bachymbyd Letters 70.
[138] NLW, Bachymbyd Letters 65.
[139] NLW, Bachymbyd Letters 70.

was careful to provide for the women in her family; money gave women some measure of power in a world of untrustworthy men. Elizabeth's bequests had the potential to increase her granddaughters' negotiating power in their own marriage settlements. In turn, this enabled better jointures, giving a widow the right to more money in the event of her husband's death. As a widow with a generous jointure and the mother of a desirable heiress, Elizabeth understood the importance of a satisfactory marriage settlement to protect the rights of women to money and property.[140] Behind the women who married into the Salesbury family, there were relatives, including mothers and fathers, who wanted to protect their daughters just as Elizabeth wanted to protect Jane. The kindred helped the Salesburys in times of adversity, but there were also wider kinship ties which attempted to ensure women were in good marriages that respected early modern ideals of the relationship between a husband and wife.

CONCLUSION

The early modern Welsh gentry were intensely kinship focused. This reflected the close link between ancestry and status in medieval Wales which continued into the early modern period. At its heart, Welsh gentility was found in a family's pedigree, both in the paternal and maternal lines. This chapter has particularly emphasised the role of women in the transfer of gentle status and their importance as partners to their husbands at the head of a gentry household. Mothers and wives were fundamental links in a world of kinship ties. However, even as ancestry continued to be a key indicator of gentility in early modern Wales, elite families like the Salesburys of Rhug and Bachymbyd recognised that wealth and landed property made it easier to display other qualities of gentility, such as generous hospitality, bardic patronage, and the

---

[140] Amy Louise Erickson, 'Common law versus common practice: the use of marriage settlements in early modern England', *Economic History Review*, 2nd series, 43 (1990), 27.

ability to hold positions of political authority. As the example of the Salesburys shows, gentry families had a responsibility to protect the patrimony and ensure the continuation of their estates, a task not always successfully achieved by the head of the Salesbury family. In many respects, their obligation to the patrimony was an extension of the Welsh gentry's kinship focus; kinship meant protecting not just the family's interests, but also the interests of future generations. The next chapter looks in more detail at how the Salesburys established themselves as a landed gentry family and used their estates at Rhug and Bachymbyd to emphasise their position as one of the leading gentry families in north Wales. Ancestry gave the Salesburys the right to claim gentle status, kinship gave them a network of associates throughout north Wales and the borders, and landed estates legitimised their ability to hold power in the local area.

2
TERRITORIAL LEGITIMACY

The Salesbury family defined themselves by their estates. They were 'of Rhug and Bachymbyd', in the same way that their cousins were the Salusburys 'of Lleweni' or 'of Erbistock'. Landholdings were a distinguishing feature and an intrinsic part of a gentry family's identity. The Wynns, for example, were 'of Gwydir', the Pulestons were 'of Emral' and the Griffiths were 'of Penryn'. Like other gentry families, the Salesburys of Rhug and Bachymbyd explicitly associated themselves with their estates, though notably they never referred to them both at the same time. In Denbighshire, the Salesburys were 'of Bachymbyd' and in Merioneth they were 'of Rhug'. Gentry estates were inextricably connected to the family's position in their local community and enabled them to hold positions of power and influence in two different counties. As a result, the Salesburys' estates established the family's sphere of influence. More practically, the estates also provided the Salesburys with an income, primarily from livestock farming and rents, but supplemented occasionally by more diverse income streams, such as mining licences. This enabled the Salesburys to maintain the standard of living expected of a gentry family and provide generous hospitality to guests in their *plastai*, or country houses. At the same time, the estates were also the Salesburys' homes, where they lived with their children and servants, and sometimes their younger siblings too. The Salesburys slept in feather beds, kept a Welsh Bible, played an Irish harp, and, by the end of the seventeenth century, owned hundreds of books. This chapter looks at the role of the Salesbury estates as places which established the Salesburys as a gentry family and connected them with their ancestors, but also at how the estates supported multiple generations of the family even in times of economic difficulty.

ESTABLISHING THE ESTATES

There were many ways for an enterprising family to acquire land in early modern England and Wales. There was a glut of monastic land on the market after the Reformation, and so the Mansels of Oxwich became the Mansels of Margam after purchasing the monastic estate of Margam Abbey in Glamorgan.[1] From the 1570s, the Spencers of Althorp, Northamptonshire, became rich through sheep-farming, which enabled them to expand their landholdings further by marrying into prosperous families.[2] Sheep-farming encouraged landholders to enclose common land, a contentious issue among their tenants, and there was also the option of improving wasteland.[3] As H. J. Habakkuk argued with regard to monastic property, it was easier for those who already had land to gain more because they had the means and money.[4] However, Wales had its own peculiarities which brought both advantages and disadvantages. Before the Acts of Union in 1536–43, Wales had two systems of land law, depending on whether land was held under Welsh tenure or English tenure. Under Welsh law, land belonged to the kindred, four generations of men, and it could not be sold or alienated.[5] Equally, *cyfran*, the Welsh system of partible inheritance, entitled all sons, legitimate and illegitimate, to a share in their father's land, which militated

---

[1] Glanmor Williams, 'Rice Mansell of Oxwich and Margam (1487–1559)', *Morgannwg*, 6 (1962), 42–4.

[2] Gordon Batho, 'Landlords in England B: Noblemen, gentlemen, and yeomen', in Joan Thirsk (ed.), *The Agrarian History of England and Wales*, vol. 4: *1500–1640* (Cambridge, 1967; 2011 edn), pp. 290–1. W. G. Hoskins, *The Making of the English Landscape* (London, 1955; 1992 edn), pp. 130–2.

[3] See, for example, Richard W. Hoyle (ed.), *Custom, Improvement, and the Landscape in Early Modern Britain* (Farnham, 2011).

[4] H. J. Habakkuk, 'The market for monastic property', *Economic History Review*, NS, 10/3 (1958), 380.

[5] See T. M. Charles-Edwards, *Early Irish and Welsh Kinship* (Oxford, 1993), chapter four.

against estate-building by gentry families. In England, partible inheritance existed in some areas, but it was predominantly associated with peasant and yeoman holdings; Welsh partible inheritance encompassed the land of elite families.[6] Families in Wales who held their land under English tenure were not subject to the same restrictions and could inherit holdings in their entirety, a significant advantage for families who wanted to build up estates.

However, opportunities developed in later medieval Wales to circumvent legal restrictions on Welsh land. For instance, Gruffudd ap Madog, the grandfather of Owain Glyndŵr, entailed some of his holdings to convert them to English tenure and pass on the estate intact, and other families illegally exchanged land or paid a fee to the lord to alienate their holdings.[7] Above all, it was possible to use a legal fiction called *tir prid*, or gage land, a system which gradually developed in the burgeoning monetary economy after the Edwardian Conquest of 1282–3 specifically to overcome the restrictions on Welsh tenure.[8] In return for a sum of money, land was mortgaged for a period of time, usually four years, and the intended buyer owned the land if the mortgage was not redeemed after four renewals.[9] There was never any intention to redeem the mortgage; the sum of money was not a loan, but consideration for the land's purchase. Nevertheless, although land could be alienated from the kindred, developing an estate was a slow process. The Maurice, or Morris, family in Caernarfonshire, for example, began consolidating their kindred's land in the early fourteenth century, but they did not complete it until the sixteenth century, when Elis Morris bought the remaining interests in the

---

[6] Richard M. Smith, 'Families and their land in an area of partible inheritance: Redgrave, Suffolk 1260–1320', in Richard M. Smith (ed.), *Land, Kinship, and Life-cycle* (Cambridge, 1985), pp. 135–95.

[7] Carr, *Gentry of North Wales*, p. 80.

[8] Llinos Beverley Smith, 'The gage and the land market in late medieval Wales', *Economic History Review*, NS, 29 (1976), 539–41; see also Llinos Beverley Smith, 'Tir prid: deeds of gage in land in late medieval Wales', *BBCS*, 27 (1976–8), 263–77.

[9] T. Jones Pierce, 'Landlords in Wales: The Nobility and the Gentry', in Thirsk, *Agrarian History*, vol. 4, p. 367.

land.[10] Families needed to be enterprising to succeed in their estate-building. The Mostyn family of Mostyn, Flintshire, built up one of the earliest purchased estates in the fourteenth century, which they then augmented through sensible marriages.[11] Equally, Maredudd ab Ieuan ap Robert, founder of the Wynns of Gwydir, Conwy, encroached on vacant bond land in Dolwyddelan, Conwy, taking advantage of the decline of villeinage in the fourteenth century, which laid the foundations for the Wynns' estates.[12] The gentry constructed their estates using different methods and the process was often slow, but the aim was the same: to have substantial landholdings inherited by the next generation, preferably the eldest son, which formed the basis for the family's power in the local area and a focus for their sense of familial identity.

The Salesburys established their estates over about a century. In the 1470s, John Salesbury (b.*c.*1450), a younger son of Thomas Salusbury of Lleweni, began the process of purchasing the Bachymbyd estate in the marcher lordships of Denbigh and Ruthin. John's family, the Salusburys of Lleweni, were an established gentry family in the lordship of Denbigh. They too built up their estates over time: in 1334, the Salusburys owned forty-four acres in Lleweni, and by 1437 their land had increased fifteenfold, to 660 acres.[13] Even today, Lleweni contains good agricultural land, and the profits from farming enabled the Salusburys to invest in land, eventually making money from rents as well as agriculture. The Salusburys arrived in Denbigh as tenants of Henry de Lacy, earl of Lincoln and first lord of Denbigh, probably from his Lancashire or Herefordshire

---

[10] T. Jones Pierce, 'The Clenennau estate', in J. Beverley Smith (ed.), *Medieval Welsh Society: Selected essays by T. Jones Pierce* (Cardiff, 1972), pp. 229–49.

[11] Carr, *Gentry of North Wales*, pp. 82–5. For the medieval development of the Mostyn estates, see Carr, 'The Mostyn family and estate, 1200–1642'.

[12] John Gwynfor Jones, 'The Wynn estate of Gwydir: Aspects of its growth and development *c.*1500–1580', *National Library of Wales Journal*, 22/2 (1981), 141–3.

[13] Carr, *Gentry of North Wales*, p. 76; D. Huw Owen, 'Clans and gentry families in the Vale of Clwyd, 1282–1536', in R. A. Griffiths and P. R. Schofield (eds), *Wales and the Welsh in the Later Middle Ages* (Cardiff, 2011), p. 154; Paul Vinogradoff and Frank Morgan (eds), *Survey of the Honour of Denbigh 1334*, vol. 1 (London, 1914), pp. 63, 66, 69.

estates.[14] Lleweni was a new-model Englishry: the English administration exchanged the lands of Welsh residents for holdings in other townships, and thus the land was not subject to the restrictions of Welsh land law and it was particularly attractive to English settlers.[15] It is likely, for example, that English settlers in Denbigh had larger holdings than their Welsh counterparts, a pattern found in the neighbouring lordship of Ruthin.[16] Consequently, John Salesbury, although a younger son, came from a wealthy family who were able to support all their children. Equally, despite their origins as English settlers, the Salusburys of Lleweni quickly married into Welsh families: Henry Salusbury, for example, the great-great-great-grandfather of John Salesbury, married Nest, the daughter of Cynwrig Fychan, whose father had been granted land at Lleweni by Edward I which had previously belonged to the princes of Gwynedd.[17] The Salusburys understood how to navigate the hybrid Anglo-Welsh world of the late medieval marcher lordships.

Unlike Lleweni, Bachymbyd was not an Englishry; it was still under Welsh tenure when John Salesbury began to purchase it. In the thirteenth century, the tenants at Bachymbyd sided against the king of England, firstly with the prince of Wales in 1282–3, then with Madog ap Llywelyn, leader of the Welsh revolt in 1294–5.[18] By 1476, the house at Bachymbyd and its demesne belonged to Madog ab Ieuan ap Madog ap Gruffudd and he leased it to John Salesbury for six years at £2 a year.[19] In 1482, Madog and John engaged in the fictional mortgage exchange of *tir prid* and Madog granted Bachymbyd to John on a renewable four-year lease for

---

[14] Smith, *Salusbury Correspondence*, p. 2–4.
[15] D. Huw Owen, 'The Englishry of Denbigh: An English colony in medieval Wales', *Transactions of the Honourable Society of Cymmrodorion* (1975), 65, 68–9. For a study of post-Conquest English settlement in the neighbouring lordship of Ruthin or Dyffryn Clwyd, see Barrell and Brown, 'A settler community in post-Conquest rural Wales', 332–55.
[16] Diane M. Korngiebel, 'English colonial ethnic discrimination in the lordship of Dyffryn Clwyd: segregation and integration, 1282–*c*.1340', *WHR*, 23/2 (2006), 15.
[17] Owen, 'Clans and gentry families', p. 155.
[18] Vinogradoff and Morgan, *Survey of Denbigh*, p. 33.
[19] NLW, Bachymbyd 168.

£20.[20] At the end of the mortgage period, Bachymbyd belonged to John, successfully alienated from Madog's kindred. In the same period, John continued to acquire more neighbouring land. On 14 December 1486, John bought the reversion of land in the commote of Colion from John Holand, a servant of Edmund Grey, earl of Kent, who had granted Holand the interest in the land which had escheated to Lord Grey because the holder had no sons to inherit.[21] As escheated land, it was automatically held by English tenure.[22] John Salesbury was successfully building an estate for his own family, but it was subject to two different legal systems and the Welsh land would have been subject to partible inheritance. It was important to John Salesbury that his estate should pass intact to his eldest son and heir or else his estate-building efforts would result in no substantial landholdings to establish and support the family. To protect his new estate, John Salesbury successfully applied for letters patent from Henry VII to convert his land at Bachymbyd to English tenure, which John received on 20 November 1487.[23] The family also carefully preserved a copy of a 1508 charter issued by Henry VII which granted that all land in the lordship of Ruthin should descend to the eldest son and heir.[24] John Salesbury, a younger son of an established gentry family, now had his very own estate at Bachymbyd, held under English tenure and inheritable in its entirety by his eldest son, Piers.

In this next generation, the Salesburys utilised another means of estate-building: marriage. Piers Salesbury (d.1548) married Margaret Wen ferch Ieuan (d.<1548), daughter and heiress of Ieuan ap Hywel ap Rhys of Rhug. The addition of

---

[20] NLW, Bachymbyd 39.

[21] NLW, Bachymbyd 5; 111; J. Y. W. Lloyd, *The History of the Princes, the Lords Marchers and the Ancient Nobility of Powys Fadog*, vol. 3 (London, 1882), p. 64.

[22] Llinos Beverley Smith, 'Family, land and inheritance in late medieval Wales: A case study of Llannerch in the lordship of Dyffryn Clwyd', *WHR*, 27/3 (2015), 424.

[23] NLW, Bachymbyd 351–2.

[24] NLW, Bachymbyd 523. This charter for the marcher lordship of Ruthin followed similar charters issued to the Principality of North Wales: see J. Beverley Smith, 'Crown and community in the principality of north Wales in the reign of Henry Tudor', *WHR*, 3 (1966), 157–9.

the Rhug estate into the Salesburys' holdings extended their influence out of the marcher lordships and into the Principality of North Wales. Rhug was fifteen miles south of Bachymbyd, but administratively very different. Rhug was part of the commote of Edeirnion, an independent lordship rewarded for its support during the Edwardian Conquest by being allowed to retain its ancient privileges, granted by the princes of Wales. As a result, the barons of Edeirnion were among the few Welsh lords to survive the Conquest. After the Conquest, they had a special tenure of *pennaeth*, or Welsh baronry, a lesser status than the marcher lords which gave the barons slightly less independence; for example, they remained under the authority of the king's coroner and escheator. Edeirnion was more conservative than the marcher lordships to the north and its residents were less interested in building estates or overcoming the restrictions on partible inheritance.[25] By the end of the fifteenth century, Rhug was not subject to such restrictions, but there are no surviving documents in the Salesbury papers which record its conversion to English tenure or the grant of any circumventions on Welsh inheritance law. This contrasts sharply with the Salesburys' Bachymbyd estate, where the Salesburys carefully preserved documents supporting the right of the eldest son and heir to inherit. Of course, the Rhug documents may have been lost, but it is also possible that the estate was converted to English tenure before Piers's marriage to Margaret. Welsh inheritance laws did not technically permit women to inherit kinship land, although there is one surviving medieval Welsh law book which did permit a daughter to inherit in the absence of sons, possibly influenced by English practices which were affecting the culture of inheritance by the later Middle Ages.[26] Indeed, there are earlier examples of elite Welsh women, a group to which Margaret Wen belonged, holding land as widows.

---

[25] Carr, 'Appendix 2: Parishes and townships in medieval Merioneth: Edeirnion', pp. 138–50. See also A. D. Carr, 'The barons of Edeirnion, 1283–1485, I and II', *Journal of the Merioneth Historical and Record Society*, 4 (1963), 187–93, 289–301.

[26] Robin Chapman Stacey, 'Gender and the social imaginary in medieval Welsh law', *Journal of the British Academy*, 8 (2020), p. 280, n.62.

This would seem to be in contradiction to Welsh law and it highlights the unknown gulf between Welsh law books and Welsh law in practice.[27] Thus, Rhug may have been a Welsh estate, and Margaret Wen inherited it from her father because he adopted English inheritance practices for his only child, taking into account that he was a local lord with little external interference in how he managed his lordship. On the other hand, Rhug may have been an English estate. There are scattered references to Welsh barons who converted their estates to English tenure or used legal devices to subvert Welsh inheritance law: for example, in 1328, Gruffydd ap Madog, lord of Glyndyfrdwy, used a fine and recovery to preserve his estate in the next generation.[28] The absence of surviving documents for Rhug is perhaps unsurprising, given the records for the commote of Edeirnion do not survive. Both options for Margaret's inheritance suggest a readiness to adopt new customs, quite possibly in response to external cultural influence, which belies Edeirnion's existing reputation as a conservative commote. Both are equally plausible, although in practice the tenure of Rhug when Piers Salesbury married Margaret Wen is irrelevant: Margaret did inherit her father's estate, and Welsh law had been abolished by the time her eldest son inherited Rhug in 1548, thus the estate could only descend according to English law.

Regardless of the tenurial status of the Rhug estate, the Salesburys adopted the title of 'barons of Edeirnion'. For example, a deed of 1526 describes Robert Salesbury (d.1550) as a 'gentylman and Baryn of the Edeirnion'.[29] The title also survived the reforms of the Acts of Union when all land became English tenure: in a deed of 20 February 1548, Robert Salesbury was still described as 'baron of Dernion' and another gentleman, Hugh Thomas Lloyd, still called himself a baron of Edeirnion in a deed

---

[27] Emma Cavell, 'Widows, native law and the long shadow of England in thirteenth-century Wales', *EHR*, 133/565 (2018), 1387–419. I am grateful to Sara Elin Roberts for our discussion on female inheritance in later medieval Wales.

[28] A. D. Carr, 'An aristocracy in decline: The native Welsh lords after the Edwardian Conquest', *WHR*, 5 (1970), 124.

[29] CRO, XD2/1109.

of 1581.[30] The status of the title was separate from the land's tenure, and a baron's lands did not need to be subject to Welsh law. In 1577, a Jenkin Gwynne, possibly an agent, wrote to John Salesbury (d.1580), who inherited Rhug from his father Robert in 1550. In the letter, Gwynne confirmed that Edeirnion was still held '*per servicium baroniae* [by baronial service] every jot of it'.[31] Through his marriage to Margaret Wen ferch Ieuan, Piers Salesbury acquired a significant estate for their children. However, it also legitimised the family's position in the local area and allowed them to assume a historical position of privilege in Edeirnion. The Salesburys, descendants in the paternal line from English settlers, became barons of Edeirnion, a title of minor Welsh nobility. It is likely that they also assumed the privileges and liberties of the title, including the right to hold a baronial court, although unfortunately the baronial court records do not survive.[32] Rhug itself was an estate of significance: it was associated with Gruffydd ap Cynan (d.1137), king of Gwynedd, who was captured by the earl of Chester at Rhug, and Owain Brogyntyn (d.1215×1218), a prince of Powys, who owned Rhug from 1170 until his death.[33] The Rhug estate was part of how the Salesburys established their territorial legitimacy, capitalising on its historical associations to assert themselves as a Welsh gentry family with a long lineage.

To validate their gentle status, the Salesburys made a conscious attempt to associate themselves with earlier, Welsh power structures in the locality. Bachymbyd was the ancestral estate, the founding house of the family. Rhug carried historical clout and gave them particular privileges as Welsh nobles, even if the position came with little weight outside Edeirnion. On 3 August 1549, Robert Salesbury, the son of Piers and Margaret Wen, bought a third small estate called the lordship of Glyndyfrdwy. In many ways, this was a sensible purchase: it neighboured the Rhug estate and extended

---

[30] CRO, XD2/1149; NLW, Bachymbyd 549.
[31] NLW, Bachymbyd Letters 1b.
[32] Carr, 'Appendix 2: Edeirnion', p. 138.
[33] Paul Russell (ed.), *Vita Griffini Filii Conani: The Medieval Latin Life of Gruffudd Ap Cynan* (Cardiff, 2012), pp. 70–3; Carr, 'Appendix 2: Edeirnion', pp. 138–9.

the Salesburys' landholdings in Merioneth east along the Dee Valley towards Llangollen.[34] Robert was an existing tenant of some of the land so he was familiar with its economic potential. Glyndyfrdwy was also another barony of Edeirnion, which further cemented the Salesburys' claim to the title. However, there was another intangible benefit: Glyndyfrdwy was the ancestral manor of Owain Glyndŵr and where he supposedly declared himself Prince of Wales on 16 September 1400. Glyndyfrdwy was not Glyndŵr's main residence, but, just like the Salesburys a century later, he recognised the cultural importance of the royal title associated with the estate.[35] When Glyndŵr was declared a traitor, his lands were attainted and reverted to the Crown; Robert bought Glyndyfrdwy in a convoluted process which required a licence from the king. The lordship was originally granted to Lord William Grey of Wilton and John Bannister for their service against the Scots and the sum of £1,015 10s., and the licence to sell to Robert was a further 26s. 8d. Glyndyfrdwy cost Robert a significant sum of money, equal to or greater than the amount paid by Lord Grey and Bannister. Robert held Glyndyfrdwy for the fourth part of a knight's fee and rent of 32s. 8d per annum.[36] It was an expensive undertaking, but one which Robert thought would enhance the Salesburys' estates and their reputation as a gentry family.

It might seem strange that the Salesburys would want to associate themselves with a known traitor. The Salesburys' future estates were at the epicentre of the Glyndŵr Revolt (1400–c. 1415), which began with an attack on Ruthin in September 1400, but the Salesburys were not yet settled at Rhug and Bachymbyd during the time of the revolt and there is no indication that the Salesburys' paternal forefathers sided with Glyndŵr.[37] Some of the Salesburys' maternal ancestors did fight for Glyndŵr, because ten barons of Edeirnion were involved in Glyndŵr's attack on Ruthin and the commote of Edeirnion supported the revolt.[38] It is

---

[34] *CPR: Edward VI*, vol. 3, pp. 60, 70.
[35] R. R. Davies, *The Revolt of Owain Glyn Dŵr* (Oxford, 1995), pp. 131, 133–5.
[36] CRO, XD2/1247.
[37] R. I. Jack, 'Owain Glyn Dŵr and the Lordship of Ruthin', *WHR*, 2 (1964), 303.
[38] Carr, 'An aristocracy in decline', 125–6.

likely that the Salesburys were aware of the connection, informed as they were about their genealogy and the history of their estates. However, the Salesburys were loyal servants of the Crown; they were associated with the stewardship of the lordship of Ruthin and Robert Salesbury was the first of many Salesbury sheriffs in 1545.[39] However, within Wales, there was cultural capital in claiming a connection to Glyndŵr, reflecting the focus on ancestry in the recognition of gentle status. For example, Gruffydd Aled Williams has identified multiple examples of early modern praise poems which celebrate different gentry families' descent from Glyndŵr.[40] The Salesburys of Rhug and Bachymbyd were one of the families who recognised a familial link; a sixteenth-century pedigree shows they were descended in the maternal line from Glyndŵr's sister, Lowri, who married Robert Puleston.[41] The Salesburys and their contemporaries were well aware of the link: in the seventeenth century, for example, Rhisiart Phylip praised William Salesbury (d.1660) for the 'fraint rhyw brogaintyn / a glynn dwr' ('honour of a lineage of [Owain] Brogyntyn and Glyndŵr').[42] As an ancestor of renown, Glyndŵr acquired neutrality, another famous Welshman to emphasise the Salesburys' claim to gentility.

However, Glyndŵr's reputation was also under revision in early modern Wales. The fifteenth- and sixteenth-century English chronicle sources of the Glyndŵr Revolt are, unsurprisingly, critical of Glyndŵr. For example, Edward Halle (c.1496–1547) wrote in his *Chronicle* of 1547 that Glyndŵr terrorised the Marches, 'robbed villages, brent tournes [burnt towns] and slew the people, and

---

[39] *LP*, vol. 20, part 2, p. 451. See Jarrett, 'Officeholding and local politics in early modern Wales', 206–32; Carr, 'An aristocracy in decline', 125–6.
[40] Gruffydd Aled Williams, 'The later Welsh poetry referencing Owen', in Michael Livingston and John K. Bollard (eds), *Owain Glyndŵr: A Casebook* (Liverpool, 2013), pp. 534–45. See also Gruffydd Aled Williams, 'Owain Glyndŵr yn ei gynefin', *Journal of the Merioneth Historical and Record Society*, 17 (2016), 229–48. I am grateful to Gruffydd Aled Williams for an illuminating discussion on this subject, with specific reference to the Salesburys of Rhug and Bachymbyd.
[41] BL, MS Stowe 669, ff. 98v–99v. Alternatively, they were descended from Glyndŵr's brother, Tudur, who married a Lowri (Williams, 'Owain Glyndŵr', 241).
[42] Hughes, 'Noddwyr y beirdd', 615.

laden with praies and bloudy handes returned again to Wales'.[43] Nevertheless, there were more neutral accounts which recognised the Welsh cultural context of the revolt. Adam Usk, for instance, a Welshman and contemporary of Glyndŵr, identified that Glyndŵr positioned himself as a prophesied leader who claimed descent from notable Welsh figures of legend, such as Cadwaladr, the seventh-century king of Gwynedd, and that Glyndŵr used Uther Pendragon's standard, as recorded in Geoffrey of Monmouth's *History of the Kings of Britain*.[44] Adam Usk did not give a favourable impression of the revolt itself, but he identified how Glyndŵr used Welsh history to cultivate his image and reputation. This might explain why sympathetic portrayals of Glyndŵr became more widespread in sixteenth-century Wales. For example, Elis Gruffudd's chronicle, completed in *c.*1552, presents a reasonably supportive portrait of Glyndŵr, who had been 'under the lash of King Richard and King Henry for as much as twelve years'.[45] Another theme in the early modern Welsh fashioning of Glyndŵr presented him as a trickster who could successfully extricate himself from difficult situations.[46] From the 1560s, there are multiple surviving copies of a poem, ostensibly contemporary and by Iolo Goch, successfully warning Glyndŵr about treachery, highlighting a late sixteenth-century interest in Glyndŵr as a plucky hero.[47]

There were still Welsh critics of Glyndŵr in the sixteenth century. Sir John Wynn (1553–1627) of Gwydir, in his *History of the Gwydir Family and Memoirs*, criticised the destruction caused

---

[43] Edward Halle, *Hall's Chronicle: Containing the history of England, during the reign of Henry the Fourth, and the succeeding monarchs, to the end of the reign of Henry the Eighth, in which are particularly described the manners and customs of those periods; carefully collated with the editions of 1548 and 1550* (London, 1809), p. 23, quoted in Alicia Marchant, *The Revolt of Owain Glyndŵr in Medieval English Chronicles* (York, 2014), p. 121. Marchant comments that 'praies' could be 'praise' or 'prizes'.

[44] 'Adam of Usk, *Chronicle, Part 3*', in Livingston and Bollard, *Owain Glyndŵr*, pp. 144–9; Marchant, *Revolt of Owain Glyndŵr*, pp. 126–7.

[45] 'Elis Gruffudd, *Chronicle*', in Livingston and Bollard, *Owain Glyndŵr*, pp. 231, 409.

[46] Dafydd Johnston, 'Shaping a heroic life: Thomas Pennant on Owen Glyndŵr', in Mary-Ann Constantine and Nigel Leask (eds), *Enlightenment Travel and British Identities: Thomas Pennant's Tours in Scotland and Wales* (London, 2017), p. 111.

[47] 'A Poem of Warning to Owain Glyndŵr', in Livingston and Bollard, *Owain Glyndŵr*, pp. 217, 398.

by the revolt.[48] Equally, David Powel commented in his *Historie of Cambria* (1584) that those who followed Glyndŵr believing he was the prophesied leader who 'might recover againe the honour and liberties of their ancestors' were misled by cunning men and brought Glyndŵr 'into such a fooles paradise . . . [that he] proceeded and made warre upon the Earle of March', and pretended to his title.[49] The Salesburys themselves understood that Glyndŵr's reputation as a traitor preceded him, particularly across the border in England. In 1574, John Salesbury (d.1580) found himself accused in the court of Star Chamber of stealing land in Burton, Denbighshire. The plaintiff alleged that John claimed the land as the descendant of a previous owner who 'was attainted of treason for favouring and furthering the Rebellyon of [Owain Glyndŵr]'.[50] John, however, who said he had not claimed the land in question, added that his ancestor had not been involved in the Revolt and 'was alyve longe after the Rebellion'.[51] John did not want to be associated with a traitor who participated in the Glyndŵr Revolt while defending himself in a London lawsuit. He may even have been telling the truth about that particular ancestor, although the Salesburys' lands in Edeirnion were in the heartland of the Revolt.[52] The suit shows, however, that the memory of the Revolt remained strong in sixteenth-century north Wales and continued to influence disputes between the local gentry.

When John Salesbury died in 1580, the poet Siôn Tudur described him as:

> Arglwydd Sion o Rûg eurglod el iddo
> hir lwyddiant a gorfod
> arglwydd henw eurgledd hynod
> Arglwydd y Glyn rhyglyddai glod.[53]

---

[48] Sir John Wynn, *The History of the Gwydir Family and Memoirs*, ed. John Gwynfor Jones (Llandysul, 1990), pp. 22, 51.
[49] David Powel, *The Historie of Cambria, now called Wales* (London, 1584), pp. 318, 386.
[50] TNA, STAC 5/L23/2, interrogatories.
[51] TNA, STAC 5/L23/2, John Salesbury's answer.
[52] Carr, 'An aristocracy in decline', 125–6.
[53] Hughes, 'Noddwyr y beirdd', 572.

[Lord John of Rhug, may he receive fine praise,
far-reaching prosperity and triumph, the renown
of a lord, he of the illustrious golden sword, Lord
of the Glyn, he deserved praise.]

The poem presented John as the heir to Welsh nobility: he was lord of Rhug and Glyndyfrdwy, a baron of Edeirnion. The Salesburys' estates conveyed historical authority and territorial legitimacy on their position in the local community. They were aware of the Glyndŵr Revolt and its epicentre on their family estates, but they also cultivated and celebrated their connection to Glyndŵr as an important figure in Welsh history who himself claimed distinguished ancestry. On the one hand, the Salesburys were a respectable gentry family, entrusted with local and national offices, who made the sensible purchase of a neighbouring estate to extend their holdings. However, they were also descendants of Owain Glyndŵr's kin and they brought the ancestral manor back into the family. Robert's acquisition of Glyndyfrdwy in 1549 purposefully associated the Salesburys with the lordship and its history, and it immediately became part of the Salesburys' identity. For example, when Robert died in 1550, Raff ap Robert's elegy included the line 'gwael ydyw bron gwlad heb wres / glyndwr galon' ('it is wretched that the bosom of the land lacks the warmth of Glyndŵr's heart').[54] The lordship remained an important and praiseworthy aspect of the Salesbury family throughout the sixteenth and seventeenth centuries. In a poem composed for Sir Robert Salesbury (d.1599), Simwnt Fychan celebrated Sir Robert as 'doeth Arglwydd o stad / Glyn Dwr' ('wise lord of Glyndŵr's estate').[55] Even as late as 1697, a pedigree collection described Owen Salesbury (d.1694) as 'Arglwydd glyndwr', or 'lord of Glyndyfrdwy'.[56] The purchase of Glyndyfrdwy was not just a sensible expansion of the Salesburys' holdings: because of

[54] Hughes, 'Noddwyr y beirdd', 567.
[55] Hughes, 'Noddwyr y beirdd', 597.
[56] NLW, Llanstephan 159D, p. 91.

its association with a famous historical figure and its legacy as an important Welsh estate, Glyndyfrdwy enhanced the Salesburys' claim to Welsh gentility. Although they were the Salesburys of Rhug and Bachymbyd, the family also prized their lordship of Glyndyfrdwy, an estate demonstrating that the Welsh gentry valued land for more than its income, and that land was intricately bound up with the cultural focus on historical connections and ancestry.

ESTATE DEVELOPMENT

Certainly, more land did bring value in terms of increasing the size and income of the Salesbury estates. Robert Salesbury purchased large tracts of lands in addition to Glyndyfrdwy, which significantly expanded the family's holdings. None of these purchases had the history or associations of Glyndyfrdwy, although there may have been relevance for contemporary society which has been lost. For example, Robert bought St Cadfan's Lands in Tywyn, Merioneth, on 17 October 1549, the same year that he acquired Glyndyfrdwy.[57] Tywyn, on the coast west of Machynlleth, is over forty miles from Rhug, and the deed for St Cadfan's Lands is the earliest surviving record of Salesbury interests so far south in Merioneth. It is probable that Robert took advantage of the glut of monastic land on the market after the Reformation. In 1545, Robert bought land in Llanarmon-yn-Iâl, Denbighshire, which formerly belonged to Valle Crucis Abbey, and he bought more Valle Crucis land on 7 March 1549 in Mwstwr, Merioneth.[58] The monastery, located in Llantysilio, Denbighshire, closed in 1537 as part of the Dissolution. These purchases were convenient and took advantage of the land market, but the addition of St Cadfan's Lands in Tywyn also suggests that Robert wanted to expand the Salesburys' influence beyond the immediate boundaries of their

[57] CRO, XD2/1241.
[58] NLW, Bachymbyd 527; CRO, XD2/932.

main estates. Tywyn was a portionary church, reflecting its status as a wealthy mother church and also a place of considerable status in medieval Wales; perhaps, as with Glyndyfrdwy, Robert also wanted a cultural association with a place of importance in Welsh history, although it is harder to ascertain the significance of Tywyn's medieval status in early modern Wales.[59]

Robert Salesbury clearly had a considerable amount of capital as well as the ambition to expand his estates. There is no surviving evidence which shows how Robert had the money to fund the expansion. Robert was in his forties when he began making substantial purchases such as Glyndyfrdwy, and his father, Piers, was still alive, dying only two years before Robert in 1548. When Robert died on 28 September 1550, he owed at least £128 to the Exchequer, but this was not a large debt compared with the cost of holdings such as Glyndyfrdwy.[60] However, in the next generation, there is evidence that the Salesburys were astute investors who diversified their income when opportunity arose. For example, on 13 May 1555, two of Robert's sons, John and Piers, purchased Clocaenog Park, Denbighshire, from William, earl of Pembroke, and William Clerke, a gentleman.[61] John (d.1580) was Robert's eldest son and heir, and Clocaenog Park was his first major purchase after reaching his majority. At the time, John lived in London where he was a student at Gray's Inn and, conveniently, a servant of the earl of Pembroke, who became president of the Council in the Marches in the same year.[62] Clocaenog Park was an investment and the initial outlay was offset slightly by the opportunity to sell on parcels of land to existing tenants, associates and relatives. For example, a month after buying Clocaenog, John Salesbury sold some tenements held by Richard Thelwall to Simon Thelwall

---

[59] A. N. Palmer, 'The portionary churches of mediaeval north Wales', *Archaeologia Cambrensis*, 5th series, 3 (1886), 175–209; Huw Pryce, 'The medieval church', in J. Beverley Smith and Llinos Beverley Smith (eds), *History of Merioneth: Vol. II – The Middle Ages* (Cardiff, 2001), pp. 261–2.
[60] TNA, WARD 9/103/82, f. 82v.
[61] NLW, Bachymbyd 543.
[62] TNA, C 1/1385/9.

and Richard himself for 50s.[63] In 1556, John and Piers sold three parcels of land to John Price of Derwen and a further four parcels of land to their first cousin, John Salesbury of Clocaenog.[64] Thus, when the brothers bought Clocaenog, they knew that there were tenants interested in buying their holdings; John Salesbury himself had inherited the lease of a pasture in Clocaenog from his father before purchasing the park.[65] However, the park was also a long-term investment for the Salesburys because they leased out holdings to tenants. In September 1555, for example, John leased fourteen acres in Clocaenog to a Foulk ap John, then in May 1556, he leased a tenement with three parcels of land to a Ieuan ap David ap Madog.[66]

Although it was a sensible purchase and possibly brokered by John's master, the earl of Pembroke, nothing survives to show how John and Piers funded the initial outlay. John made no further substantial purchases until the 1570s when he once again began to expand the Salesbury estates. On 13 July 1573, John leased the manor of Dinmael from Robert Dudley, earl of Leicester, for twenty-one years. In return for an annual rent of £5 2s. and John's best beast as heriot, John received the demesne and farmlands of Dinmael, the rents of the tenants, and all courts, services and liberties.[67] John also made a number of purchases with Henry Dynne of Heydon Hall, Norfolk, an auditor of the Exchequer. Henry Dynne had connections to the earl of Leicester; in 1569, for example, he heard an inquisition into the extent of Leicester's lands in Denbigh.[68] With Henry Dynne, John bought a significant amount of land scattered across Anglesey, Caernarfonshire, Merioneth and Montgomeryshire, some of which formerly belonged to the priory of Beddgelert.[69] Former monastic land was still influencing the market in north Wales thirty years after

[63] NLW, Bachymbyd 543; DRO, DD/WY/113.
[64] NLW, Bachymbyd 301; 364.
[65] NLW, Bachymbyd 527.
[66] NLW, Bachymbyd 178; 544.
[67] NLW, Bachymbyd 426.
[68] NLW, Bachymbyd 84.
[69] CRO, XD2/1337; NLW, Bachymbyd Letters 48.

the Dissolution; John and Dynne also bought land in Llanelltyd, Merioneth, which previously belonged to Cymer Abbey.[70] The involvement of noblemen in all John's major purchases may be a coincidence, but this is unlikely, and it suggests that the sixteenth-century Welsh gentry were aided by patrons in their acquisition of substantial landholdings. However, John's enthusiasm for buying and leasing land in the 1570s also suggests he had a good income. In 1568, John ventured into quarrying, acquiring a twenty-one-year lease for all the royal quarries in Anglesey, Caernarfonshire and Merioneth.[71] John paid a sizeable yearly rent of £10 3s. 4d, but clearly thought it a lucrative endeavour, and the expansion of the Salesburys holdings in the 1570s suggests that he was successful. On 25 April 1575, for example, he bought Segrwyd Park, Denbighshire, on the border of the Bachymbyd estate.[72] This was the year that John's second son was born, and John later bequeathed Segrwyd Park to him in his will; it is plausible that John bought the park, worth £60 per annum, to support his younger son.[73] John also extended the family's holdings in Glyndyfrdwy and Dinmael.[74]

When John Salesbury died in 1580, the Salesbury estates had expanded significantly from the original demesnes at Rhug and Bachymbyd. The family had land throughout the Vale of Clwyd, stretching from Ruthin in Denbighshire to the north, down to Corwen in Merioneth, then west through the Dee Valley towards Llangollen. They also had interests further afield near Dolgellau and Machynlleth, as well as stretches of ex-monastic land in Anglesey, Caernarfonshire and Montgomeryshire. The Salesburys were a successful Welsh gentry family, risen to become significant landowners with holdings though north Wales. For much of the sixteenth century, the Salesburys consolidated their original estates at Rhug and Bachymbyd and expanded their influence in their

[70] CRO, XD2/428.
[71] *CPR: Elizabeth I*, vol. 4, p. 232.
[72] NLW, Bachymbyd 18.
[73] TNA, PROB 11/63/70.
[74] CRO, XD2/953; XD2/1258.

main counties of Denbighshire and Merioneth. Partly this was due to good fortune, particularly their ability to take advantage of the availability of monastic land after the Dissolution, as well as their connections to powerful nobles like the earls of Pembroke and Leicester. However, it also depended on the skill and care of the family, particularly the paterfamilias, and the ability to make sound investments. In the absence of good financial management, there was no guarantee that a gentry family's estates would survive into the next generation. In fact, although John Salesbury left a prosperous and extensive patrimony to his thirteen-year-old son, the future Sir Robert (d. 1599), John's death heralded a prolonged period of crisis for the Salesbury estates which did not recover until his youngest son, William (d. 1660), inherited the patrimony and began to undo the mistakes of his older brothers.

Sir Robert Salesbury was not the most competent head of the Salesbury family. As we shall explore in chapter five, he was distracted by his attempts to achieve martial glory in Ireland, and the expense of soldiering meant he died with debts of over £1,000. This was partly the result of his early death, and there is evidence that he worked hard to make his estates more profitable.[75] His debts encumbered the estates, but they were manageable and a diligent gentleman could have recovered the situation. When Sir Robert Salesbury died in 1599, the estates passed to his infant son, John. Unfortunately, John held the estates for only a handful of years and he died, aged ten, on 1 January 1608.[76] The boy's uncle, John Salesbury, inherited the Salesbury patrimony and, in his four years as paterfamilias, he single-handedly almost ruined it. Within six months of his nephew's death, John borrowed £1,500 from a London goldsmith called John Williams, and he had spent the entire sum within four months.[77] John Williams refused to loan John a further £1,500 in early November 1608, but he agreed to a mortgage on John's Bachymbyd estate.[78] John

---

[75] See below, pp. 95–100.
[76] NLW, Bachymbyd 490.
[77] NLW, Bachymbyd 964; 719.
[78] NLW, Bachymbyd 720.

needed his younger brother's agreement as heir presumptive and William later claimed that he acquiesced only because John swore to redeem the mortgage. John promised that 'he would not for all the world suffer [Bachymbyd] to be forfeited'.[79]

However, John's financial issues continued. By December 1609, John had incurred further debts of £4,000 and William agreed to discharge them. In return, John granted him all his lands in Denbighshire, except Clocaenog Park and the mortgaged Bachymbyd estate. On 30 December 1609, the brothers entailed the Merioneth lands in William's name as John's heir presumptive and John promised to arrange a marriage between William and Margaret Salusbury, daughter of Thomas Salusbury of Lleweni, a wealthy heiress who inherited the Berain estate from her grandmother, Katherine of Berain.[80] John himself 'was fully resolved never to marie', thus guaranteeing that William would inherit the Salesbury patrimony.[81] This all suggests that, although John was profligate, he was still trying to keep the Salesbury estates together and protect his brother's inheritance. However, at some point between December 1609, when John granted land to William, and December 1611, when John died, he came under the influence of a group of local gentry who slowly obtained land and favour from him. William Salesbury related the events in two concurrent Chancery cases, one against the group of gentry and one against John Williams, the London moneylender. As a result, William presented John as a victim and the gentry as nefarious men and one stereotypically convenient, conniving woman who took advantage of him. However, as we shall see, it is also possible that these were John's friends, and John's actions were the result of them lending him money and requiring recompense.

John was an ill man in the final few years of his life. In the spring or summer of 1608, he became very sick and nearly died;

---

[79] NLW, Bachymbyd 719.
[80] NLW, Bachymbyd 514–15; NLW, Bachymbyd 719. For a recent study of Katherine of Berain, see Helen Williams-Ellis, 'Delweddu Catrin o Ferain Mewn Llun a Gair' (unpublished PhD thesis, Bangor University, 2020).
[81] NLW, Bachymbyd 719.

it may have damaged his health permanently or it may have been another episode of an extended illness.[82] John fell ill again after he mortgaged Bachymbyd in November 1608 and went to convalesce at the Salesburys' Pool Park estate, where they had a small farmhouse. However, at some point, he relocated to the home of John and Ellen Owen because Ellen offered to nurse him. William accused Ellen of working with her husband, as well as Piers Griffith of Penrhyn, Thomas Vaughan, John Wyn Salusbury and Piers Lloyd, to obtain John's land and money for themselves, knowing that John had recently received a large sum from the mortgage of Bachymbyd. At their behest, John sold lands worth £2,000 and gave the money to Ellen or some of the gentlemen. William also alleged that they poisoned John against his younger brother, who was not only John's heir but also the executor of his will. They told John that William 'loves not him . . . and that he had spoken words of disgust of the said John Salesbury touching him deeply in his reputacion'. When William visited, John refused to see him. John would not consent to the marriage between William and Margaret Salusbury of Lleweni, nor would he convey any lands to William.

On 15 November 1610, John leased a large proportion of his estate to Piers Griffith and John Owen for thirty years. William said that John blackmailed him into consenting to the lease, threatening to release the condition of redemption for Bachymbyd to John Williams, essentially selling Bachymbyd to the moneylender. John also said that he would disinherit William of the reversion of the leased land. William was not a witness to the lease, which John granted 'for and in consideration of the especial trust and Confidence which the said John Salusburie doth repose in the said Peirs [*sic*] Griffith and John Owen' and the sum of £10.[83] Piers Griffith and John Owen also promised to pay John's

---

[82] TNA, STAC 8/201/24.
[83] NLW, Bachymbyd 656. There is no year on the deed, but 1610 is likely, given the details in the Chancery suit.

debts, except the Bachymbyd mortgage and money owed to Sir John Conwy and Evan Lloyd of Bodidris.

John recovered from his bout of sickness. However, on 10 January 1611, he sold the condition of redemption to John Williams for £3,300 and gave the money to Piers Griffith. William Salesbury received none of the £7,000 received for the Bachymbyd mortgage and release, which was divided between John's friends. When John fell ill again, he changed his will and made Piers Griffith his sole executor. The codicils confirmed the validity of all John's leases and bargains, isolating a large proportion of the Salesbury estate for decades.

In the judgment of William's Chancery case, the Lord Chancellor said one lease was held in trust for Ellen and her children. William blamed Ellen and her associates for forcing John to change his will and claimed that they refused to allow John's friends to visit him when he was ill; Ellen said John was in no fit state to receive visitors. At John's death in December 1611, John Williams the moneylender owned Bachymbyd, William's widowed sister-in-law held the Rhug estate as her jointure, and Owen Lloyd had the lease of Pool Park. Owen Lloyd also had a lease of Bottegir, Denbighshire, for a thousand years and Piers Griffith leased Clocaenog Park. John had sold land worth £24 per annum in Trevalyn to Sir John Trevor of Trevalyn.[84] He had also leased a substantial amount of land in Uwchmynydd to their older sister, Margaret, for thirty-one years.[85] John Salesbury was a reckless and destructive paterfamilias who alienated almost all the Salesburys' landholdings from his heir's control. The Lord Chancellor, the Salesburys' patron Thomas Egerton, found in William's favour. In the final judgment, Egerton ruled that the defendants took advantage of John in his 'weakness and great Infirmytie' and that William Salesbury should receive the land leased to Piers Griffith and John Owen, the lease to which William consented under duress, 'as a younger brother upon pretence'.

---

[84] William outlined the state of his inheritance in NLW, Bachymbyd Letters 48.
[85] FRO, D/PT/397.

Egerton restricted Piers Griffith as executor of John's will to dispensing charitable bequests and adhering to legal suits brought in his name to recover John's personal estate.[86]

John may have been influenced by Ellen Owen and Piers Griffith, and the other gentry, who saw an opportunity to gain power over a sick and frail man. John may have been a victim, helpless to the machinations of people he believed were his friends. This is the story that William had to narrate in his Chancery suit because he wanted to secure his inheritance and thus he needed to demonstrate that the defendants maliciously conspired to deprive him of it and gain for themselves. Nevertheless, John's threats to William over the lease to Piers Griffith and John Owen suggest that John was not so helpless and he was willing to blackmail his younger brother. Given that the conditions of the lease included the responsibility to repay John's debts, it is likely that John felt he had no choice but to alienate parts of the Salesbury patrimony to deal with his spiralling debts. This also explains why he sold the condition of redemption in January 1611: because he needed the money. John could never control his profligacy; when he died, his debts included £80 owed to his tailor, demonstrating that not even the escalating damage to the Salesbury patrimony could curb his spending.[87] Far from being the stereotype of a conniving woman, Ellen Owen may well have been John's nurse in his illness, which was certainly debilitating, and which eventually killed him; the lease in trust for Ellen and her children was possibly recompense for her care, not the successful conclusion of Ellen's scheme. In *c.*1652, Godfrey Goodman, bishop of Gloucester, who knew the Salesbury family well, said that John Salesbury had 'loved Peirce Griffith as a brother'.[88] This suggests that William's nefarious plotters were actually John's friends. John himself caused the ruination of the Salesbury patrimony, and William, who once refused to serve in his older brother's company as a soldier, was bitterly aware of it.[89]

[86] NLW, Bachymbyd 720.
[87] NLW, Bachymbyd Letters 48.
[88] NLW, Bachymbyd Letters 47.
[89] NLW, Bachymbyd Letters 48.

William Salesbury did not repeat his older brothers' mistakes. He was an outstanding steward of the Salesbury patrimony and diligently pieced it back together after Sir Robert and John lost substantial landholdings. Although he never knew his father and could find no model paterfamilias in Sir Robert and John, William understood his responsibilities as the head of the Salesbury family. William's mission to reclaim his family estates required patience, determination and financial acumen. For example, on 2 July 1614, William won a suit in the Council in the Marches which granted him the reversion of estates which formerly belonged to the Priory of Beddgelert in Anglesey, Caernarfonshire, Merioneth and Montgomeryshire, the lands which William's father, John, had co-purchased in the 1570s with Henry Dynne of Heydon.[90] William also successfully challenged Richard Nanney in Chancery for holdings in Llanelltyd, Merioneth, another of the ex-monastic landholdings purchased by John Salesbury and Henry Dynne.[91] William's struggles highlight his brothers' failures as administrators of the Salesbury patrimony. Henry Dynne outlived John Salesbury and so Henry's heir, Frances, inherited all the land and sold parts of it to other people. If Sir Robert Salesbury had challenged Frances Dynne, the Salesburys would have retained their interest in the land and William could have avoided two expensive lawsuits.

William's greatest success, however, was reclaiming the Bachymbyd estate from the moneylender John Williams. The Chancery suit took three years and cost William £749 18s. 8d, 'besides losse of tyme and vexacion'.[92] The estate also became a major financial burden for William, which restricted his finances until the 1630s. Thomas Egerton, the Lord Chancellor, did his best to help William, but he could not overcome the facts of the suit: irrefutably, John Salesbury had mortgaged the estate and sold the redemption to John Williams. Egerton continually delayed

---

[90] CRO, XD2/1342–3.
[91] CRO, XD2/426–8.
[92] CRO, XD2/498.

proceedings until, as later related by Sir Edward Bagot, father-in-law of William's granddaughter Jane, John Williams, 'growing weary of it in a passion wished in court he had his money and the other his land'.[93] John Williams regretted his outburst, but the Lord Chancellor rapidly agreed to the compromise and warned the moneylender that 'he should not play Childrens play at fast and loose in the Court'. As a result, on 28 May 1614, the court required William to pay £6,800 to John Williams: £3,000 within three weeks and the remainder paid by 1 August 1615. In return, John Williams released Bachymbyd on 25 November 1615 and William once again owned Bachymbyd.[94] However, although William met some of the expense by selling lands worth £126 a year, William still needed to borrow £3,000. As a result, he mortgaged Bachymbyd almost immediately to cover the repayment costs, first to Richard Parry, bishop of St Asaph, in January 1616, then to Thomas Lloyd of Milton, Kent, in May 1619, then to the Denbighshire gentlemen Sir Bevis Thelwall, Sir Eubule Thelwall and John Thelwall on 1 October 1626.[95] Three months later, on 4 December 1626, the Thelwalls leased Bachymbyd to William for seven years and William never again mortgaged the estate, which suggests he finally repaid the money by 1633.[96]

Rescuing the Salesbury estates was a slow process. Although geographically the same estates as those held by his forefathers, William's estates were virtually of his own making. This perhaps explains his willingness to divide his holdings in the next generation between his sons; he felt less responsibility to maintain the ancestral estates when he had worked so hard to reclaim them. However, William's fiscal responsibility did not outweigh his loyalty to the king. Just a decade or so after finally repaying the mortgage on Bachymbyd, William once again endangered the Salesbury estates, through his participation in the Civil Wars of 1642–51. In November 1643, Charles I appointed William as governor

---

[93] NLW, Bachymbyd Letters 93.
[94] NLW, Bachymbyd 719.
[95] NLW, Bachymbyd 623; 641–3; 645; 491; Bachymbyd Letters 9b.
[96] NLW, Bachymbyd 975.

of Denbigh Castle and William only surrendered it at the king's express command in September 1646. For three years, William spent nearly £2,000 of his own money to supply his regiment with victuals and undertake repairs on the castle.[97] On the losing side at the end of the war, there was no one to fulfil Charles I's promise to recompense William for his efforts. Worse still, on 4 May 1647, William compounded £781 for his estate, which did not include Rhug because he had sold it to his son Owen in 1640.[98] Despite his years of financial stringency, William reached his mid-sixties with debts of £1,900 plus interest. In order to discharge the debt, William conveyed all his lands in Denbighshire, which included Bachymbyd, to his son Charles, and Charles paid William an annuity for life from the Denbighshire lands.[99] When William died on 19 June 1660, he left all his remaining lands and goods to Charles.[100] Bachymbyd and the Denbighshire holdings then passed to Jane Salesbury and her husband, Sir Walter Bagot.

Through William's elder son, Owen, the Salesbury family retained ownership of the Rhug estate. They were no longer Salesburys of Rhug and Bachymbyd, but Owen's marriage to Mary Goodman significantly enhanced the Salesbury patrimony. Mary was the heiress of both her father, Gabriel Goodman, and her uncle, Godfrey Goodman, bishop of Gloucester. As a result, the Salesburys acquired the substantial Goodman holdings in north Wales, primarily around Wrexham with a capital messuage at Trevalyn. These lands included the estate at Plas Issa, Wrexham, which Mary retained during her life, leasing it to a tenant with her mother.[101] When Owen Salesbury died in 1694, the family still held Plas Issa, but the inventory contains no mention of a house, only livestock; possibly they only farmed the demesne. The Trevalyn estate came to be used as jointure for the Salesbury wives,

---

[97] CRO, XD2/463.
[98] Mary Anne Everett Green (ed.), *Calendar, Committee for Compounding: Part 3* (London, 1891), p. 1723.
[99] NLW, Bachymbyd 321.
[100] DRO, DD/DM/1647, f. 26r; TNA, PROB 11/302/545.
[101] CRO, XD2/799; CRO, XD2/800.

replacing the function of the Pool Park estate in Denbighshire. For example, when Roger Salesbury married Jane, daughter of Howell Vaughan of Glanllyn, Merioneth, the marriage settlement conveyed the Trevalyn estate and Plas Issa in trust for Jane's jointure.[102] Thus, Owen Salesbury's marriage to Mary Goodman enabled the Salesbury family to retain a significant estate in north Wales, despite the loss of Bachymbyd. They still had the income from two holdings and their sphere of influence continued to extend across Merioneth and Denbighshire. As demonstrated by the Chancery suits between the Salesburys and the Bagots, the separation of Bachymbyd still rankled for the Salesburys of Rhug, particularly after it was inherited by Charles Salesbury's daughter, Jane, and they never identified as the Salesburys of Rhug and Trevalyn.[103] The division of Rhug and Bachymbyd attacked the Salesburys' pride and identity as a gentry family, but economically they continued to be a prosperous local family.

ESTATE INCOME

Despite forays into quarrying, the Salesburys primarily made their money from farming and rents. The estates were large enough and geographically varied enough to allow a diverse farming portfolio. In the lowland fields, it was possible to grow arable crops and, in a valuation of 1668, the Salesburys grew rye, wheat, oats and barley on their Rhug estate.[104] There was a dovecote and an orchard ('Y Berllan') on the demesne, as well as a hop-yard, demonstrating that the family engaged with the comparatively new crop of hops. Equally, there were rich pastures to support livestock, and the same valuation says that the Salesburys had seventy-eight cows, thirty-three pigs and eighteen horses, including two bay coach horses.[105]

[102] DRO, DD/WY/6521.
[103] TNA, C 5/447/83; C 5/446/5; C 10/173/11; C 5/550/32; C 5/446/195; C 8/202/58.
[104] CRO, XD2/1391.
[105] CRO, XD2/1391.

In 1668, the total value of produce from the Rhug demesne was £390 18s., but the cattle were easily the most valuable part of the business at £249 12s. Cattle were an important part of the local economy and it is likely that the Salesburys' ability to keep cows contributed significantly to their wealth.[106] In 1635, William Salesbury (d.1660) asked his son Owen to monitor the beef market in London, which suggests the Salesburys sold their cattle in the capital as part of the vibrant Welsh cattle trade with England.[107] Up on the hills, the Salesburys kept 289 sheep. The Salesburys valued their sheep primarily for wool; in 1621, William Salesbury, reflecting his personal interest in the Welsh wool trade, spoke in the House of Commons to object to the monopoly of Shropshire drapers.[108] The family also owned meadows to provide hay and woodland for timber, all of which could be sold. The timber rights were an important and valuable part of the estate; when William Salesbury sold Rhug to Owen in 1640, William kept the timber rights.[109] In 1668, two field names referenced saplings, or *gwiail*, so woodland management was a sustainable farming practice. Nevertheless, despite these glimmers of insight, the records for the Salesburys' estates are extremely patchy, with no surviving evidence for the Salesburys' farming interests before the seventeenth century. The level of debt charged on the estates when William Salesbury inherited in 1611 might suggest that the estates were not always especially lucrative, particularly when prices rose in the second half of the sixteenth century.[110] However, it is equally plausible that the head of the Salesbury family did not always live within his means and that the estates were reasonably prosperous. The Salesburys were not wealthy by the standards of many gentry families in England, but they were certainly comfortable within their own community in north Wales.

[106] Caroline Skeel, 'The cattle trade between Wales and England from the fifteenth to the nineteenth centuries', *Transactions of the Royal Historical Society*, 9 (1926), 135–41.
[107] NLW, Bachymbyd Letters 25.
[108] Simon Healy, *HPO (1604–1629)*: 'Salesbury, William (1580/1–1660)'.
[109] NLW, Bachymbyd 322–3; 516; 677.
[110] N. J. Mayhew, 'Prices in England, 1170–1750', *Past and Present*, 219 (2013), table 1.

In addition to farming their demesne, the Salesburys also received an income by leasing land to tenants. In 1583, the entire annual income of the Salesbury estates was £377.[111] The two demesnes at Rhug and Bachymbyd were worth £138 6s. 9d, so nearly two-thirds of the Salesburys' income in this period came from rents. However, this was a time of increasing economic pressure and the Salesburys and their estates were not immune to it. In the sixteenth century, the new idea of improvement came to describe attempts by landlords to increase the income of their estates by achieving the full market value in rent.[112] R. H. Tawney viewed improving landlords as rapacious extortionists, but more recent research has also recognised that farming needed to be more productive to increase the food supply for a growing population and an economy suffering from inflation.[113] Until the 1590s, there is no particular evidence that the Salesburys were improving landlords. In fact, their rental income was substantially lower than the potential market value. When John Salesbury died in 1580, the earl of Warwick, at John's request, bought the wardship of John's son and heir, the future Sir Robert. Warwick also undertook a valuation in 1583 of John's estates.[114] Warwick's agent predicted that the Salesbury estates could achieve an estimated yearly income of £602 if the land was properly exploited, a considerable increase on the £377 yearly income under John Salesbury. The problem was partly low rents and partly long leases. Many of the tenants held leases for multiple lives, restricting the Salesburys' ability to increase rents or change the terms of the tenancy, and even leases for years were for long periods: Thomas ap Thomas,

---

[111] CRO, XD2/1284.

[112] Paul Ward, 'The Idea of Improvement, c.1520–1700', in R. W. Hoyle (ed.), *Custom, Improvement and the Landscape in Early Modern Britain* (Farnham, 2011), pp. 127–48.

[113] R. H. Tawney, *The Agrarian Problem in the Sixteenth Century* (London, 1912; repr. Oxford, 1967), Part III, chapter one; Elizabeth Griffiths, 'Improving Landlords or Villains of the Peace?: A Case Study of Early Seventeenth-Century Norfolk', in Jane Whittle (ed.), *Landlords and Tenants in Britain, 1440–1660: Tawney's Agrarian Problem Revisited* (Woodbridge, 2013), p. 166.

[114] CRO, XD2/1834.

for example had forty-three years remaining on his lease of a fulling mill.

When Sir Robert Salesbury gained control of his inheritance, he followed the advice of his former guardian and worked to increase the income of the estates. In the 1590s, Sir Robert instructed an agent to compile a document which compared current rents with the market value of the tenancies on his estates.[115] There were significant discrepancies: for example, Evan ap Siôn Tudur held sixteen acres of arable land and two acres of woodland for 6s. 8d per annum, but it was valued at £4. Equally, Robert Wyn Salesbury held forty acres of arable land and three acres of meadow for £2 per annum, but it was valued at £20. Importantly, this exercise was not merely theoretical; it was part of a wider project which transformed the income of the Salesbury estates. Sir Robert died in 1599, and his administrators undertook another valuation of the Salesbury estates two years later, in 1601.[116] This shows that the income of the estates had risen from £377 to £707 12s. 1d, an increase of over £330, or 87.5 per cent. Even allowing for inflation, this was a considerable improvement. Rather than increasing the rents of existing tenants, the 1601 valuation suggests that Sir Robert took on new tenants who paid higher rents. Glyndyfrdwy provides a good example. In 1583, Warwick's agent noted that the fourteen tenancies at Glyndyfrdwy Park brought in £7 a year in rent, but were worth a potential £20 a year, once the existing leases expired and the tenants for life died. By 1601, the rental income from the park had increased to £26 10d a year; Sir Robert had implemented Warwick's advice and improved Glyndyfrdwy Park. Although there were still fourteen tenancies, the tenants themselves had all changed.

Some of the tenants may have died, but it is also probable that some tenants refused to renew their leases at the new rate. This raises the question of what happened to those previous tenants: maybe they leased multiple holdings from different landlords, so

---

[115] BL, Add. MS 14974, ff. 88r–99v.
[116] THL, Ellesmere MS 1782e.

the loss of the Salesbury tenancy had little effect on them; maybe they could obtain a cheaper lease elsewhere; or maybe they lost their primary income when they could not afford the new rent. However, the tenants were certainly not passive recipients of rent increases.[117] The 1590s valuation recorded that David Lloyd ap Robert held thirteen acres in Clocaenog and paid 5s. per annum for it. In 1601, David ap Robert still held land in Clocaenog and still paid 5s. for it, but his name was included with a list of five other tenants who were in dispute with Sir Robert over the amount of rent they paid. The tenants were able to make decisions about their leases and their holdings: in 1601, for example, David ap David had been a tenant for a year in Glyndyfrdwy where he paid £3 for a stretch of meadow, but he refused to renew the lease. In 1601, the administrators of Sir Robert's estate found that tenants took advantage of the uncertainty caused by Sir Robert's death by claiming to hold their land under more favourable terms. Symond ap Ellis, for example, admitted that he and his mother, Margaret ferch David, had paid Sir Robert and his brother John Salesbury £3 6s. 8d for their tenement, but he refused to pay it now because he claimed they were copyholders. Harry ap John Foulk leased one tenement from John Salesbury and paid an annual rent of £3; Harry said that he never paid more than 13s. 4d a year and 'refuceth to paie anie more'.

However, rent increases were not the only way that Sir Robert managed his tenancies. In 1583, Robert ap Thomas Vaughan was a tenant at will in Clocaenog, paying 13s. 4d a year in rent. A tenant at will was vulnerable to the vagaries of his or her landlord. However, in 1601, Robert ap Thomas Vaughan still held land in Clocaenog and he still paid rent of 13s. 4d, but now he had a fee farm lease. This new lease provided more security for the tenant, but it limited the landlord's ability to increase the rent, making the estate vulnerable to inflation over time. Nevertheless,

---

[117] See, for example, the resistance of customary tenants on the Hornby Castle estate, Lancashire, in Jennifer S. Holt, 'The financial rewards of winning the battle for secure customary tenure', in Whittle, *Landlords and Tenants in Britain*, pp. 133–49.

the fine to enter the lease would have provided some immediate income for the estate, suggesting that Sir Robert had to balance the competing priorities of cash flow with future income. Other tenants also converted their tenancies at will to tenancies by fee farm without increasing their rent payments, but even tenants at will did not necessarily experience increased rents. For example, in 1583, William ap John and his wife were tenants at will, paying 19s. 8d. In 1601, William ap John lived alone, but he still held his tenancy at will and still paid 19s. 8d. Sir Robert evidently managed his relationship with his tenants and not always to the obvious benefit of the estates. Sir Robert significantly improved his estates, but he did not endeavour to extract as much money as possible from his tenants.

The ability of tenants to refuse to renew their leases or even refuse to pay their rents suggests that there were limits to Sir Robert's ability to make money from rent. Sir Robert's father had not improved his estate, but that still enabled him to make considerable expansions to his holdings, such as the lease of the manor of Dinmael and the purchase of ex-monastic land. Sir Robert's improvement activity was the direct result of the earl of Warwick's advice and Warwick was responding to the economic conditions in England. Given the trade connections with the border counties of Cheshire and Shropshire, as well as London, it is a reasonable assumption that the north Wales economy was influenced by England's, particularly the economies of the neighbouring English counties. However, there is also the possibility of notable difference. For example, the Salesbury estates did not experience the same demographic pressure as estates in England; the population was not increasing to the extent that it was restricting the amount of land available. In 1601, the administrators of the Salesbury estates decreased the rent of a vacant tenement in order to find tenants for it. Equally, they could not find any tenants willing to take on a particular holding on the Pool Park estate, so it remained part of the Salesbury demesne. This is a useful reminder that land is only worth what someone will pay for it, and clearly the Salesburys did not have a surplus of tenants at the turn of the seventeenth century.

The various rentals and valuations also fail to capture many of the personal relationships involved in the transactions and the fact that the tenants knew their landlord. For example, a Salesbury steward called Richard Worrall owned considerable amounts of land between 1583 and 1601 and he paid either no rent or peppercorn rents. However, Worrall was a valued member of the Salesbury household and a foster father to Sir Robert's two younger brothers.[118] The Salesbury paterfamilias was also constrained by the wills of his predecessors which remitted rents for loyal service. Sir Robert, for example, made various such decrees in his will, including that Robert Wyn Salesbury could hold the park at Bachymbyd while Sir Robert's heir was under age.[119] Immediate family also limited the profit that could be made on an estate. In the 1590s, William Salesbury, Sir Robert's youngest brother, paid no rent while he held Pool Park, which contained a farmhouse and nearly a thousand acres of land. In 1601, Sir Robert's middle brother, John, held a hay pasture and, if he did not want it again, it was reserved for Sir Robert's widow, Elinor, who needed it for her geldings. The head of the Salesbury family had responsibilities to his kin, servants and tenants, which meant he had to make considerations beyond the economic value of his estates.

Despite Sir Robert's successful improvement of the Salesbury estates, he did not bring about any sort of financial stability. In fact, the family entered a period of crisis which was not fully resolved until William Salesbury finally repaid the mortgage on Bachymbyd in the 1630s. Although living costs were higher in the early seventeenth century, the levels of debt created by Sir Robert and his brother John, coupled with the increased income of the estates, suggest that the two Salesbury patriarchs lived significantly

---

[118] John Salesbury (d.1611) left money to his foster father, Richard Worrall, in his will. TNA, PROB 11/118/503.
[119] TNA, PROB 11/96/125.

beyond their means. Both men were active as soldiers, but the debt demonstrates that they could not afford their lifestyles.[120] When the family no longer had a profligate paterfamilias, the estate income kept increasing. From the 1640s, the two estates were divided and no meaningful run of records exists for both Rhug and Bachymbyd to allow for any significant comparisons. However, in 1668, the Rhug demesne alone was worth approximately £556, excluding any rents from the rest of the estate.[121] When Owen Salesbury died in 1694, the value of the Rhug estate excluding the demesne was £545; these figures are twenty-six years apart, but it suggests that when Roger Salesbury inherited from his brother, the Rhug estate was worth over £1,000 a year.[122] In addition, this valuation does not take into account any income from the rest of the Salesbury holdings, which included the substantial Goodman land around Wrexham. At the same time, there was a general understanding that the Salesburys as landlords kept rents low. In the Chancery suit over the portions of Elizabeth and Margaret Salesbury, a number of depositions claimed that Roger Salesbury had not increased the rents when he inherited from his brother Owen, and this was agreed by deponents for both sides. Thomas Foulk, who worked as an agent for Roger Salesbury in 1695, said that he had heard from 'severall persons that the family of Ruge never used to enhance their rents but suffered their tenants to hold and enjoy their lands att the old and accustomed rents'.[123] The Salesburys increased their income from their estates, but they were widely considered to be fair landlords.

By 1685, the Bachymbyd estate belonged to William Salesbury's granddaughter, Jane Salesbury, and her husband, Sir Walter Bagot. Bachymbyd alone now had a rental income of £673 8s. 9d, almost the same amount as the two Salesbury estates combined in 1601. This does not include the value of

[120] Rhys Morgan, *The Welsh and the Shaping of Modern Ireland, 1558–1641* (Woodbridge, 2014), pp. 114, 193.
[121] CRO, XD2/1391. The document is damaged, preventing more accurate calculations.
[122] TNA, C 22/1005/53.
[123] TNA, C 22/1005/53.

the demesne and it is plausible that Bachymbyd was also worth over £1,000 a year; at the turn of the seventeenth century, Bachymbyd's demesne was larger and more valuable than Rhug's. As with Rhug, this amount does not account for the Bagots' estate at Blithfield Hall, Staffordshire, or any of their other holdings and it is likely that the family's income was much higher. Thus, by the end of the seventeenth century, Rhug and Bachymbyd were worth over £2,000 a year and played a key part in supporting two gentry families, the Salesburys and the Bagots. This was a remarkable survival, given the turmoil of the early seventeenth century, when the family temporarily lost Bachymbyd and William Salesbury had an annual income of only £34. By the end of the seventeenth century, the Salesburys had wealth and they were a secure landed gentry family. Bachymbyd remained part of the Bagot family's estates until the family sold it during the agricultural recession of the nineteenth century. The new owners cultivated the land for timber, before it was redeveloped by a new family as a dairy farm, which still exists today. Rhug remained an agricultural estate, bequeathed by Elizabeth Salesbury's granddaughter, Maria Charlotta Pugh (d.1780), to her cousin, Colonel Edward Williames Vaughan (d.1807), before passing to the Wynn family in the nineteenth century, who eventually reinvented the estate in the twenty-first century as an organic farming enterprise.[124]

HOUSES

The Salesbury estates were also the family's home. There are sufficient early modern gentry houses still standing in north Wales to appreciate that they were large and imposing buildings with numerous decorative references to the family's status and identity. They include Gwydir Castle, Llanrwst; Plas Mawr, Conwy; Vaenol Old Hall, Y Felinheli; Nantclwyd y Dre, Ruthin; Plas Coch, Llanedwen; Mostyn Hall, Mostyn; Cors y Gedol Hall,

---

[124] See Rhug Estate at *https://rhug.co.uk* (accessed 14 April 2022).

Dyffryn Ardudwy; and Plas Rhiwaedog, Bala. Unfortunately, none of the original Salesbury houses survive: the current house at Rhug was built in the early nineteenth century and Charles Salesbury (d.1666) completed the construction of a new house at Bachymbyd in the year of his death. The house at Pool Park, the estate traditionally used to provide a jointure for the Salesbury wives, was also demolished and rebuilt in the nineteenth century. However, it is still possible to build a picture of how the Salesburys lived and how their homes reflected their status as a gentry family. Early modern Wales was a place of architectural change as the Welsh gentry, with some regional differences, began to draw on Renaissance fashions and emphasise the front of the house, building storeyed houses instead of medieval hall-houses.[125] Sometimes the gentry constructed new houses, like Sir Richard Clough (*c.*1530–70), who built Plas Clough and Bachegraig in 1567 when he married Katherine of Berain, but other houses, such as Gwydir Castle, developed gradually, a reflection of the family's time, money and inclination.

The earliest recorded building in the vicinity of the house at Rhug was a motte-and-bailey castle, called the castle of Edeirnion in 1160. It has been extensively studied by the Royal Commission on the Ancient and Historical Monuments of Wales and subject to archaeological digs since the nineteenth century.[126] The motte, however, utilised a prehistoric funerary monument, which the Salesburys incorporated much later into the design of their garden. The original house at Rhug grew around a medieval hall-house, built adjacent to the castle. Thus, Rhug shared similarities with other *plastai* in Merioneth which were also built near castles, such as nearby Crogen; it may suggest that elite houses could be unfortified because the castle provided protection or, which is

---

[125] Peter Smith, *Houses of the Welsh Countryside: A study in historical geography* (London, 1975), pp. 228–31; Mark Baker, 'The development of the Welsh country house' (unpublished PhD thesis, Cardiff University, 2015), 86–91.

[126] RCAHMW, 'Rug Castle Mount and Prehistoric Funerary Monument', available at *https://coflein.govx.uk/en/site/306598?term=rug%20mound* (accessed 29 March 2022). Today, the mound is a scheduled monument, but in the nineteenth century the estate used it as an ice-house.

more likely, the need for a fortified home was no longer necessary. The Salesburys occupied a landscape that had been inhabited for millennia; in addition to the prehistoric mound, the hills above the house contained the Iron Age hillfort of Caer Drewyn. Giving a fleeting insight into how the Salesburys might have viewed the ancient structures in their vicinity, the first recorded mention of the site comes from around 1600 and claims that the fort was built by a giant called Drewyn Gawr.[127]

In addition to the medieval core of the house, Rhug also had numerous extensions, added at different times. This suggests that the Salesburys generally followed the approach of the Wynns of Gwydir, rather than Sir Richard Clough, and extended their houses when they had the money and inclination. A 1601 inventory confirms the existence of the hall, with a high and low parlour on either side, and a great chamber upstairs, as well as the sprawling rooms and buildings around the central core.[128] The earliest pictorial evidence for the Salesburys' houses survives from the eighteenth century and the images reflect the ramshackle design implied by the inventory.[129] With all the extensions, the Salesburys' house at Rhug was very large, reflecting the desire for a *plasty* to be an impressive building, but also representative of the size of the household it supported and the need for outbuildings, such as the family's brewhouse, dairy house, granary and stables, in addition to living space. The house overlooked a small lake, used for boating in the eighteenth century, but also valuable for keeping fish. The interior of the house was also luxurious. In 1601, the family lived at Bachymbyd rather than Rhug. However, the house at Rhug still contained eight bedsteads and truckle beds, including four expensive feather mattresses. There were also blankets, quilts, pillows, bolsters, tables, chests, cupboards, and chairs with velvet seats and embroidered backs. The great chamber had four

[127] RCAHMW, 'Caer Drewyn', available at *https://coflein.gov.uk/en/site/95431/* (accessed 29 March 2022).
[128] THL, Ellesmere MS 1782g.
[129] H.W.L., 'Old Rûg', *Archaeologia Cambrensis*, 5th series, 4 (1887), plate; CRO, XD2/3913; Thomas Pennant, *A Tour in Wales*, vol. 6 (London, 1781), p. 68/2.

framed maps and pictures. When Owen Salesbury died in 1694, the standard of living had increased further.[130] The master of the house had a four-poster bed worth £30, and even the maids' chamber contained four bedsteads with feather mattresses and nine blankets. The high or great parlour contained seven framed pictures and two unframed pictures, while the passageway had pictures and maps. The study, used as a storeroom in the 1601 inventory for Rhug, contained 609 books 'of all sorts'. Rhug was a very comfortable house. The family were surrounded by decorative items such as wall-hangings, rugs and embroidered cushions; they ate well on stores of meat, grain and beer; and they kept warm in winter with fireplaces, warming pans and lots of blankets.

When Charles Salesbury inherited Bachymbyd, he built a new house on the site. However, although the new house was constructed in a fashionable style and made of brick, the fact that Charles kept the old house as additional space across the courtyard implies that the family also needed more room. The older building does not survive today, but it is visible in a watercolour painting by Moses Griffiths for Thomas Pennant's *A Tour in Wales* (London, 1781).[131] One of the chimneys is located where a cross-passage would be found, suggesting that Bachymbyd also originated as a medieval hall-house. The 1601 inventory duly records that Bachymbyd had a hall and a parlour, as well as a chamber over the parlour. Like Rhug, Bachymbyd also had a number of outbuildings, including a dairy, a brewhouse, a stable and a fifteenth-century barn, the only building described which still survives today.[132] There was also a 'New Building', which contained a hall, two chambers, a parlour, a kitchen, a little larder and an empty room, thus the family had, at some point, already tried to expand the house at Bachymbyd, but all the cooking equipment was in the main house. The resident family was quite small at the time of the inventory;

---

[130] TNA, C 6/474/15.
[131] Pennant, *Tour in Wales*, p. 58/2.
[132] Cadw, 'Reference No. 22147: T-shaped Agricultural Range at Bachymbyd Fawr', Full Report for Listed Buildings, available at *https://cadwpublic-api.azurewebsites.net/reports/listedbuilding/FullReport?lang=&id=22147* (accessed 29 March 2022).

only Elinor Bagnall and her young son lived permanently at Bachymbyd. However, they still had a high standard of living. For entertainment, there was an Irish harp in the parlour and an old pair of playing tables in the hall. Upstairs, the main bedchamber contained a four-poster bed with red and green curtains and there was a window seat covered with red silk. Altogether, there were nineteen beds or mattresses, including eleven feather beds, to support a large household. They had quilts, blankets, tablecloths, embroidered cushions, and carpets. Fifteen candlesticks provided light into the evenings and enabled the household to extend its activities past daylight hours.

The Salesburys' third house was at their Pool Park estate. This was not a main family residence as it was primarily reserved for Salesbury widows. Pool Park, rather than Bachymbyd, became the main Welsh estate for the Bagot family after they inherited the Salesburys' Denbighshire lands through Sir Walter Bagot's marriage to Jane Salesbury, and the house at Pool Park was demolished and rebuilt in 1826–9 by William Bagot (1773–1856), second Lord Bagot. However, once again, an image of the Salesburys' house survives in a painting by Moses Griffiths for Thomas Pennant's *A Tour in Wales*.[133] In the eighteenth century, Pool Park was a large and extensive house, reflecting the Bagots' investment in the jointure estate. However, the original core of the house was built with typical Tudor rectangular windows, which corresponds to the purchase of Pool Park by Robert Salesbury and Katherine ferch Ieuan on 11 July 1545.[134] The bargain and sale does not include a dwelling place, though it specifies them at other lands purchased in the same deed. Thus, Robert and Katherine, or Robert's heir, John, built a small house at Pool Park. The 1601 inventory shows that it had a parlour, chamber and a buttery downstairs, but no hall, and two chambers and a loft over the porch upstairs.[135] There was also a kitchen in a

---

[133] Pennant, *A Tour in Wales*, vol. 6, p. 58/2.
[134] NLW, Bachymbyd 527.
[135] THL, Ellesmere MS 1782g.

separate building with two chambers attached. In 1613, William Salesbury described Pool Park as a 'litle farme house'; its use as a farm is supported by the 1601 inventory, which says the demesne contained fifty-eight sheep, four horses, a family of peacocks, and 5,600 faggots, suggesting significant woodlands.[136]

For almost all the seventeenth century, Pool Park was used as a jointure for Salesbury widows: first, Elinor Bagnall (d.1656), wife of Sir Robert Salesbury (d.1599), then Elizabeth Thelwall (d.1693), wife of Charles Salesbury (d.1666). During Elinor's widowhood, Pool Park was primarily used to provide an annuity for Elinor; in the 1640s, Elinor complained to the commissioners of array for Cheshire, Denbighshire and Flintshire that William Salesbury had not paid her annuity because he claimed he needed the money for the war effort.[137] However, after Elizabeth Salesbury died in 1693, the inventory of her estate shows that Pool Park had undergone a significant transformation.[138] It now contained a hall and hall chamber, a parlour and parlour chamber, a study, a garden room, and various other chambers used as bedrooms. There was a gateway with accommodation either side and numerous service buildings, including a larder, buttery, dairy, kitchen, brewhouse, slaughterhouse, washhouse and henhouse, as well as two granaries and a barn. These agricultural buildings supported a significant increase in the demesne: the livestock now included fifty-eight cattle, two bulls, eight oxen, six mares, sixteen pigs and 262 sheep, valued at £205 9s., almost half the total value of the inventory of £449 14s. The description of the house more closely matches the depiction of Pool Park in Moses Griffiths's watercolour; it is large and sprawling, a country house which corresponded with the reputation of the Salesbury and Bagot families. Once again, the inventory shows the high standard of living enjoyed by the family: Elizabeth had a mirror, two pictures, and a 'grate fire'

---

[136] NLW, Bachymbyd 720; THL, Ellesmere MS 1782g.
[137] NLW, Bachymbyd Letters 37.
[138] NLW, Bachymbyd 251–3.

in the parlour; a 'large Welsh Bible' and a Book of Common Prayer in the hall, and outside there was a coach and chariot, as well as harnesses for four horses. In one of the garrets, Elizabeth kept old trunks and chests filled with tablecloths, napkins, sheets and pillowcases. It was a spacious and comfortable home.

The Salesbury houses, like the Salesbury estates, were not static and there was significant change over time. In the earliest decades of the Salesburys' tenure at Rhug and Bachymbyd, they lived in medieval hall-houses, but, as the family's income grew, their houses grew with them. This reflected the fashions of the day, but also the need for a gentleman's house to reflect his status in society. The *plastai* were the nuclei of the Welsh gentry's spheres of influence, places where they administered their estates, distributed hospitality, and lived with their families. As the surviving *plastai* in north Wales show, the gentry's houses were impressive and imposing buildings which enabled the gentry to fulfil their function as governors of their local community. The family did not always need so much space; in 1601, only Bachymbyd was occupied and Rhug was used for storage. However, the houses also connected the Salesburys with past and future generations; the paterfamilias grew up in those houses and he lived there with his wife, raising their children together, ideally keeping the estates profitable so that the family could survive long into the future. The Salesburys had a high standard of living which must have contrasted with the poverty that surrounded them; the family supported almshouses and gave money to the poor in their wills.[139] However, the feather beds, the tableware for large numbers of guests, the candlesticks and the decorative furnishings also demonstrated the Salesburys' status and emphasised that they were a gentry family. They lived in their ancestral houses on their ancestral estates and benefited from their ancestors' accumulated holdings and wealth.

[139] DRO, PD/90/5/9.

CONCLUSION

In early modern Wales, landed estates became key drivers of the Welsh economy. They brought gentry families significant wealth, even though their estates were often smaller and less profitable than gentry estates in England. However, estates were also cultural and social centres. The gentry's *plastai* were fulcrums of the local communities, places of administration where the gentry interacted with their tenants, but also places of hospitality where tenants could expect to receive food and entertainment on allocated days of the year. Estates needed tenants and labourers to be profitable and they were not passive entities docilely willing to accept the orders of their landlord; estates were living places of interpersonal relationships. Through the provision of hospitality, the Welsh gentry cemented their network of tenants and kin, but also connections with their fellow gentry across north Wales and the English border counties. The Salesburys of Rhug and Bachymbyd understood the economic and cultural power conveyed by their estates. They were a vital part of their identity as a gentry family; the loss of Bachymbyd to the Bagots of Blithfield Hall was not about money, which was more than compensated by the Goodman holdings, but the intangible social and cultural qualities associated with owning the Salesburys' 'ancient Inherytaunce', as William Salesbury (d.1660) once called it when he was trying to piece together his father's patrimony.[140] The division of Rhug and Bachymbyd fundamentally changed the Salesburys' sense of self, even though they suffered no financial loss. In addition to wealth, landed estates brought their owners influence and cultural power, a valuable commodity in status-driven Welsh gentry society. The next chapter will explore how the Salesburys used their estates' sphere of influence to cultivate relationships with their tenants and servants, and how it brought them into the orbit of powerful, noble patrons.

---

[140] NLW, Bachymbyd 720.

3

NETWORKS OF POWER

As an elite gentry family, the Salesburys of Rhug and Bachymbyd were embedded in their local communities. Their two estates enabled them to hold positions of authority across Merioneth and Denbighshire and they were the lynchpins of their local network of power. At the same time, they were also part of national networks across England and Wales, woven into the web of noble influence which stretched over the realm. Noble patronage, as this chapter will show, could be a valuable commodity for a gentry family, enabling its members to gain power and depend on their patron's support. However, patronage could also be a source of tension in local communities, the cause of factionalism between elite families. At a local level, the Salesburys themselves were patrons, dispensing their favour and collecting their own band of loyal followers. This included tenants and labourers from their estates, as well as household servants, who could often be relied upon to support their masters when factionalism broke out, increasing the likelihood of violent disputes. This chapter examines how noble patrons influenced the Salesburys' lives, but it also looks at how the nobility affected the Salesburys' own communities. Noble patronage could be highly disruptive, heightening tensions between the gentry and their followers. The Welsh gentry were intensely status-driven and conscious of the need to promote and maintain their position in local society. Power and authority in early modern Wales, as elsewhere, was fundamentally about status. Factions developed when one family felt another threatened or usurped its position, with an inevitable domino effect as kinship and allegiance divided gentry society into different family groupings poised against each other. This chapter is largely about men: men who held public offices; men who followed noble patrons to war; men who engaged in violent brawls in the churchyard. However, as I have explored elsewhere, this does not mean that gentlewomen failed to care about their family's status, or their own personal position in society, but that they had different means of protecting their status and different standards for respectability.[1]

NOBLE PATRONAGE

The local lord, although not necessarily resident, could be a valuable patron for a gentry family, providing opportunities to gain offices and influences in the community. This could bring some measure of stability to the area, keeping control of the avaricious tendencies of local families. However, the nobility were also sources of disruption, establishing and maintaining rivalries between families which could last generations. The Salesburys of Rhug and Bachymbyd understood the complex relations which governed their world. Cultivating the favour of a noble patron brought the possibility of holding authority on their lord's behalf and obtaining a measure of power in the local community. In the earliest evidence for the Salesburys' service to the nobility, Piers Salesbury (d.1548) was steward of the lordship of Ruthin and thus a servant of Henry Fitzroy (1519–36), duke of Richmond and Somerset and lord of Ruthin. Henry Fitzroy was the illegitimate son of Henry VIII and son-in-law to Thomas Howard, duke of Norfolk, a powerful patron for the Salesbury family. However, Fitzroy died in 1536 and Piers sent his condolences to Norfolk, 'for the dredffull losse' of 'my speciall goode lorde and master my lorde of Richmond'.[2] As a gift, Piers sent Norfolk a leash

---

[1] For an examination of behavioural standards for Welsh gentlewomen, see Jarrett, '"By reason of her sex and widowhood"', pp. 79–96.
[2] TNA, SP 1/105/251a.

of greyhounds, and Piers's son, Robert (d.1550), sent a leash of merlins to Norfolk's son, Henry Howard, earl of Surrey. Animals were an appropriate gift to a noble patron, emphasising loyal service.[3]

In 1536, the same year that Fitzroy died, the marcher lordships were absorbed into Wales's extended shire system. The Salesburys stayed associated with the stewardship of Ruthin, which, in effect, became a manor. However, in 1563, Elizabeth I granted the lordships of Denbigh and Chirk to Robert Dudley, earl of Leicester, and in 1564, she granted the lordship of Ruthin to his older brother, Ambrose Dudley, earl of Warwick, and their powers intentionally reflected those of a marcher lord.[4] John Salesbury (d.1580) was steward of Warwick's lordship of Ruthin, and John was loyal to his lord, or at least, he understood how to maintain his lord's favour. For example, during John's stewardship, Warwick sent an agent to enclose a common called Y Ffrith Faenol. Some of the tenants of the lordship attacked the agent, significantly damaging Warwick's relationship with his tenants. John persuaded the tenants to pay a collective annuity of £120 to Warwick and his wife, Anne, for the duration of their lives.[5] The incident shows not only Warwick's anger with the tenants, but John's power in the local community and his desire to retain Warwick's support. Remembering the incident many years later in an Exchequer case about the lordship, a deponent recalled that John was 'powerful . . . and of great kindred and alliance'.[6] John was also a tenant himself, almost certainly subject to the same annuity, and it was in the lordship's interest to cultivate good relations with the lord. It was also in John's own interest. When John died in 1580 and his thirteen-year-old son, the future Sir Robert (d.1599), inherited the Salesbury estates, Warwick became Sir Robert's guardian. John wrote a letter on his deathbed to Anne, countess of Warwick, and

---

[3] Felicity Heal, *The Power of Gifts: Gift exchange in early modern England* (Oxford, 2014), p. 52.
[4] Simon Adams, *Leicester and the Court: Essays on Elizabethan politics* (Manchester, 2002), pp. 258, 295.
[5] TNA, E 134/16CHAS1/EAST13; E 134/16CHAS1/TRIN7.
[6] TNA, E 134/16CHAS1/EAST13.

Anne wrote a touching reply that she hoped John would live to see his son grow to be a man, but promised that her husband would endeavour to raise Sir Robert as John intended.[7] In John's last will and testament, and possibly in a response to Anne's letter that does not survive, John asked Warwick to grant Sir Robert's wardship to George Bromley, justice of Chester, and Warwick duly complied with John's request.[8] Warwick was a trustworthy and reliable patron and, as Anne promised, he followed John's wishes for his son's upbringing. Noble patronage came with benefits for the gentry, and John's 'faythfull and honest' service was rewarded by the knowledge that his patron would continue to protect his heir's interests.[9]

Individual patronage could thus give power, influence and a measure of security to a gentry family. However, noble patronage could also be a source of instability, particularly when families competed to earn the favour of the lord and factionalism developed. This was a problem throughout England and Wales. For example, sixteenth-century Sussex was dominated by the influence of noblemen such as Anthony Brown (1528–92), Viscount Montague, and Thomas Sackville (1536–1608), earl of Dorset, who promoted their own candidates to run the county administration, with ensuing complaints among other gentry families.[10] Equally, the execution of Thomas Howard, duke of Norfolk, in 1572 exposed fault lines in Norfolk society as the gentry competed amongst themselves for local offices and drew on long-standing grievances, capitalising on the sudden vacuum of leadership in the county.[11] The gentry of north Wales were similarly prone to divisive politics, often played out in the law

---

[7] NLW, Bachymbyd Letters 3. It was a valued letter in the family: William Salesbury (1580–1660) endorsed it as 'from the L. and lady Warwik to my Father upon his Death bedd'.

[8] TNA, PROB 11/63/70; NLW, Bachymbyd 983.

[9] NLW, Bachymbyd Letters 3.

[10] Anthony Fletcher, *A County Community in Peace and War: Sussex 1600–1660* (London, 1975), pp. 23–4.

[11] A. Hassell Smith, *County and Court: Government and Politics in Norfolk, 1558–1603* (Oxford, 1974), chapter nine.

courts of Ludlow and London, but also easily spilling over into violence. In the second half of the sixteenth century, for example, the Salesburys had an enduring rivalry with the Owens of Llwyn and the Prices of Rhiwlas and Plas Iolyn. In the early 1550s, the Merioneth parliamentary seat alternated between Lewis Owen of Llwyn and John Salesbury (d.1580), an early suggestion of rivalry between the two families. At the time of his election in 1553, John was a servant of William Herbert, earl of Pembroke, who was also president of the Council in the Marches, a sufficiently powerful patron to help John secure the seat.[12] The Salesburys were not alone in their dislike for the Owen and Price faction; Lewis Owen, when sheriff of Merioneth in 1555, was murdered by bandits from the lordship of Mawddwy, the so-called 'Red Bandits of Mawddwy', in retaliation for Owen's efforts to prevent crime in the county.[13] The Owens and Prices held all the major offices in Merioneth, a problem for Merioneth families who wanted access to the status and influence of officeholding, but less problematic for the Salesburys, who had their second estate at Bachymbyd in Denbighshire.[14] John Salesbury was close to his powerful cousins, the Salusburys of Lleweni, who had considerable influence in Denbighshire politics, and John married Elizabeth, the daughter of Sir John Salusbury of Lleweni. John was able to access public offices in Denbighshire, holding Denbigh Boroughs in April 1554 and January 1558, and the shire seat in January 1559.[15] Officeholding was a key indicator of gentility in early modern England and Wales, but it had additional importance for the Welsh gentry, who were historically restricted in the offices they could hold.[16]

---

[12] TNA, C 1/1385/9.

[13] John Gwynfor Jones, 'Lewis Owen, sheriff of Merioneth, and the "Gwylliaid Cochion" of Mawddwy in 1554–55', *Journal of the Merioneth Historical and Record Society*, 12 (1994–7), 221–40.

[14] H. G. Owen, 'Family politics in Elizabethan Merionethshire', *BBCS*, 18/2 (1959), 86–91.

[15] P. S. Edwards, *HPO (c.1509–58)*: 'Salesbury, John (1533–1580)'.

[16] See Jarrett, 'Officeholding and local politics in early modern Wales', 206–32.

However, the introduction of the Dudley brothers into north Wales politics caused significant disruption. Robert Dudley, earl of Leicester, supported the Owen and Price faction: he appointed Dr Ellis Price of Plas Iolyn as his steward, cementing the families' power in Merioneth. Eventually, Price's ambitions were rewarded with an appointment to the Council in the Marches.[17] With the stewardship of Denbigh, Price also gained considerable influence over other gentry families. For example, Leicester was made chief forester of the Forest of Snowdon, a position he exploited for financial gain by investigating encroachments into the Forest by families illegally obtaining more land, and it was Price who oversaw Leicester's investigation.[18] It highlights the dilemma facing gentry families who needed to protect their own lands and interests, but did not want to alienate a powerful nobleman. The Salesburys doubtless disliked the power granted to their rival, but they could not risk offending Leicester, firstly because of his position, but also because of his fraternal relationship to the Salesburys' own lord, the earl of Warwick. For example, in 1566, Sir John Salusbury of Lleweni, Dr Ellis Price and Robert Wyn Cadwallader were the commissioners in an inquiry into the rents paid in the old marcher lordship of Denbigh, and John Salesbury of Rhug and Bachymbyd was the leader of the jury.[19] John and Ellis Price were also commissioners at the 1567 Caerwys eisteddfod, and the Council in the Marches named them in a miscellaneous commission of 1570, an appointment they shared with Sir John Salusbury of Lleweni and John Lloyd of Bodidris.[20]

[17] Penry Williams, *The Council in the Marches of Wales under Elizabeth I* (Cardiff, 1958), p. 274.
[18] Madeleine Gray, 'Power, patronage and politics: office-holding and administration on the Crown's estate in Wales', in R. W. Hoyle (ed.), *The Estates of the English Crown, 1558–1640* (Cambridge, 1992), p. 150; E. D. Evans, 'Politics and parliamentary representation in Merioneth, 1536–1644: Part 1', *Journal of the Merioneth Historical and Record Society*, 15 (2006), 14.
[19] NLW, Gogerddan LB2/1.
[20] HMC, *Report on Manuscripts in the Welsh Language*, vol. 1 (London, 1898), pp. 291–2; Ralph Flenley, *A Calendar of the Register of the Queen's Majesty's Council in the Dominion and Principality of Wales and the Marches of the Same [1535] 1569–1591 from the Bodley MS. no. 904* (London, 1916), p. 69.

The latter two men were close associates of John; no doubt Sir John's power aided his son-in-law's ambitions to hold local offices, and John's daughter, Margaret, married the grandson of John Lloyd of Bodidris. John Salesbury had protection and support in Denbighshire and he was able to work with Dr Ellis Price when it was in his own interest.

In Merioneth, the situation was more fraught. In 1571, John Salesbury stood against Hugh Owen of Caerberllan, the son of Lewis Owen, the murdered sheriff, whose candidacy Ellis Price supported. The very existence of a contested election shows the extent of the disagreement between the parties; the selection of a candidate could be contentious and riddled with corruption, but the gentry usually agreed on the new MP before the election was held.[21] Crucially, the Welsh gentry coveted the office of MP; it had been introduced in Wales by the Acts of Union and families soon viewed it as one of the most superior of the county offices.[22] When John stood against Hugh Owen, it would have already been clear from the early negotiations that Owen would win the seat, but John evidently wanted to make his opposition to Owen especially public. On the face of it, this was a dispute between gentry families. However, it also encompassed the earl of Leicester as the local lord, and Owen and Price's faction felt they had the upper hand. The election dispute was part of an ongoing disagreement about the lease of the township of Dolgellau, Merioneth. Ellis Price's associate, John Owen, granted the lease to Price's nephew, Hugh Lloyd, who was also one of Leicester's servants. In the meantime, one Sir Robert Constable bought the lease and gave half of it to John Salesbury. Ellis Price complained to Leicester that John Salesbury hired Constable to buy the lease on his behalf: Constable used 'some malicous procurement'.[23]

---

[21] Emyr Gwynne Jones, 'Country politics and electioneering 1558–1625', *Transactions of the Caernarvonshire Historical Society*, 1 (1939), 37–46.
[22] J. E. Neale, 'Three Elizabethan elections', *EHR*, 46 (1931), 211.
[23] Dudley Papers II/307, in G. Dyfnallt Owen, *Calendar of the Manuscripts of the Most Honourable The Marquess of Bath*, vol. 5: *Talbot, Dudley and Devereux Papers 1533–1659* (London, 1980), pp. 188–9.

Price said that John resented him and his friends for their success in the parliamentary election, and that John Salesbury, 'as is not unknowen in England and Wales, hath of long tyme, as also of late, bourne unto me malice and displeasure and to my ffrend John Owen'. The gentry families of Merioneth were already prone to rivalry as they competed for status, land and a finite number of offices. Leicester's arrival in 1563 introduced a new layer of factionalism into north Wales politics as his patronage secured certain families, namely the Owens and the Prices in Merioneth, dominance over their rivals.

The factionalism caused by Leicester even destroyed the relationship between the Salesburys and their cousins at Lleweni, despite the marriage of John Salesbury to Elizabeth Salusbury of Lleweni and the close support of John's father-in-law for his career. The Salusburys of Lleweni resented how Leicester's agents dominated local offices, to the extent that this influenced the decision of the eldest son of the family, Thomas Salusbury, to participate in the 1586 Babington Plot, a failed attempt to secure the English throne for Mary, Queen of Scots.[24] Thomas Salusbury was arrested and executed for treason in September 1586. By this point, John Salesbury had been dead for eight years and his eldest son and heir, Sir Robert, was nineteen, enrolled at Gray's Inn as a law student, and about to participate as MP for Denbighshire in the October 1586 Parliament. The Salesburys of Rhug and Bachymbyd, loyal to Warwick and thus also loyal to his brother, Leicester, were manoeuvring for power just as the Salusburys of Lleweni were disgraced by their own heir. However, the earl of Leicester died in 1588 and the earl of Warwick in 1590. The noblemen's absence created a vacuum in local politics, which the Salusburys of Lleweni desperately wanted to fill in order to repair their damaged reputation. Thomas Salusbury's younger brother, the future Sir John Salusbury (c. 1565–1612), succeeded him as the Salusbury heir and, in a concerted effort to demonstrate his

---

[24] Adams, *Leicester and the Court*, p. 304.

own loyalty to the Crown, he sought to prove himself as a diligent public officer.

Emphasising the importance placed on officeholding by the Welsh gentry, Sir John's ambitions brought him into conflict with his first cousin, Sir Robert Salesbury. Notably, Sir Robert's father had held the position of alderman in 1579–80 in the borough of Denbigh, but Sir Robert himself did not hold any offices in the borough, only county offices.[25] The loss of Leicester's and Warwick's patronage affected the Salesburys' ability to obtain local offices. As a result, Sir Robert instigated a campaign against his cousin to restrict his officeholding. In 1598, according to a letter sent by one John Lloyd Rossendale to Sir John Salusbury, Sir Robert went to dinner at Greenwich Palace with the Lord Keeper Thomas Egerton, an influential patron in north Wales society; Sir Thomas Myddelton (*c*.1556–1631), a north Wales merchant with political ambitions of his own; Thomas Sackville, Lord Buckhurst; and Sir John Fortescue, Chancellor of the Exchequer.[26] Apparently, the men plotted a letter-writing campaign to ruin Sir John Salusbury's reputation; Rossendale said that 'ther maleice still encresith more venemus then the stinge of aders', and they wanted to remove him as a Justice of the Peace and prevent him from becoming Deputy Lieutenant. If true, Sir John Salusbury had powerful enemies and Sir Robert had powerful friends, although Sir John continued as a Justice of the Peace and became Deputy Lieutenant in 1602.[27] At the same time, it is difficult to understand the extent to which personal feelings influenced gentry factionalism. Sir Robert's father had been a close ally of the Salusburys of Lleweni and the family were equally not free of Leicester's patronage; the ill-fated Thomas Salusbury had been Leicester's ward. The fractious atmosphere and the jostling for position among the north Wales gentry was a source of animosity between families.

---

[25] Adams, *Leicester and the Court*, Table 4.2, pp. 300–1.
[26] NLW, Lleweni 23, in Smith, *Salusbury Correspondence*, pp. 38–9.
[27] A. H. Dodd, *HPO (1558–1603)*: 'Salusbury, Sir John (*c*.1565–1612)'.

As Sir Robert's dinner at Greenwich highlights, the Salesburys continued to court noble patrons after Warwick's death. In particular, the Salesburys obtained the favour of Thomas Egerton (1540–1617), who became Baron Ellesmere in 1603. Ellesmere supported numerous gentry families across north Wales, Cheshire and the Marches, including the Breretons, Grosvenors, Pulestons, Mostyns and Ravenscrofts.[28] Ellesmere was also closely involved with the Salesburys and he knew their business well; he was a commissioner at the inquisition post mortem of John Salesbury (1533–80).[29] John's son, Sir Robert, attended Brasenose College, Oxford, which happened to be Ellesmere's old college; Ellesmere's influence in Sir Robert's life may well be apparent here, because no other Salesbury attended Brasenose and Ellesmere was an enthusiastic supporter of the college and its members.[30] Egerton was an evangelical Protestant, particularly committed to supporting preachers, anti-Catholic scholars and Calvinist theologians, and the gentry families who received his patronage shared his religious and political views.[31] It is thus unsurprising that he disliked the Salusburys of Lleweni, tarred by their association with a Catholic plot to unseat the queen, and thus supported Sir Robert Salesbury against them. Factionalism was thus tied into the confessional politics which, as Peter Lake has argued, developed in England after the Reformation.[32] The gentry of north Wales, however, did not necessarily form their allegiances along religious lines and Sarah Ward Clavier has proposed that the Welsh gentry were more inclined to trust Catholics than Puritans.[33] Thus, they did not follow what Lake calls the 'conventional view' that

---

[28] Louis A. Knafla, 'The "County Chancellor": The patronage of Thomas Egerton, Baron Ellesmere', in French R. Fogle and Louis A. Knafla (eds), *Patronage in Late Renaissance England* (Los Angeles, 1983), pp. 66–8.

[29] TNA, WARD 7/20/173.

[30] *Al. Oxon*; Knafla, 'The "County Chancellor"', p. 55.

[31] Knafla, 'The "County Chancellor"', pp. 40–7.

[32] Peter Lake, 'Post-Reformation Politics, or on Not Looking for the Long-Term Causes of the English Civil War', in Michael J. Braddick (ed.), *The Oxford Handbook of the English Revolution* (Oxford, 2015), pp. 21–40.

[33] Clavier, *Royalism*, pp. 115–16.

Catholicism was more dangerous.[34] The Welsh gentry's tolerance for Catholicism will be discussed in the next chapter, but the example of Ellesmere's patronage highlights the close relationship between religion and politics in early modern Britain.[35]

Mirroring the earl of Warwick's relationship with John Salesbury, Ellesmere protected the Salesburys' interests after Sir Robert's death in 1599. Sir Robert's last will and testament asked Egerton to oversee the executors of his will and administer the annuities granted to Sir Robert's younger brothers, John and William.[36] Three months after Sir Robert's death, John and William petitioned Egerton for their money: 'our meanes are but weak and our expenc is great . . . it will please your honore to remember our brothers wille for our maintenance during the mynoritye of our nephye and afterwards'.[37] The Salesbury brothers succeeded in their petition because John and William continued to live at Bachymbyd and a rental of 6 April 1601 says that Bachymbyd had never been let, implying that they did not pay rent and the brothers were not considered tenants.[38] In the rental, multiple tenants held land from John Salesbury, including Thomas ap Robert Matthew, Robert ap Robert and Harry Lloyd. John also held the seven acres of Dol yr Ychen, the small meadow, in the demesne of Bachymbyd, but 'if he hath noe use for it this yeere', then it would be rented by David Salesbury and Ieuan ap Harry, the former tenants. When John Salesbury was imprisoned in the Marshalsea for his involvement in the Essex Revolt, he complained to Robert Cecil 'that the Lord Keeper [Egerton], from whom he derives his chief maintenance, takes occasion upon this his restraint, to restrain him from the benefit [of his late brother's will]'. John worried that, without his freedom, his friends would be discouraged and fail to ensure that Egerton performed

---

[34] Lake, 'Post-Reformation Politics', p. 25.
[35] See below, pp. 187, 190–3.
[36] TNA, PROB 11/96/125.
[37] SA, 212/364/1. There is no date on the letter, but it includes a signed declaration of 26 September 1599 by witnesses testifying to the brothers' right to money from Sir Robert's estate.
[38] THL, Ellesmere MS 1782e.

the conditions of the will.[39] Until this point, then, Egerton had paid maintenance to John and William, as stipulated in their older brother's will, and there is no evidence to suggest that Egerton ever stopped.

However, while John was imprisoned, Egerton arranged for an inventory of Sir Robert's goods and chattels on 15 June 1601, and this may well have prompted John's concern about his own income.[40] It is noteworthy that Egerton delayed the inventory of Sir Robert's estate until two years after Sir Robert's death and coinciding with John's imprisonment, and it is possible that Egerton believed John to be an impediment to his nephew's inheritance.[41] On the other hand, on 6 June 1601, just a week before the inventory, John leased the Crown's share of the Salesbury estates, and this transfer of land may have prompted the need for an inventory of Sir Robert's goods.[42] John's letter to Cecil implies he had friends working on his behalf, which may explain how he managed to lease Crown land while imprisoned for participating in a revolt. John and William's 1599 petition to Egerton suggests that Egerton had firm control over their nephew's affairs. John, however, became heavily involved in his young nephew's wardship, paying the security on behalf of his nephew's guardian, administering his nephew's estates, and leasing the Crown's third of his lands. Given Egerton's formidable character and local power, it seems unlikely, though not impossible, that John could have been so integrated into his nephew's life and estate without Egerton's permission. John also trusted Egerton; John himself had delivered his nephew into Egerton's protection after Sir Robert died.[43]

Egerton was a diligent overseer of Sir Robert Salesbury's will and he took his responsibilities to the Salesbury family seriously.

---

[39] R. A. Roberts (ed.), 'Cecil Papers: July 1601, 16–31', in *Calendar of the Cecil Papers in Hatfield House: Volume 11, 1601* (London, 1906), pp. 287–313. *British History Online*, available at *http://www.british-history.ac.uk/cal-cecil-papers/vol11/pp287-313* (accessed 3 August 2022).

[40] THL, Ellesmere MS 1782g.

[41] This is the view proposed by W. J. Smith in his 'Three Salesbury mansions in 1601', *BBCS*, 15/4 (1954), 294.

[42] TNA, WARD 9/120, f. 177v.

[43] SA, 212/364/1.

In 1603, Egerton became Lord Chancellor and he used his position to assist William Salesbury when he needed to rebuild the family estates after he inherited from John in 1611. In the Chancery suit against John Williams the moneylender, Egerton could not help William directly, but he frustrated William's opponent by delaying the court proceedings and then refused to let John Williams withdraw his offer to give William back his estate if William repaid the money.[44] It was useful for a gentry family to have friends in high places, and Egerton achieved one of the most useful high places of all. At the same time, Egerton was not corrupt, and he never wrongfully interpreted the law to help William. William still needed to prove his case in court and repay a substantial sum of money to John Williams, which financially hindered his estates for two decades. By overseeing the family's affairs through the young John's wardship and using his position as Lord Chancellor to support William in his various Chancery suits, Egerton worked to preserve the Salesbury patrimony, unlike William's profligate brother John, who nearly destroyed the patrimony during his four years as head of the family. Egerton was perhaps more suspicious of John than of Sir Robert or William, and this suggestion of reticence in Egerton's relationship with him may well indicate Egerton's opinion of John's attitude to money and, after 1601, of his involvement in the Essex Revolt.

John Salesbury was a loyal servant of Robert Devereux, 2nd earl of Essex, who was a major influence on John's youth. Egerton may well have been the connection between the two men. Essex was Egerton's friend, and Egerton's eldest son, Sir Thomas, fought with Essex in Ireland, where Sir Thomas died in August 1599.[45] John Salesbury was a friend of Sir Thomas, 'uppon who I relied only next to my master [the earl of Essex]'.[46] Essex was an important and divisive figure in the lives of the

---

[44] NLW, Bachymbyd Letters 93.
[45] J. H. Baker, 'Egerton, Thomas, first Viscount Brackley (1540–1617)', *ODNB* (2004).
[46] SA, 212/364/1.

late sixteenth-century north Wales gentry.[47] According to A. H. Dodd, Essex recruited dissatisfied men, those who resented their exclusion from local administration by the dominance of the Salusburys of Lleweni, those who had not been favoured by the previous noble, the earl of Leicester, and those who had Catholic sympathies. Dodd notes that Essex's party went on to cause further problems for the government, including the riotous 1601 Denbighshire election, discussed below.[48] However, a gentleman did not need to be of a rebellious nature to recognise that Essex was a powerful noble, and he attracted men who wanted a patron to support and protect them. For example, Essex was also patron to Owen Salusbury of Holt, a cousin of the Salesburys of Rhug and Bachymbyd, who was a gentleman of limited financial means, but very conscious of his honour and status.[49] Like John Salesbury, Owen earned his living as a soldier. It is plausible that John followed his cousin into soldiering and possibly Essex's service. By 1596, Owen and John Salesbury had commissions to muster men for Essex's expedition to Cadiz, and John was later accused in Star Chamber of abusing the commission.[50] The commission demonstrates that John had joined the earl of Essex by 1596, aged around twenty-one. By 1599, John and Owen were both serving Essex in his campaign in Ireland, where Essex was attempting, as Lord Lieutenant of Ireland, to put down a revolt by the earl of Tyrone.[51] Younger sons of the gentry were particularly attracted to serve in Ireland to obtain honour and a good reputation, but, like all younger sons, they were also attracted by potential financial gain.[52] The earl of Essex's patronage thus brought the opportunity to gain money, honour and status. It also brought trouble.

---

[47] Despite some errors, the seminal work on this subject remains A. H. Dodd, 'North Wales in the Essex Revolt of 1601', *EHR*, 59/235 (1944), 348–70.

[48] Dodd, 'North Wales', 369.

[49] BL, Lansdowne MS 99, ff. 256–8.

[50] TNA, STAC 5/T7/31.

[51] For details of the Salesburys' campaigning, see chapter five.

[52] Rhys Morgan, *The Welsh and the Shaping of Modern Ireland, 1558–1641* (Woodbridge, 2014), pp. 47–9.

Essex's campaign was a disaster. After failing to make progress, and against the wishes of the queen, Essex agreed a truce with the earl of Tyrone and returned to England on 28 September 1599, narrowly escaping charges of treason.[53] His followers were free to disperse, but John and Owen stayed loyal to their lord. The earl of Essex was desperate to regain the queen's favour and became convinced that her ministers, particularly Robert Cecil, were the source of his continued ostracism from court after his return from Ireland. The Essex Revolt in February 1601 was a desperate and misguided attempt to regain the queen's favour. In the months leading up to the revolt, Essex summoned his followers from across the country to Essex House on the Strand in London. The examination of Sir John Lloyd of Bodidris after the revolt reveals the closely linked network of Essex's followers. Sir John Lloyd was John Salesbury's brother-in-law, married to John's sister, Margaret.[54] Sir John said that prior to the revolt, there were 'divers meetings and private confidences' between Sir John himself, John Salesbury, Owen Salusbury and Peter Wynne, a fellow Welsh gentleman soldier. While John was staying in Sir John Lloyd's house a fortnight before Christmas 1600, he received a letter from Essex summoning him to London and Sir John gave him the money to travel. John was away for about a week and, during this time, he went to Northamptonshire to see Reverend Edward Puleston, a member of another local Welsh gentry family whose brother had served in John Salesbury's company in Ireland. Afterwards, John returned to Sir John Lloyd's house at Bodidris. Evidently, John was using his own contacts to rally support for Essex's cause.

By Christmas 1600, John and his cousin Owen had taken lodgings on the Strand near Essex House, where they lived with Peter Wynne and Francis Meyrick, a younger son of Rowland

---

[53] For more on the earl of Essex in Ireland, see below, pp. 121–3.
[54] R. A. Roberts (ed.), 'Cecil Papers: February 1601, 21–28', in *Calendar of the Cecil Papers in Hatfield House: Volume 11, 1601*, pp. 75–100. *British History Online*, available at *http://www.british-history.ac.uk/cal-cecil-papers/vol11/pp75-100* (accessed 3 August 2022).

Meyrick, bishop of Bangor.[55] The lodgings were organised by Francis's older brother, Sir Gelly Meyrick, who had been a follower of the earl of Essex since the 1580s. When trying to find lodgings, Sir Gelly told one reluctant landlord that 'it was the Earl of Essex's pleasure to have his friends lie about him'. On 11 February 1601, three days after the revolt, Richard Hughes, one of the queen's footmen and previously a servant of the earl of Essex, gave a detailed testimony of his involvement, saying he himself was never 'one day absent from their lodging either at dinner or supper'.[56] On 29 January 1601, John Salesbury invited Hughes to have supper at their lodgings with Owen Salesbury and the future Sir Francis Leigh, son-in-law of Thomas Egerton. Hughes denied any knowledge of a revolt and insisted he 'had no communication but of ordinary matters with any of them'. After supper, John and Hughes went to Essex House and Owen joined them a quarter of an hour later, but went to talk with other people. Hughes said he never saw Owen again and, although he often met John, claimed they never discussed anything about Essex. Whether true or not, the examination of Essex's followers highlights the close-knit network of the Welsh diaspora in London. People knew each other and their families. It is a brief insight into the Salesburys' involvement in national events and it demonstrates the complicated web of their social relations with connections throughout Wales, England and Ireland, and on the continent.

The activities of Essex's followers centred on Essex House. On the morning of Sunday 8 February 1601, Thomas Egerton arrived at Essex House along with Sir William Knollys, earl of Banbury; Edward Somerset, earl of Worcester; and Sir John Popham, Lord Chief Justice. Under instruction from the queen, the lords came to assure Essex that she wanted to address his concerns. The courtyard of Essex House, however, was crowded with Essex's followers, 'a very tumultuous sort', according to

[55] R. A. Roberts (ed.), 'Cecil Papers: February 1601, 11–15', in *Calendar of the Cecil Papers in Hatfield House: Volume 11, 1601*, pp. 40–57. *British History Online*, available at http://www.british-history.ac.uk/cal-cecil-papers/vol11/pp40-57 (accessed 3 August 2022)

[56] Roberts, 'Cecil Papers: February 1601, 11–15'.

Egerton's later testimony.[57] These followers locked the gates of the courtyard, preventing the nobles' exit and doubtless presenting an intimidating front. In the midst of the hostile gathering, Egerton attempted to speak with Essex, but Essex's followers were too loud and uncooperative. Egerton instructed the men to depart and requested a private audience with Essex. As the lords followed Essex into the house, his followers shouted 'Kill them', 'Cast the great seal out of the window', and 'Let us shop them up'. The aggression displayed by Essex's followers might well explain any later sense of animosity between Thomas Egerton and John Salesbury. The reception was no less frosty inside. Essex followed his men's advice to 'shop them up' and he imprisoned the noblemen in his study. Owen Salusbury was placed in charge of the musketeers guarding the door, an extremely enthusiastic participant in the revolt. Owen told Sir Gelly Meyrick that if Essex's followers lost control of the house, 'he and they above [the lords] would all go to God together'.[58] Unlike his cousin, Owen Salusbury did not survive the revolt and he died in the gallery, shot from outside in the street.[59]

Essex had insufficient weapons and no real promise of any additional support. Even the term 'revolt' somewhat overstates the circumstances of 8 February 1601; Essex wanted the queen's attention rather than to overthrow the government. His band of armed followers, many of them experienced soldiers, helped the situation to spiral into violence. Having left Essex House after imprisoning his fellow nobles, Essex attempted to persuade the City of London to rise in his support. He and a splinter group of followers, including John Salesbury, reached Ludgate, but it was defended by the bishop of London's men, who shot at them and forced a retreat. After a rather pathetic attempt to enter the City, Essex and fifty of his followers, again including John Salesbury,

[57] *CSP Dom., 1598–1601*, pp. 585–6.
[58] R. A. Roberts (ed.), 'Cecil Papers: March 1601, 11–20', in *Calendar of the Cecil Papers in Hatfield House: Volume 11, 1601*, pp. 119–36. *British History Online*, available at *http://www.british-history.ac.uk/cal-cecil-papers/vol11/pp119-136* (accessed 3 August 2022).
[59] NLW, Plas Nantglyn MS 1, p. 53.

took boats at Queenhithe and returned to Essex House.[60] They ran chaotically for the boats and William Parker, Lord Monteagle, nearly drowned in the melée, but John Salesbury saved his life.[61] Back at Essex House, Sir John Davies (1560–1625), a scholar and soldier who had, like other followers, fought under Essex at Cadiz, engaged Essex's wife and sister to make polite conversation with the hostages in the study.[62] Just before Essex arrived back at the house, Sir Ferdinando Gorges, a formerly loyal servant of Essex, successfully persuaded Sir Gelly Meyrick and Sir John Davies that Essex had ordered the release of the prisoners.[63] It was an ignominious end to a disorganised and incomprehensible attempt at a rising.

Although Essex was executed on 25 February 1601, many of his followers received only light punishments.[64] John Salesbury was imprisoned in the Marshalsea for less than ten months and continually sent petitions for his release to Robert Cecil.[65] Sir Thomas Gerard (1560–1621), a northern Catholic gentleman, carried the petitions for John, despite having no obvious connections to him. Sir Thomas, however, did matriculate at Brasenose College, Oxford, around six years before John's older brother, Sir Robert; this might be the link between the two men.[66] John's petitions to Cecil highlight one of the dangers of serving a noble patron. John said that he acted only out of 'the love he bare to his dead Lord, bound by the many favours he [Essex] did him'. John was 'resolve[d] and willing to undergo with him and for him all fortunes', but he regretted 'the danger his Lord had drawn him into'. John thus claimed that he did not follow Essex for political reasons and had no wish to rebel against the queen; Essex was his

---

[60] Alexandra Gajda, *The Earl of Essex and Late Elizabethan Political Culture* (Oxford, 2012), pp. 29–31.
[61] *CSP Dom., 1598–1601*, pp. 574–5.
[62] J. J. N. McGurk, 'Davies [Davis], Sir John', *ODNB* (2004).
[63] Robert Lacey, *Robert Earl of Essex: An Elizabethan Icarus* (London, 1971), pp. 294–5; Charles E. Clark, 'Gorges, Sir Ferdinando', *ODNB* (2004).
[64] *CSP Dom., 1598–1601*, pp. 574–5; Lacey, *Robert Earl of Essex*, pp. 294–5.
[65] Roberts, 'Cecil Papers: July 1601, 16–31'.
[66] *Al. Oxon.*

lord and master and he was honour-bound to obey his orders. This language of hierarchical obedience was easily comprehensible in early modern England and Wales. John argued that he was not a conspirator in the revolt, only a servant obeying his master, which explains why so many of Essex's followers escaped with only light reprimands. Robert Cecil eventually relented and released John, requiring him to pay a fine of £40 for participating in the revolt. John was free by October 1601, when he was involved in further altercations at home in Denbighshire.[67]

John Salesbury's involvement in treasonous activity contrasted sharply with the experience of his cousin, Thomas Salusbury of Lleweni. As a family, the Salesburys of Rhug and Bachymbyd received little damage to their reputation through John's involvement in the Essex Revolt, unlike the loss in status for the Salusburys of Lleweni after Thomas Salusbury's execution as a conspirator in the 1586 Babington Plot. Whether true or not, John claimed that he was only involved in the revolt because he followed the commands of his lord, to whom he was bound by shared loyalty: John did what Essex wanted and, in return, Essex did 'many favours' for John. Thomas Salusbury, in contrast, was a co-conspirator in a Catholic plot to assassinate Elizabeth I, not merely a follower of Anthony Babington. There was honour in John's behaviour: he was a gentleman who understood his duty, even if he was led astray. Disobedience violated the gentleman's code of honour. In this respect, John's involvement in the Essex Revolt was a treasonous mirror of his younger brother's loyalty to Charles I in the Civil Wars of 1642–51. In early modern England and Wales, a gentleman's code of honour involved mutual obligations.[68] John and Essex had their own responsibilities towards each other, but similar duties existed in other relationships, such as between kinsmen. Wales even had its own cultural concept of *pwyth*, or obligation, which formalised such relationships,

---

[67] See below, pp. 123–7.
[68] Jerrilyn Greene Marston, 'Gentry, honor and royalism in early Stuart England', *Journal of British Studies*, 13/1 (1973), 23.

although unlike honour, it also encompassed men of lower status, who formed crucial parts of the Salesburys' networks of power and influence.[69]

LOCAL NETWORKS

Thus far, this chapter has examined how the Salesburys gained and used power through their relationships with noble patrons. However, the Salesburys also negotiated complex relationships within their local communities. Other gentry families provided friends as well as allies, and the Salesburys also interacted with their tenants, servants and labourers, and those of their fellow gentry. They were part of the close-knit and complex world of early modern north Wales and the border counties of Cheshire and Shropshire. Friendship in early modern society was conceptualised as a perfect ideal between people of equal rank and status.[70] More practically, the word 'friend' denoted a place within a complex social network: a friend could be a patron, a tenant or an ally.[71] Friendship could also form what Alan Bray termed 'voluntary kinship', a pertinent term in the kin-focused world of the early modern Welsh gentry.[72] Friendship thus extended the bonds of kinship beyond immediate family and, in the large kinship groups of the Welsh gentry, provided a mechanism to tighten relationships with their vast number of 'cousins'. It is notable that this section includes virtually no information about the friendships of women. This is a problem of the sources, which are scant even for the Salesbury men. The Salesbury women, who left few records beyond a handful of letters to their male relatives, doubtless engaged in female sociability, which included activities

---

[69] Evans, 'Politics and parliamentary representation', 8.
[70] Alexandra Shepard, *Meanings of Manhood in Early Modern England* (Oxford, 2003), pp. 122–3.
[71] Alan Bray, 'Homosexuality and the signs of male friendship in Elizabethan England', *History Workshop Journal*, 29 (1990), 3–4.
[72] Alan Bray, *The Friend* (London and Chicago, 2003), p. 104.

such as gift exchange, correspondence with other women, and the provision of health advice.[73] With no further information, however, this section focuses on male sociability and the wide range of friendships maintained by the Salesbury men.

Friendship between early modern gentlemen came with responsibilities and obligations. As a formal relationship between equals, it involved the complex gentry qualities of honour and duty. One incident in 1572 involving John Salesbury (d.1580) and Robert Lloyd, a Denbighshire JP, illustrates the bonds of friendship which criss-crossed gentry society, sometimes to the detriment of friendly relations with other families. In 1574, Roger and John Lloyd brought a suit in Star Chamber against John Salesbury, Ellis Powell and various other defendants for the murder of their brother, Robert.[74] This had been preceded by an investigation at the Coroner's Inquest of Denbighshire, and the Lloyd brothers had also brought suits at the assizes of Denbighshire, the assizes of Shropshire and the Council in the Marches, as well as a suit in Star Chamber against the Shropshire assizes jury for corruption.[75] Robert Lloyd's death was the result of a protracted disagreement involving the daughters of one Roger Roydon, who lived in Burton, Denbighshire. In 1569, Ellis Powell married Margaret Roydon, one of Roger's underage daughters. He tendered to sue her livery on her behalf in the court of Wards and he duly entered into her share of Roger Roydon's lands. However, as John Salesbury said in his answer to the Lloyd brothers' suit, there was discontent that Powell received the profits of the land. In particular, opposition came from fellow Denbighshire gentlemen Owen Brereton of Borras, Evan Lloyd of Bodidris, John Trevor of Trevalyn and Edward Billett. According to John, they made threats against Powell that they would take the farm for themselves and put Powell in gaol.[76] Powell, meanwhile, had the support of John Salesbury of Rhug and

---

[73] See Amanda E. Herbert, *Female Alliances: Gender, Identity, and Friendship in Early Modern Britain* (London, 2014).
[74] TNA, STAC 5/L21/24; STAC 5/L23/2; STAC 5/L48/7; STAC 7/4/2.
[75] TNA, STAC 5/L48/7; 7/4/2.
[76] TNA, STAC 7/4/2, John Salesbury's answer.

Bachymbyd, John Hanmer of Hanmer, Flintshire, and Lancelot Bostock, as well as other unnamed friends. Like Powell, Lancelot Bostock had also married a daughter of Roger Roydon, in around 1565.[77] Ellis Powell claimed that John Trevor of Trevalyn wanted a third of the land in question, which Powell disputed.[78] The plaintiffs claimed that Ellis Powell and John Salesbury with their confederates harassed Roger Roydon's widow to gain possession of the farm.[79] The plaintiffs also argued that John Salesbury wanted the farm for himself and bought the title of the farm from Ellis Powell, even though they alleged that Powell had no lawful claim to it. This could have been a red herring, or Ellis may have promised the messuage to John in return for his support. Importantly, however, the gentlemen involved all had their own allies, followers and servants, increasing the numbers involved and the potential for factional violence.

The two sides first attempted to resolve their dispute in court. On 12 February 1572, the Denbighshire Great Sessions declared that the ownership of the land should be settled 'by mediacion of friendes'.[80] The gentlemen met at Gresford, Denbighshire, nine days later on 21 February. However, neither side could reach an agreement and they departed when night began to fall. According to Powell, one of Brereton's party said as they were leaving, 'What is the daye broken, I laye a wager then, there wilbe many a broken head on to morowe at night about the matter'. Thus, mediation failed, there was an undercurrent of violence, and Ellis Powell still controlled the farmhouse. At this point, John Salesbury sent men to Burton to help Powell 'keape his possessions'. John Salesbury admitted sending the men, but denied inciting violence and denied any claims to the property himself.[81] According to the plaintiffs, John gave the men weapons, provisions and 'one grete mastiffe dogge' to keep the farm by force. If anyone attempted to remove them and retake the house, John told them that 'they

---

[77] W.J.J., *HPO (1558–1603)*: 'Bostock, Lancelot (bef.1533–*c.*88)'.
[78] TNA, STAC 7/4/2, Ellis Powell's answer.
[79] TNA, STAC 7/4/2, bill.
[80] TNA, STAC 7/4/2, Ellis Powell's answer.
[81] TNA, STAC 7/4/2, John Salesbury's answer.

should either kill or be killed'.[82] The men swore an oath to keep possession of the farm and John promised to bring reinforcements if they needed further help.

The dispute was evidently large enough and with sufficient potential for unrest to attract the attention of the Council in the Marches, who sent a commission to end the armed occupation of the farmhouse. On 22 February 1572, the day after the failed mediation at Gresford, Robert Lloyd and John Lloyd arrived at the farm in their roles as commissioners from the Council in the Marches and Denbighshire JPs. The commissioners persuaded the men in the house to let them come to the window and deliver the Council's instructions. The plaintiffs claimed that they read the commission 'with gentle words and persuaswns'. The defendants said that the commissioners brought their own servants and followers to engage in an armed conflict; John Salesbury said that the commissioners 'demeaned themselves . . . in unruly manner'.[83] However, both parties to the suit agreed that after the commissioners delivered the Council's instructions, there was a violent altercation between the men occupying the farmhouse and the men who accompanied the commissioners. From within the farmhouse, the men shot through windows 'and holes made for that purpose', injuring sixteen of the commissioners' servants, which gives some sense of the scale of the numbers involved.[84] In the melée, thirty-year-old John ap Robert ap Howell, a common labourer and the son of one of John Salesbury's tenants, struck Robert Lloyd over the head, and Lloyd died of his wounds on 25 February 1572.

No one denied that the fight took place: Robert Lloyd's death was irrefutable. It was also accidental, in the sense that he was not a particular target, but caught up in the attack. John Salesbury said that he did not 'beare any malice to the said Robert . . . the said Robert Lloid was not only [John's] kynsman . . . but also his Friende as this Defendant was also the Frinde of the said Robert Lloid'.[85]

[82] TNA, STAC 5/L23/2, interrogatories for John Salesbury, Ellis Powell and others.
[83] TNA, STAC 7/4/2, replication of Roger and John Lloyd.
[84] TNA, STAC 5/L23/2, interrogatories for John Salesbury, Ellis Powell and others.
[85] TNA, STAC 7/4/2, John Salesbury's answer.

Lloyd's brothers failed to secure a conviction in Denbighshire and took their case to Shropshire, where the jury found John ap Robert ap Howell, John Lloyd Maylor and William ap William guilty of manslaughter.[86] The jury could not convict for murder because the evidence was too uncertain: it was produced long after Robert Lloyd's death, some of the witnesses were of 'smal and light creddit', and they heard 'diverse Weltchmen out of Wales . . . suche as the moste of them cowlde not speake any englishe att all', so they were forced to have a bilingual witness translate, which compromised the quality of the evidence in the eyes of the jury. The convicted men all claimed benefit of clergy because they could read and escaped significant punishment. Ultimately, Robert Lloyd's death was caused by the entangled alliances and rivalries of the Denbighshire gentry and their division into factions over a land dispute. John Salesbury said that Ellis Powell needed help at the farmhouse because Powell 'was but a strainger at Burton farre from his frindes'. Powell came to John 'to stand his good Frend and kinsman . . . and to helpe him with his advise and Counsaill'. John continually emphasised in his answer that he was a friend of Powell. He told another of Powell's associates that 'the said Ellis was [his] kinsman and frende and that [John] himseelf wold do for the said Ellice any thinge that laye in his power and that he might Lawfully and convenyently do'.[87] However, the bonds of friendship tied the plaintiffs too. One of the defendants, John Salesbury's former steward, Hugh Salesbury, complained that the suit only existed because of the 'malice and evill will borne towards hym by the said Complainants theire friends and confedrates'.[88] Few of the gentlemen involved in the dispute actually had a claim on the property or thought their claim had been violated; instead, they felt an obligation to aid their friend. Sometimes, friendship in sixteenth-century Denbighshire meant helping someone defend their property by force, whatever the cost incurred.

[86] TNA, STAC 5/L48/7, answer of Thomas Ludlow, John Lee and Thomas Fewtrell.
[87] TNA, STAC 7/4/2, John Salesbury's answer.
[88] TNA, STAC 7/4/2, Hugh Salesbury's answer.

Friendship was an important and meaningful bond for the early modern Welsh gentry, part of the web of alliances and faction that characterised local society. However, the gentry's social relations were also fluid and changed over the generations. Highlighting the gentry's complicated loyalties, the Lloyds of Bodidris and the Trevors of Trevalyn, antagonists in the Star Chamber suit over the farmhouse at Burton, were close allies of the next generation of Salesburys. Evan Lloyd's son, for example, Sir John Lloyd, married John Salesbury's daughter, Margaret, sometime after John's death, and he was especially close to John's namesake second son, John (d.1611). In his deposition taken after the Essex Revolt, Sir John Lloyd described John, with Owen Salusbury of Holt and Peter Wynne, as 'the greatest friends and the inwardest that [he] had'.[89] John Salesbury and Sir John Lloyd formed a close alliance with Sir Richard Trevor (1558–1638) of Trevalyn, John Trevor's eldest son. The three gentlemen particularly opposed the election of Sir John Salusbury (1565–1612) of Lleweni to the office of MP for Denbighshire in October 1601, resulting in a brawl in a Wrexham churchyard between the two factions and a postponed poll. The relationship between the Salesburys of Rhug and Bachymbyd and their cousins, the Salusburys of Lleweni, was, as discussed above, another casualty of the ever-shifting landscape of gentry alliances. Soured by the Salesburys' ambitions after the Babington Plot, the situation deteriorated further because of John Salesbury's own treasonous activity in the Essex Revolt. Sir John Salusbury described his cousin as 'lately so insolent an actor against Her Royal Highness' person and estate (being much ashamed such to be of my name)'.[90]

The events of the 1601 Denbighshire election were part of the local fallout from the Essex Revolt. John Salesbury was a known follower of Essex who participated in the revolt. Sir

---

[89] Roberts, 'Cecil Papers: February 1601, 21–28', pp. 75–100.
[90] R. A. Roberts (ed.), 'Cecil Papers: April 1602, 16–30', in *Calendar of the Cecil Papers in Hatfield House: Volume 12, 1602–1603* (London, 1910), pp. 109–36. *British History Online*, available at *http://www.british-history.ac.uk/cal-cecil-papers/vol12/pp109-136* (accessed 3 August 2022).

Richard Trevor's brother fought under Essex in Ireland.[91] Sir John Lloyd was knighted by Essex.[92] Sir John Salusbury of Lleweni, meanwhile, received his knighthood from the queen herself for aiding in the suppression of the Essex Revolt. He was an utterly loyal servant of Elizabeth I, appointed an Esquire of the Body in March 1595.[93] The precise series of events which resulted in the Wrexham brawl is unknown, but there was doubtless extreme tension between old rivals and the two respective factions of the Salusburys of Lleweni and the Trevors of Trevalyn. Sir John Salusbury had the support of various Salusbury kin, including Roger Salusbury of Bachegraig, Flintshire, and Thomas Salusbury of Denbigh, as well as other leading gentry families, such as the Thelwalls of Plas y Ward, historically allies of the Salesburys of Rhug and Bachymbyd.[94] In Sir Richard Trevor's faction, meanwhile, there were Sir John Lloyd, John Salesbury, Thomas Price and Thomas Trafford, all of whom except John Salesbury had been Denbighshire JPs. Sir John Salusbury also accused the sheriff, Owen Vaughan, who would one day be father-in-law to John Salesbury's younger brother William, of colluding with Sir Richard's party.[95] No one was injured or killed during the subsequent confrontation at the election in Wrexham, and the gentry's subsequent retellings to the Privy Council and Star Chamber strongly suggest that it was a posturing display of force which spilled over into violence.[96]

---

[91] H.G.O., *HPO (1558–1603)*: 'Trevor, Sir Richard (1558–1638)'.
[92] Roberts, 'Cecil Papers: February 1601, 21–28'.
[93] Carleton Brown (ed.), *Poems by Sir John Salusbury and Robert Chester* (Bryn Mawr, PA, 1913), p. xvi.
[94] TNA, STAC 5/T15/33, Sir Richard Trevor's bill.
[95] TNA, STAC 5/S51/14, Sir John Salusbury's bill.
[96] TNA, STAC 5/A55/34; STAC 5/Addenda 15/54; STAC 5/S28/6; STAC 5/S45/29 (missing at TNA in 2021 and not orderable); STAC 5/S51/14; STAC 5/S59/2; STAC 5/T9/31; STAC 5/T15/33; STAC 5/T30/18; STAC 7/15/54; John Roche Dasent (ed.), *Acts of the Privy Council of England Volume 32, 1601–1604* (London, 1907), pp. 342–3; R. A. Roberts (ed.), 'Cecil Papers: October 1601, 21–31', *Calendar of the Cecil Papers in Hatfield House: Volume 11*, pp. 440–65. *British History Online*, available at http://www.british-history.ac.uk/cal-cecil-papers/vol11/pp440-465 (accessed 3 August 2022).

Fundamentally, Sir Richard Trevor and his party did not want Sir John Salusbury, a powerful rival, to become MP for the county. According to Sir Richard Trevor's bill against Sir John Salusbury, the dispute began over a question of honour. Sir John Salusbury claimed to be a better man than Sir Richard or Sir John Lloyd because he, Salusbury, had been knighted by the queen for his service against the earl of Essex, but Sir John Lloyd was knighted by the 'traitor' himself, and Sir Richard by Sir William Russell as Lord Deputy in Ireland.[97] Attacks on a gentleman's honour and reputation were legitimate causes for dispute.[98] However, the argument also encompassed the gentry's followers and the correct use of authority. Sir Richard and Sir John Salusbury both accused the other of abusing a commission to muster soldiers to fight in Ireland. Sir John said that, three days before the election, Sir Richard proclaimed a general muster in Wrexham of all the inhabitants of the hundred of Bromfield and threatened to compel any freeholder who did not vote for him to serve in Ireland.[99] The freeholders refused to comply and so Sir Richard pressed numerous men into service to prevent 'their masters and friends' from voting in the election, and some of the freeholders were remanded on pain of death to stay in Wrexham, where the election was to take place. According to Sir John, the election was purposefully delayed by Owen Vaughan from 23 September 1601 to 21 October 1601 to give Sir Richard's party time to influence the votes. Sir Richard, however, said that it was Sir John Salusbury who abused his commission by delaying a muster and threatening to send the 'sons, servants, kinsmen and friends' of freeholders to the wars in Ireland.[100] The similarity in their accounts suggest that at least one, possibly both, of the gentlemen were misusing their authority to call a muster and blackmailing freeholders in the election.

---

[97] TNA, STAC 5/T15/33, Sir Richard Trevor's bill.
[98] Bowen, *Anatomy of a Duel*, pp. 80–1.
[99] TNA, STAC 5/S51/14, Sir John Salusbury's bill.
[100] TNA, STAC 5/T15/33, Sir Richard Trevor's bill.

Sir Richard claimed that Sir John Salusbury wanted to deny Sir Richard and Sir John Lloyd the office of MP, one of the pre-eminent county positions in the office-obsessed world of the Welsh gentry. Sir John, however, said that Sir Richard's party conspired to prevent him winning the election because 'I am your majesty's sworn servant . . . and one that all they greatly hated as one not lyking their Courses'. According to Sir John, Sir Richard's party attempted to persuade William Middleton, the sheriff's kinsman, to stand for election and offered him a bribe of £50 above the knight's fee 'to animate him'. Middleton, however, refused the offer when he discovered the plot because he did not want 'to stir up some striefe' with Sir John Salusbury, then Middleton told his friends to vote for Sir John.[101] As Sir Richard's party were unsuccessful in their attempt to stand a rival candidate, they gathered their supporters to march on Wrexham on election day. Sir John claimed that Sir Richard, Sir John Lloyd and Owen Vaughan, who were commissioners of oyer and terminer for Flintshire, Denbighshire and Montgomeryshire, used their positions to assemble 'willfull and disordered persones . . . ydle persones [who] comitt any villainie whatsoever'. In total, he accused Sir Richard's party of assembling 570 armed men, a small army, including fifty men from the Salesburys' estate at Bachymbyd. Sir Richard Trevor obtained weapons from Chester and the army marched to Wrexham, where Sir Richard dispersed groups of armed men throughout the town.

Both parties agreed that they were involved in a brawl on the election day in Wrexham and a dispute evidently occurred, because the election was officially delayed by three days. Sir John Salusbury claimed that he went to walk in the church at Wrexham, presumably St Giles, the parish church, with two elderly gentlemen and six other friends. In the churchyard, Sir John met Sir Richard Trevor, Thomas Trafford and others, around twenty men in total, all armed. This group passed Sir John and went to whisper together in the place where the election was to be held later in

[101] TNA, STAC 5/S51/14, Sir John Salusbury's bill.

the day, before they returned to the churchyard, still armed. Sir Richard ordered the men to lock the church doors with Sir John outside and placed armed men in the churchyard. Sir John asked them to keep the queen's peace, but he was forced back on to the church wall and there were swords around him before he could draw his own sword to defend himself.[102] Sir Richard claimed that he, not Sir John, called for peace, but he was forced to draw his sword when he noticed Sir John's hand on his sword hilt.[103] One of Sir Richard's men fired a shot to summon the rest of the party and they arrived, again with weapons. One of them was John Salesbury, armed with sword and buckler, who 'asked where the villaine [Sir John Salusbury] was . . . that he would shoot him through'. By the time Owen Vaughan calmed the situation, it was too late to hold the election and Vaughan postponed it. Sir Richard did not give any details of the brawl itself in his bill, preferring to emphasise that Sir John was a disreputable official who abused his positions, terrorised the local community with his illegal retinue, and did not abide by the standards expected of a gentleman.

On 5 November 1601, the Privy Council summoned Sir John Salusbury, Sir Richard Trevor, Sir John Lloyd and 'the rest that had part in that factious disorder' to appear before them in person because they had been 'informed of a very great and tumultious disorder that happened in that county of Denbigh'.[104] The Council in the Marches was also concerned about the deteriorating situation in Denbighshire. Soon after the election day brawl, Sir Richard Lewkenor, Chief Justice of Chester and a member of the Council, wrote to Robert Cecil and said that he had previously attempted to pacify relations between Sir John Salusbury, Sir Richard Trevor and Sir John Lloyd, but the latter two felt they had been wronged by Sir John Salusbury.[105] However, Sir Richard Lewkenor believed he left them on reasonably good terms and he was surprised that

---
[102] TNA, STAC 5/S51/14, Sir John Salusbury's bill.
[103] TNA, STAC 5/T15/33, Sir Richard Trevor's bill.
[104] Dasent, *Acts of the Privy Council, 1601–1604*, pp. 342–3.
[105] Roberts, 'Cecil Papers: October 1601, 21–31'.

it erupted into violence during the election. He worried that the rivalry 'will breed such dissension in the shire, where the people are factious and ready to follow those they do affect in all actions, without respect to the lawfulness or unlawfulness thereof, as justice will hardly be administered or the people kept in quiet'. In reality, however, there were very few consequences for the men involved in the dispute. John Salesbury of Rhug and Bachymbyd delivered a writ of *supersedeas*, intended to delay proceedings, in April 1602, which outraged Sir John Salusbury and prompted another letter to the Privy Council.[106] On 7 July 1602, John Lewis Gwyn, a 'servant and kinsman' of Sir John Salusbury, was murdered by followers of Sir John Salusbury's 'adversaries', the servants of Foulk Lloyd.[107] Sir John complained to Robert Cecil that 'for want of an indifferent sheriff the few offenders brought in take no indifferent trial'.[108] Indeed, according to Sir John, the offenders thought they would be pardoned because John Salesbury of Rhug and Bachymbyd came to solicit on their behalf. Sir John asked Cecil to ensure 'an indifferent man be appointed' sheriff next year so that there could be a fair trial. The issue was still unresolved on 5 November 1604 when Sir John Salusbury received a letter from his lawyer in London reporting on the case. His lawyer had visited the president of the Council in the Marches to petition for a neutral sheriff; the sheriff in 1604 was one John Lloyd of Faenol, not an impartial surname in the dispute.[109]

With too many families competing for a limited number of seats, the Welsh gentry were no strangers to contested parliamentary elections.[110] However, the failed election on 21 October 1601 was unusually violent and protracted, as well as a source of concern for the authorities. Gentlemen felt compelled

---

[106] Roberts, 'Cecil Papers: April 1602, 16–30'.

[107] Brown, *Poems by Sir John Salusbury*, p. xxii; R. A. Roberts, 'Cecil Papers: November 1602, 1–15', in *Calendar of the Cecil Papers in Hatfield House: Volume 12, 1602–1603*, pp. 460–73. *British History Online*, available at *http://www.british-history.ac.uk/cal-cecil-papers/vol12/pp460-473* (accessed 3 August 2022).

[108] Roberts, 'Cecil Papers: November 1602, 1–15'.

[109] NLW, Lleweni 33, in Smith, *Salusbury Correspondence*, p. 47–8.

[110] Bowen, *Politics in the Principality*, chapter one.

to defend their honour and take umbrage at slights to their reputation, and disliked seeing their rivals gain advantage over them. The tension between Sir John Salusbury, Sir Richard Trevor and Sir John Lloyd, as well as their friends and followers, demonstrates the potential for long-term discontent among the factions of the local gentry, and unresolved disputes damaged relationships between gentry families and their rivals. The shadow of friendship was faction; an argument could spread from one gentleman to his friends and all their servants and followers. The lawsuits over the brawl are notable for their continual mention of friends. Early modern Wales was less violent than in previous centuries, but there was still opportunity for armed disputes, although it is notable that no one was hurt at Wrexham. However, as Sir Richard Lewkenor's letter to Robert Cecil demonstrates, there was contemporary concern about the levels of factionalism in Denbighshire, which could be expressed in endless lawsuits as well as brawls in the street. Factionalism was caused by rivalry and argument, but it also indicated the strength of the bonds between a gentleman and his friends.

RETAINERS AND SERVANTS

The gentry's retainers were a major contributor to factionalism in north Wales. In medieval Wales, possession of a *plaid*, or a retinue, was an important cultural indicator of a gentry family's status, and having a group of armed followers also came in useful when engaging in rivalries with other families.[111] Although the sources for the Salesbury family do not use the term *plaid*, it is used here to reflect the Welsh cultural context of maintaining retinues. Retaining continued to be a problem in England and Wales throughout the fifteenth and sixteenth centuries and the government repeatedly introduced legislation to prevent the practice. In 1572, for example, the Vagabond Act banned all retainers, with the exception of

[111] Carr, *Gentry of North Wales*, pp. 133–4.

household servants.[112] The example of the Salesburys and other gentry families, such as the Mostyns of Mostyn, suggests that the Welsh gentry continued to maintain their *pleidiau* into the seventeenth century, and the Star Chamber suits discussed above reinforce the government's concern that retinues were a source of disorder in local communities.[113] For instance, in the 1574 Star Chamber suit brought by the Lloyd brothers against John Salesbury (d.1580) and Ellis Powell, John Salesbury denied that he kept retainers, which was, of course, illegal and thus not readily admitted in a law court. Nevertheless, there is strong evidence that the defence of the farm at Burton involved John Salesbury's *plaid* and it highlights the retinue's intense loyalty to their master. The depositions in the 1574 suit show that some of the men at the farm were John Salesbury's tenants and servants and, according to the plaintiffs, they disagreed with Ellis Powell and his own men about how to handle the arrival of the commissioners from the Council in the Marches.[114] John Salesbury's men refused to yield control of the farm and allegedly told the commissioners that their master had promised to pay their legal costs and 'if any of us fortune to be slaine the losse is finall it is But a knave out the way and wee are promisd to serve for suche a purpose'.[115] This may or may not have accurately characterised the relationship between John and his men, but it was a suitable argument in a court of law of how a gentleman regarded his followers.

John Salesbury's followers were diverse in age and status. Erasmus Griffith was the youngest defendant at eighteen years old, Robert ap Howell Vaughan was twenty-four, then Raffe Gwyneth was twenty-eight, John ap Robert ap Howell was thirty, Thomas ap David was thirty-six, David ap John Griffith was forty-

---

[112] Peter Roberts, 'Elizabethan players and minstrels and the legislation of 1572 against retainers and vagabonds', in Anthony Fletcher and Peter Roberts (eds), *Religion, Culture and Society in Early Modern Britain: Essays in honour of Patrick Collinson* (Cambridge, 1994), pp. 30–1.

[113] Jarrett, '"By reason of her sex and widowhood"', pp. 92–3; Evans, '"To contynue in my bloud and name"', chapter two.

[114] TNA, STAC 7/4/2.

[115] TNA, STAC 5/L23/2, interrogatories.

eight, and John Lloyd Maylor was the oldest at forty-nine.[116] Hugh Salesbury was a tenant and former steward of John Salesbury, and they shared a common surname, suggesting a kinship relationship, something meaningful to the Welsh gentry, however distant the degree. John ap Robert ap Howell was a common labourer and the son of John Salesbury's tenant, demonstrating the various extended bonds that connected people to the Salesbury family. They were also Welsh speakers who claimed not to understand English, a source of frustration for the Shropshire jury who heard the murder charge. David ap John Griffith said that the commissioners from the Council in the Marches came to the window of the house to speak with Ellis Powell and 'theare they talked in the english tong . . . which this Deponent understandeth not'.[117] The gentry, however, were evidently bilingual in English and Welsh, able to speak English on official business, but also able to communicate with their servants and tenants in Welsh. John Salesbury, a JP himself and educated at Gray's Inn in London, was competent in English, but Welsh was the language of his estates, reflected in the monolingualism of his followers.

A gentleman's *plaid* was fiercely loyal and willing to defend their master's interests to the death. A relationship with a *plaid*, however, came with obligations for the gentry, a reflection of the hierarchy which governed social relations in early modern England and Wales, mirroring the relationship between the gentry and their noble patrons. A gentleman had a responsibility to look after his *plaid*. John Salesbury (d. 1611), for example, made bequests to retainers in his will, giving them land and annuities and cancelling debts. Some of the names in John Salesbury's will overlap with defendants in a Star Chamber suit brought against him by his older sister, Margaret, who accused him of sending his followers to take her and her young son by force from a house in Llanrhaeadr-yng-Nghinmeirch, Denbighshire.[118] It is also

---

[116] TNA, STAC 7/4/2, depositions of seven defendants.
[117] TNA, STAC 7/4/2, depositions of seven defendants.
[118] Jarrett, '"By reason of her sex and widowhood"', pp. 79–96.

likely that the Salesburys rewarded their followers through other means, such as security of tenure and the provision of hospitality in the Salesbury houses.[119] There is no further evidence of a Salesbury *plaid* after John Salesbury's death in 1611; the next paterfamilias, William Salesbury (d.1660) was not accused of involving his servants in armed disputes with his neighbours, and it is possible that the practice of maintaining a *plaid* was receding in north Wales. This might have reflected a wider change in tenurial relationships which had begun earlier across the border; from the mid-sixteenth century, tenants in England, for example, started to deny obligations to partake in military service for their lord.[120]

The Salesburys' household servants are not well documented. Some of them, like Hugh Salesbury, the former steward, might have been members of the *plaid*, but the household was a separate, formalised space that also included women. For example, Sir Robert Salesbury (d.1599) bequeathed a lifetime annuity of forty shillings to his servant Margaret ferch Thomas in his will.[121] Bequests rewarded good service and annuities provided some measure of security in a servant's old age.[122] William Salesbury (d.1660) thus granted land, including a new cow house, to his household servant, Edward ab Ieuan Lloyd.[123] It is clear, however, that servants could be important and deeply trusted members of the household. For example, Richard Worrall (b.1529), the Salesburys' steward, was a vital connection between two generations of the family and served four Salesbury patriarchs. A steward was a position of some status, though the term encompassed different roles: the Salesburys, for example, were stewards of the lordship of Ruthin, overseeing the manorial

---

[119] Heal, *Hospitality*, pp. 66–7, 154.
[120] Jeremy Goring, 'Social change and military decline in mid-Tudor England', *History*, 60 (1975), 189–90.
[121] TNA, PROB 11/96/125.
[122] R. C. Richardson, *Household Servants in Early Modern England* (Manchester, 2010), pp. 78–9.
[123] CRO, XD2/975.

courts.[124] It is likely that Richard Worrall, who was unable to write, if not illiterate, oversaw the Salesburys' household. When John Salesbury died in 1580, he left Worrall all his lands in Llanfwrog and Caerserwyd, Denbighshire, for the term of Worrall's life, first receiving the rents from the existing tenants, then holding the land himself when the tenancy expired for the chief rent of 13s. 4d.[125] John was survived by four children, and his sons at least maintained a close connection with Worrall. He became a foster father to John (d.1611) and William (d.1660) and remained an important presence in their lives. John Salesbury described him as his foster father in his 1611 will and bequeathed Worrall an annuity of £20.[126] It is notable that their father's will made no mention of a guardianship arrangement for the younger children, but there were evidently informal agreements in place and Worrall took responsibility for the younger sons. Looking at later medieval Wales, Llinos Beverley Smith suggested a link between wet nurses and foster fathers, and it is possible that Richard Worrall's wife was the children's nurse.[127]

When Sir Robert Salesbury died, and John and William petitioned Thomas Egerton as overseer of their brother's will for money and the right to live at Bachymbyd, Richard Worrall made his mark to witness every statement supporting their claim to money.[128] He also testified in the petition himself that he had delivered £140 to Sir Robert in order that Sir Robert could purchase his wardship from Sir George Bromley, and that the money rightfully belonged to John and William under the terms of their father's will. Sir Robert had his own connection to Richard Worrall because Worrall's daughter, Elizabeth, was the mother

---

[124] D. R. Hainsworth, *Stewards, Lords, and People: The estate steward and his world in later Stuart England* (Cambridge, 1992), pp. 10–11. For the early modern estate steward in Wales, see Sarah Ward Clavier, 'Accounting for lives: autobiography and biography in the accounts of Sir Thomas Myddelton, 1642–1666', *The Seventeenth Century*, 35/4 (2020), 453–72.

[125] TNA, PROB 11/63/70.

[126] TNA, PROB 11/118/503.

[127] Llinos Beverley Smith, 'Fosterage, adoption and god-parenthood: Ritual and fictive kinship in medieval Wales', *WHR*, 16/1 (1992), 11–12.

[128] SA, 212/364/1.

of Sir Robert's illegitimate daughter, also called Elizabeth.[129] It is impossible to know if Sir Robert took advantage of his power over his steward and his steward's family, although it is worth bearing in mind that the gentry could abuse their positions in their households and fail to live up to the expectations of the ideal gentleman.[130] On the other hand, Worrall remained a faithful servant to the family and Sir Robert acknowledged his daughter, thus perhaps Elizabeth Worrall had some agency in the situation, although that did not change the power dynamics involved. In Sir Robert's will, he bequeathed an annuity of £10 'to my base daughter Elizabeth Salisbury' and £100 towards her marriage; she married Robert Lloyd of Hendreforfydd, Corwen.[131] He bequeathed Richard Worrall all the rents and services due under his lease, giving him a free tenancy for the rest of his life. Subsequently, in the rental compiled by Sir Thomas Egerton as part of the inventory of Sir Robert's will, Richard Worrall held land worth £1 11s. 8d and more than twenty-two acres in the demesne of Bachymbyd, but he refused to pay the rent, 'alledging it was remitted by Sir Roberts will'.[132] Worrall paid rent of £4 a year for four acres of pasture and his half-share of eight acres of meadow of £8 a year, suggesting that he knew which tenancies had rent remittals under the terms of the will. The inventory also included Worrall's land from John Salesbury: Worrall held one tenement and the Wern Ddu, a woodland if the name matched the holding, by lease from John Salesbury (d.1580), paying chief rent to the queen of 13s. 4d.

However, these administrative documents do not capture any sense of the relationships between Worrall and the Salesburys. In May 1601, William Salesbury, aged twenty, was caught up in a suit in the Denbighshire Great Sessions over the killing of one Lewis Jones, alias John Lewis, a servant and trumpeter of Sir

[129] DRO, DD/DM/1647, f. 26.
[130] Richardson, *Household Servants*, pp. 203–7.
[131] DRO, DD/DM/1647, f. 26.
[132] THL, Ellesmere MS 1782e.

John Lloyd of Bodidris.[133] The defendants, John Price of Derwen, William Price, Jeffrey ap John Lloyd and others, were charged with murdering Lewis Jones, although in the end William Price was the only one found guilty, though he was cleared of murder and escaped significant punishment by claiming benefit of clergy. The suit centred on a brawl which occurred in Ruthin on 5 May 1600, where Lewis Jones was injured and later died of his wounds. The quarrel was similar to the other factional disputes discussed above which plagued the Denbighshire gentry; this time it centred on a disagreement between Thomas Thelwall and the servants of Sir John Lloyd. Thelwall accused Lewis Jones of robbing him on the highway, which Jones denied. This in itself was part of an ongoing quarrel between the two men. According to Richard Worrall, he was at home on 5 May when Sir John Lloyd sent his cook to ask Worrall to see what William Salesbury was doing in Ruthin and to bring William and Sir John's men home. Sir John evidently suspected trouble. Worrall found William with three of Sir John's servants, Owen Lloyd, Richard Jones and Lewis Jones, in the house of Thomas Jones of Ruthin, a mercer. They were visiting the deputy sheriff, Evan Lloyd, who was unwell. When Worrall had been in the house less than an hour, Thomas Thelwall arrived and confronted Lewis Jones about the robbery, which Jones denied. Thelwall threatened to complain to Jones's master, Sir John Lloyd, and Jones 'earnestlie desiered him not to complaine', offering to duel Thelwall if Thelwall believed he had wronged him. Thelwall refused the duel and reiterated that he would complain to Sir John Lloyd.

After this, Worrall said that all the men then drank together 'in loving and kinde maner as seemed to this deponent, without any evill or hotte words passing betweene them'. However, when Thelwall was about to depart, the argument resumed, although Worrall conveniently claimed he 'remembreth not' what was said. The exchange prompted Thelwall to focus his ire on William

[133] NLW, Great Sessions 4/12/1. I am very grateful to Sharon Howard for bringing this reference to my attention and generously sharing her previous work on the material.

Salesbury and he told William that 'he was as good a gentlman as he the saied Salusburie was'. William then accused Thelwall of being the son of a woman of low morals and Thelwall left the house. Other witnesses said that William disparaged Thelwall's father as well as his mother. Evan Lloyd, the deputy sheriff who had been ill in Thomas Jones's house, said Thelwall told William that his father was 'a gentleman and a priste and had whipped the said Salusbury his eldest brother and better men then he was', then Thelwall declared 'in a great rage and fury' that he was going to kill William. Everyone else stayed in the house until Robert Wyn Salesbury arrived and Worrall felt he was 'sufficientlie provided to bring the said Salusburie and the rest of his compenie out of the towne towards home'. Robert Wyn was another voice of reason in the subsequent brawl. The men had all gone as far as the churchyard when Lewis Jones declared that he would not continue without 'his felow' Owen Lloyd, who had stayed behind in the house, and Robert Wyn promised to get him. While they were waiting, Thomas Thelwall came into the churchyard and drew his sword, followed by Jeffrey ap John Lloyd, John Price of Derwen, and many others. All the men drew their weapons and a brawl ensued which killed Lewis Jones. Worrall, however, said that he was unable to describe the events in question because he had 'speciall care of mr William Salusburie being his master['s] brother'. He grabbed hold of William 'and helde him and with the helpe of another caried him into the church by force', keeping him there until the fight was over. Other witnesses corroborated Worrall's account. Griffith ap Rees ab Ieuan, a gentleman of Glyndyfrdwy, was in the market at Ruthin when he heard about the brawl in the churchyard against William Salesbury and hurried to get there, but realised that William had been 'put into the church' by Richard Worrall. Evan Lloyd said all the men were involved in the brawl, except William Salesbury who 'had bene carryed to the churche theare by his foster father for his save gard'.

These were disputes of reputation. Rees Salusbury of Llanfwrog said that, in the previous March, there was a quarrel between John Price of Derwen and Robert ap Thomas, who had been a servant of Sir Robert Salesbury. John Price disparaged the gentle status of John Salesbury, the middle brother, who was imprisoned at the time for the Essex Revolt, and William Salesbury subsequently argued with two of Price's brothers when they met in Ruthin shortly afterwards. The participants in the brawl of May 1601 were hot-headed young men who had been drinking. They believed that they were protecting their and their family's reputation. Unlike the disputes involving heads of households discussed above, it was not a disagreement over who would be MP or who would own a profitable farm, quarrels which, to a modern audience, have some sort of substance to them. However, this was a society exquisitely sensitive to status, honour and reputation, and the young men, not heads of households themselves, were involved in an intangible jostling to prove their place in the social hierarchy above their opponents. William Salesbury, who seemed very much the source of the quarrel even in the depositions of his family's supporters, was a youngest son, born after the death of his father, and pushed further down the social ladder of his family by the birth of his nephew, John. The infant John had owned the Salesbury patrimony since the death of William's eldest brother, Sir Robert, in July 1599, less than a year before the arguments took place. Younger sons and youths, or unmarried men, were especially prone to these sorts of disputes, as Lloyd Bowen has shown in his analysis of the duel between Sir John Egerton and Edward Morgan in 1610.[134] By casting aspersions on the parentage of other gentlemen and defending his middle brother's reputation, William was asserting his own status as the son of a prominent gentry family, aggressively defending his claim to be a gentleman even as his fortunes changed. Perhaps it is unsurprising that William became a privateer a couple of years later to make his own money in the New World and escape the claustrophobic

[134] Bowen, *Anatomy of a Duel*, chapter three.

environment of the competitive, status-obsessed north Wales gentry.[135]

Richard Worrall knew his foster son well. It is telling that Sir John Lloyd, hot-headed himself, perhaps, but concerned about the excesses of youth, sent his servant to Worrall and asked him to quell the situation and bring William home. Sir John knew that Worrall had a close relationship with William. It seems that Worrall could not or would not persuade William to leave Ruthin until Robert Wyn Salusbury arrived for additional support, but all the young men eventually left with him. When the brawl began in the churchyard, Worrall's sole concern was William's protection and he forced him into the church where he could not get involved in the fight which killed a man. Worrall's language in his deposition suggests that William did not approve of Worrall's behaviour; Worrall 'helde him' and took him into the church 'by force', before remaining in the church 'holding the said William Salusburie'. It is easy to picture the twenty-year-old William, struggling against Worrall to engage in a brawl against the enemies who slighted his family's reputation and thus defend his honour in armed combat. The other youths in the fight did not have their fathers or father-figures to prevent them engaging in violence, but the actions of Sir John Lloyd and Richard Worrall suggest that older men worried about their sons and servants fighting each other and endeavoured to prevent it. Worrall kept William safe during the brawl and it had the additional purpose of protecting William from legal action; no deponent accused William of participating in the brawl, although many are clear about his contribution to the tension leading up to it. The incident did not, it seems, do any damage to William and Worrall's relationship; in 1602, they sold some parcels of land together.[136] It highlights, however, that servants could hold special positions in a gentry family's household. It was widely known that the Salesbury steward acted as a foster father to the family's younger sons, two

---

[135] See below, pp. 218–23.
[136] NLW, Bachymbyd 693.

young men who lost their own father aged five and before birth, respectively. Worrall was not a gentleman himself, but he fostered two who had a strong sense of their own gentle status. It raises important questions about knowledge transmission within the family, guardianship arrangements, and the extent of Worrall's role in raising the boys, questions which cannot be answered within the limits of the existing sources.

CONCLUSION

The Salesburys of Rhug and Bachymbyd were part of local, regional and national networks of power. Through their noble patrons, the Salesburys were connected to the political life of the realm and the common association gave them a network of other gentry followers throughout England and Wales. However, they remained deeply embedded in their local society. They fought feuds with rival gentry families to maintain and protect their status, feuds which had little relevance outside the enclosed world of the north Wales gentry and flummoxed authorities which despaired at their factionalism. The Salesburys maintained their own groups of tenants, servants and labourers to protect their interests and, in return, the Salesburys provided for them with hospitality, employment and secure tenures, fulfilling their role as the lynchpin of the local community. The continued existence of the *plaid* and engagement with local people emphasises that the Salesburys had a deep knowledge of Welsh society and culture. They spoke both English and Welsh, the former as officeholders for the realm like the JPs who arrived at the farmhouse in Burton, and the latter to their tenants and servants in their households as well as between themselves. When William Salesbury argued with Thomas Thelwall about his brothers' status as gentlemen, witnesses reported that they spoke in Welsh. The Salesburys of Rhug and Bachymbyd were specifically a Welsh gentry family, part of their north Wales community, and they understood how to navigate the social norms and expectations of their world. The next chapter builds on this cultural understanding to look at the Salesburys' engagement with Welsh scholarship and their continued interest in Welsh-language culture throughout the sixteenth and seventeenth centuries.

4
CULTURE, SCHOLARSHIP AND RELIGION

The Salesburys of Rhug and Bachymbyd lived in the cradle of the early modern Welsh renaissance.[1] Their estates were in the Vale of Clwyd, a historically important region of bardic patronage due to the large numbers of gentry families with the ability and inclination to support poets. These families also had the time and money to engage with new humanist ideas arriving from continental Europe.[2] As a result, the Vale of Clwyd and its environs became an important source of early modern Welsh scholarship, producing scholars such as the cartographer and antiquary Humphrey Llwyd (1527–68), Gabriel Goodman (1528–1601), dean of Westminster, and William Salesbury (<1520–*c*.1580) of Plas Isaf, who translated the New Testament into Welsh. This list does not conventionally include the Salesburys of Rhug and Bachymbyd, who are not remembered for their great contribution to scholarship. In some ways, this is unsurprising, because even their most prolific scholar, William Salesbury (1580–1660), did not produce any particularly brilliant works of literature. Unlike the famous gentry scholarship collections at Hengwrt or Mostyn, the Salesburys' library is not recorded in an extant catalogue nor has it become part of modern archive collections; it was dispersed at some point after the death

---

[1] See G. J. Williams, 'Traddodiad llenyddol Dyffryn Clwyd a'r cyffiniau', *Transactions of the Denbighshire Historical Society*, 1 (1952), 20–32.

[2] Enid Roberts, 'The Renaissance in the Vale of Clwyd', *Flintshire Historical Society Journal*, 15 (1954–55), 52–63.

of Owen Salesbury in 1694 and only a few items survive today.[3] Other branches of the Salusbury kindred were well-known for their scholarship: in addition to William Salesbury of Plas Isaf, Sir John Salusbury (*c*.1565–1612) of Lleweni is remembered for his poetry and a possible association with William Shakespeare, while other noted scholars in the wider Salusbury kindred include Henry Salusbury (1651–*c*.1632) of Dolbelydr, a Welsh grammarian, and the genealogist John Salisbury (*fl*. 1650) of Erbistock.[4]

Nevertheless, the Salesburys were a scholarly family. They were patrons of the arts, they engaged in scholarship production, and they had a significant manuscript collection in their houses. They were also full members of the scholarly community in north Wales, lending and borrowing texts, writing about scholarly pursuits in their correspondence, and welcoming visiting scholars to their houses. Engagement with scholarship was a vital demonstration of the Salesburys' identity as a Welsh gentry family. Scholarship showed that a gentleman had an education and he could be both a competent official and a sound administrator of his estates. By the late seventeenth century, book and manuscript collections were a key feature of gentry houses across England and Wales. These collections shared similar interests: they often contained multiple copies of the Bible and a focus on classical works and theology, but there was also scope for the family's own interests to shape their composition.[5] This chapter begins by exploring how the Salesburys obtained their education, before considering how they put this education into practice through their scholarly interests.

---

[3] See Daniel Huws, *Medieval Welsh Manuscripts* (Cardiff, 2000), pp. 287–316; and Mary Chadwick and Shaun Evans, '"Ye Best Tast of Books & Learning of Any Other Country Gentn": The Library of Thomas Mostyn of Gloddaith, *c*.1676–1692', in Annika Bautz and James Gregory (eds), *Libraries, Books and Collectors of Texts, 1600–1900* (London, 2018), pp. 87–103.

[4] For Sir John's poems, see Brown, *Poems by Sir John Salusbury and Robert Chester*.

[5] David Pearson, 'Patterns of book ownership in late seventeenth-century England', *The Library*, 11/2 (2010), 144–53.

EDUCATION

The second half of the sixteenth century was a time of intensification for gentry education, with increased access to the universities and the Inns of Court for gentry families across England and Wales.[6] This included the Welsh gentry, and there was a notable increase in the numbers of Welsh students at Oxford, Cambridge and the Inns of Court.[7] The Welsh gentry's education away from Wales introduced them to scholarship beyond their own culture, while also inculcating an appreciation for vernacular Welsh literature. For contemporaries, travel was no threat to Welsh language or culture. Welsh poets praised their patrons for obtaining an education in England and it was seen as an important stage in a young man's development.[8] For the humanists of the Protestant Reformation, Welsh was a vehicle for disseminating New Learning, and the Welsh gentry had a thriving interest in international scholarship.[9] The Reformation had a major impact on educational provision, stimulating the need for literacy to read the Bible and also fuelling religious scholarship. The number of endowed schools increased in Wales, almost all connected in some way, whether through founder or endowment, to the new English Church.[10] These schools were thus educating their pupils in the reformed religion and promoting the humanist principles of duty and service to the commonwealth. Before the Reformation, there was less choice, but gentry children almost certainly received a basic education in their own households or at informal local schools run by clerics.

---

[6] Rosemary O'Day, *Education and Society 1500–1800: The social foundations of education in early modern Britain* (London, 1982), pp. 81–8.

[7] Griffith, *Learning, Law and Religion*, fig. 1, p. 15.

[8] John Gwynfor Jones, 'The Welsh poets and their patrons, c.1550–1640', *WHR*, 9 (1978), 263.

[9] R. Geraint Gruffydd, 'Wales and the Renaissance', in A. J. Roderick (ed.), *Wales through the Ages II* (1960), pp. 43–7; Chadwick and Evans, '"Ye Best Tast of Books & Learning"', pp. 87–8.

[10] W. P. Griffith, 'Schooling and Society', in John Gwynfor Jones (ed.), *Class, Community and Culture in Tudor Wales* (Cardiff, 1989), pp. 83–4.

Grammar school education, providing a competent command of Latin, was much rarer.[11]

John Salesbury (b.*c.*1450), the first head of the Salesbury family, received a grammar school education.[12] He attended school with two of his brothers, Foulk and Henry, all younger sons of Thomas Salusbury (d.1491) of Lleweni. Foulk, the second son, became dean of St Asaph, a key clerical position in north Wales which required Latin literacy and a good education. Henry, the third or fourth son, married Margaret, daughter of Gruffudd ap Rhys ap Madog Gloddaeth, and they established a successful cadet branch of the Salusbury family at Llanrhaeadr. It was expensive to educate multiple sons, and the surviving accounts include purchases of coal, candles, ink, paper, material to make gowns, and money for the manciple's stipend. The school itself is unknown, but the accounts suggest that the boys boarded. It gives an indication of the wealth of the Salusburys of Lleweni and their desire to invest in their sons' future. It enabled them to have successful careers in the Church or run their own estates with skill and competence, even the younger sons who would not inherit the Lleweni estates. W. P. Griffith believes that the boys were at a university, but it was reasonably rare for medieval Welshmen to attend university: there were just 260 Welsh students at Oxford in the fifteenth century, mainly churchmen, and very few at Cambridge.[13] Equally, no Salesbury, or a variation thereof, appears in the registers of Oxford or Cambridge for the fifteenth century.[14] Thus, John Salesbury and his brothers were away at school, where they received an education appropriate for a prosperous, fifteenth-century Welsh gentleman. This education enabled John

---

[11] Nicholas Orme, 'Education in Medieval Wales', *WHR*, 27/4 (2015), 625–9.

[12] NLW, Lleweni 674.

[13] W. P. Griffith, 'Welsh students at Oxford, Cambridge and the Inns of Court during the sixteenth and early seventeenth centuries' (unpublished PhD thesis, University of Wales, Bangor, 1981), 27; Rhys W. Hays, 'Welsh Students at Oxford and Cambridge Universities in the Middle Ages', *WHR*, 4 (1968), 327, 350.

[14] A. B. Emden (ed.), *A Biographical Register of the University of Cambridge to 1500* (Cambridge, 1963); A. B. Emden (ed.), *A Biographical Register of the University of Oxford to 1500*, vol. 3 (Oxford, 1959).

to navigate the legal maze of the north Wales marcher lordships and gain his own estate at Bachymbyd, establishing his own cadet branch of the Salusbury kindred and greatly profiting from his family's investment in his education.

It is possible that the Salusbury boys attended Ruthin School. There was a collegiate church and school at Ruthin from the end of the thirteenth century and the Salusburys, by the fifteenth century, were part of the school's likely demographic.[15] The school almost certainly provided a standard medieval education in Latin grammar.[16] John Salesbury's estate at Bachymbyd was located in the parish of Llanynys, which had a close association with the collegiate church in Ruthin, and one of the rectors of Llanynys church may have been a teacher at the school in 1455.[17] Thus, even if John Salesbury and his brothers did not attend Ruthin School, there is a strong possibility that John sent his own sons there. His eldest son, Piers Salesbury (d.1548), could read and write in English, as evidenced by his surviving writings.[18] Piers was also steward of the lordship of Ruthin so he needed administrative competence. It is probable that he was also literate in Latin, given the nature of fifteenth-century education, although this was not guaranteed: the fifteenth-century Welsh gentleman John Edwards of Chirk, for example, was educated in English, as was his son.[19] The evidence for the Salesburys' education in this period is limited, but Piers's eldest son, Robert (d.1550), also held offices and thus he was presumably literate, like his father. There is no evidence that John, Piers or Robert went on to higher education, either at the universities of Oxford or Cambridge, or the Inns of Court. Their time at school, which may have been Ruthin, was sufficient for their purposes, primarily running their estates and undertaking local administration.

---

[15] Keith M. Thomas, *Ruthin School: The First Seven Centuries* (Ruthin, 1974), pp. 54–6.
[16] For the curriculum in medieval Wales, see Orme, 'Education', 635–9.
[17] Thomas, *Ruthin School*, p. 62.
[18] See, for example, TNA, SP 1/236, f. 378.
[19] Llinos Beverley Smith, 'The grammar and commonplace books of John Edwards of Chirk', *BBCS*, 34 (1987), 182–3.

The next generation of Salesburys attended school after the Reformation. Robert Salesbury took advantage of the upheaval by buying the former lands in Llanynys of the collegiate church at Ruthin, highlighting the close connection between the foundation and the Salesburys' estates.[20] However, Ruthin School survived the religious changes, so it remained an option for the education of the Salesbury sons.[21] Nevertheless, there were other schooling options available to the gentry of north Wales in the sixteenth century. John Salusbury of Lleweni (d.1566), for example, was a pupil at Winchester College, Hampshire, and Dafydd ap Huw of Plas Coch, Anglesey, went to Hereford Cathedral School in the 1530s.[22] Wherever John Salesbury (d.1580) attended school, he was sufficiently prepared to become a student at Gray's Inn, London, in 1550, when he was around seventeen.[23] It is unlikely that John intended to become a lawyer. A spell at one of the Inns of Court was an important part of the early modern gentleman's education, giving him adequate knowledge of the law to administer his estates, enact his duties as a local officeholder, and understand legal suits brought by or against him.[24] It also enabled John to spend time in London and extend his social network. For example, while a student at Gray's Inn, John was a servant of the earl of Pembroke. Education was not just about learning to read or acquiring legal nous; it also taught young gentlemen the social skills to navigate their position in society.

John Salesbury was a friend of Gabriel Goodman (1528–1601), dean of Westminster. In 1574, Goodman re-founded Ruthin School and firmly established it as a grammar school for the local gentry.[25] The school emphasised pious study of the classics and endeavoured to give its pupils a firm grounding in

---

[20] Thomas, *Ruthin School*, pp. 71.
[21] Thomas, *Ruthin School*, pp. 68–72.
[22] NLW, 1565C, pp. 48–9; Grove-White, *A Prism for His Times*, p. 12.
[23] Foster, *Admissions to Gray's Inn*, p. 20.
[24] Wilfrid Prest, 'Legal education of the gentry at the Inns of Court, 1560–1640', *Past and Present*, 38 (1967), 20–39.
[25] Thomas, *Ruthin School*, pp. 24–5. See also R. Newcome, *A Memoir of Gabriel Goodman, with some account of Ruthin School* (Ruthin, 1825).

Greek and Latin.[26] At the time of the school's re-founding, John's eldest son, the future Sir Robert (1567–99), was around seven years old and so he was a likely candidate as a pupil. It was a large school of up to 120 pupils, mainly drawn from the Vale of Clwyd, and with a graded scale of payments depending on income; the Salesburys would have paid an admission fee of 2s. 6d and yearly tuition of 8s.[27] As an adult, Sir Robert gave six and a half acres of land in Llanynys, worth ten guineas a year, towards the school's endowment and, like his father, Sir Robert was a close associate of Gabriel Goodman. When Sir Robert became fatally ill in 1599, Goodman accompanied him home from London.[28] Sir Robert's education enabled him to matriculate at Brasenose College, Oxford, on 31 January 1584, aged seventeen.[29] Two years later, he followed in his father's footsteps to Gray's Inn, where he was admitted on 31 January 1586.[30]

It is probable that John (d.1611), Sir Robert's middle brother, also attended Ruthin School. John did not pursue higher education, instead developing a career as a soldier. However, the youngest brother, William (d.1660), became an enthusiastic scholar. He is the only Salesbury for whom there exists firm evidence of his attendance at Ruthin School, where he was a contemporary of Godfrey Goodman (1583–1656), the future bishop of Gloucester and nephew of Gabriel Goodman. In the early 1650s, Godfrey Goodman wrote to William complaining about William's refusal to bestow his entire estate on his eldest son, Owen Salesbury, who had married Goodman's niece, Mary. Goodman said that he wrote 'as a priest with Relacion to your owne good who must be accomptable to god . . . and our time can not be longe for it is nowe above three score yeares since we were schoolfellowes'.[31] William gave short shrift to the rather

[26] Thomas, *Ruthin School*, p. 83–6.
[27] Griffith, 'Schooling and Society', p. 90.
[28] Thomas, *Ruthin School*, p. 88; Roberts, *Calendar of the Cecil Papers: Volume 9* (London, 1902), p. 181.
[29] *Al. Oxon.*
[30] Foster, *Admissions to Gray's Inn*, p. 68.
[31] NLW, Bachymbyd Letters 43.

patronising letter, confident in his relationship with his God and his own ability to dispose of his estates as he pleased. Godfrey Goodman attended Westminster School, presumably joining his uncle, the dean of Westminster, from 1592/3, so William was at Ruthin School before this date. Much later, Eubule Thelwall remembered William saying that Sir Robert sent him to school, so his oldest brother oversaw his education.[32] However, Thelwall also said that Sir Robert took William from school and 'forced [William] to waite at his brother's table with a trencher', which caused William to leave his family home and become a soldier in Ireland. Nevertheless, William later matriculated at Oriel College, Oxford, on 19 October 1599, four months after his brother's death, where he stayed for one year.[33] This does suggest that Sir Robert was in some way a barrier to William's education and it is probable that money was the issue. After Sir Robert died, William petitioned Thomas Egerton as the overseer of his will to grant William the money owed to him from Sir Robert's estate. William claimed that he had not received the annual sum of twenty marks granted to him under the terms of his father's will. William had only received £30 for his year at Oxford and 'some small exhibicion for few yeares in the Countrey Schooles'. Discounting the cost of his education, Sir Robert owed William a total sum of £186 13s. 4d.[34] William's father had provided him with money for his education and maintenance, but William struggled to access it.

William's situation illustrates the difficulties facing orphaned younger sons who relied on their eldest brother for support and, in the Salesburys' case, to abide by the terms of their father's will. William's experience as a younger son contributed heavily to his decision to provide secure futures for his children. Perhaps reflecting his own struggle to access it, education was important to William and he sent his children, sons and daughters, to boarding schools. Owen,

---

[32] CRO, XD2/463.
[33] *Al. Oxon.*
[34] SA, 212/364/1.

the eldest son, attended Winchester College, Hampshire, where Owen was a commoner and paid fees.[35] Even with the Bachymbyd estate mortgaged, William prioritised the money to educate his children. Owen was at Winchester by 29 September 1627, aged fifteen, but he had not recently arrived; he wrote to tell his father that he had been 'put into a higher booke [form] than I was in'.[36] It is likely that he had arrived in 1625, aged twelve, and left four years later at sixteen.[37] Before Owen went to Winchester, he may have attended Ruthin School for a basic education. Winchester is a considerable distance from Rhug, and in the school holidays, Owen stayed with one of his teachers, former headmaster Hugh Robinson (d.1655), Doctor of Divinity and a Welshman from Anglesey, son of Nicholas Robinson (d.1585), bishop of Bangor.[38] This Welsh connection may partially explain William's decision to send Owen to Winchester. Robinson, and a Welsh predecessor, Hugh Lloyd, both oversaw an increase in pupils from north Wales.[39] There was also a familial precedent: as mentioned above, William's uncle, John Salusbury of Lleweni, had attended Winchester, although John died before William was born. Owen's letters home illuminate some aspects of his life at school. In one, he asked William to pay the bearer forty shillings because Owen borrowed it from him 'to buy some bookes which are needefull for me to use'.[40] On 10 February 1629, Owen wrote that he understood William planned to visit him in the spring 'which . . . will make mee rejoice veri much'.[41] There was a hiatus in the correspondence after the February letter and it seems that William wrote to Owen to complain about the absence of communication. On 24 June, Owen sent his father some tobacco

---

[35] Owen Salesbury does not appear in Winchester College's Registers of Scholars, which begins in 1393: Winchester College, *Registrum Primum 1393–1687*. I am grateful to Suzanne Foster for her assistance with this source.

[36] NLW, Bachymbyd Letters 18.

[37] Griffiths, 'Welsh Students', 357.

[38] NLW, Bachymbyd Letters 39; Arthur F. Leach, *A History of Winchester College* (London, 1899), p. 329.

[39] Griffith, 'Welsh Students', 357.

[40] NLW, Bachymbyd Letters 18.

[41] NLW, Bachymbyd Letters 19.

as an apology and explained that he had not written because he thought William was going to visit soon: 'I wold have written unto you longe since If I had not had a sure hope by your letter of comeinge'.[42] William and Owen were two hundred miles apart, but William enjoyed staying in touch with his son.

By 14 October 1629, aged sixteen, Owen had left Winchester and moved to Oxford.[43] There is no matriculation record for him so he did not formally join the university as an undergraduate. Instead, Owen received tutoring from Richard Lloyd, described in his October letter home as his cousin, although in the vast sprawl of Welsh gentry kinship, the description is not especially helpful. It may have been Richard Lloyd (c.1594–1659) of Henblas, Anglesey, who matriculated at Oriel College, Oxford, in 1612, notably the same college as Owen's father. Lloyd received his Bachelor of Divinity on 7 May 1628, thus it is feasible that he was still in Oxford when Owen arrived in October 1629 and the Oriel connection may be an important clue. Alternatively, he may have been Richard Lloyd, the son of Margaret Salesbury (1565–1650), William's eldest sister; if so, there is no record of his matriculation either, thus Richard Lloyd of Henblas is the more plausible candidate. Connections, including familial ones, were a useful and important feature of life in the universities and Welsh students were often associated with Welsh tutors.[44] Owen studied in Oxford during a time of considerable growth for the university. The early modern undergraduate population, growing steadily since the mid-sixteenth century, reached its peak in the 1630s.[45] It was an education tailored for the sons of the nobility and the gentry, albeit with a primary focus on classical language and literature.[46] Owen told his father that he hoped to 'profit in a smalle space that heerafter I may be a comfort to you and all the

[42] NLW, Bachymbyd Letters 20.
[43] NLW, Bachymbyd Letters 22.
[44] Griffith, 'Welsh Students', 408–9.
[45] Nicholas Tyacke, 'Introduction', in Nicholas Tyacke (ed.), *The History of the University of Oxford*, vol. 4: *The Seventeenth Century* (Oxford, 1997), p. 2.
[46] For an overview of the BA curriculum, see Griffith, *Learning, Law and Religion*, pp. 103–10.

rest of my freindes'.[47] Owen recognised that his education was a practical pursuit, intended to give him the necessary skills to run his affairs as a gentleman.

On 7 June 1632, after two and a half years in Oxford, Owen, like his uncle and grandfather before him, became a student at Gray's Inn. Attendance at an Inn of Court was an expensive endeavour; it required negotiating and paying for one of the chambers, which were in high demand, as well as payment of a fine for admission.[48] William also gave Owen £40 a year in maintenance, but Owen complained that he needed more, telling his father that it is 'more than I deserve yet it is more then I can doe to live therewith'.[49] Owen studied in the chamber of John Jones, a solicitor from Ffestiniog, once again demonstrating the Welsh connections within English educational institutions and exemplifying the informal tuition commonly arranged at the Inns of Court.[50] Educating a son in London required family resources and connections. However, there were also particular advantages. For example, much of William and Owen's correspondence in this period is concerned with lawsuits. On 19 January 1635, William sent Owen information on various suits, including a Star Chamber suit involving one John Thomas, the wardship of one Robert Lloyd's son, and a process served on a tenant whom William wanted to replace.[51] Owen had to repay some of his father's investment by undertaking the family's legal business while in London. Owen also provided a connection between Wales and London. He promised to tell William the rate 'where there is any beef solde here in London', maintaining William's knowledge of the beef market and the value of his cattle.[52] He also regularly sent goods in response to his father's requests, including sugar, seeds for medicinal plants, a box of cordial, and two plates and trays 'to boile fish'.[53]

---

[47] NLW, Bachymbyd Letters 22.
[48] Griffith, *Learning, Law and Religion*, p. 153.
[49] NLW, Bachymbyd Letters 26.
[50] Griffith, *Learning, Law and Religion*, p. 184.
[51] CRO, XD2/14.
[52] NLW, Bachymbyd Letters 25.
[53] NLW, Bachymbyd Letters 23; 26; CRO, XD2/14.

By 1635, William's second son, John, was also in London. The details of his early schooling are unknown, but William was evidently determined to set him up in a respectable career as a merchant. This was a traditional choice for the younger sons of the gentry, enabling them to have a secure future while also providing useful connections for their family.[54] John was destined to be a draper or a cloth merchant, a pertinent choice, given the Salesburys' economic interest in the wool trade. Unsurprisingly, William took great care over John's employment and he enlisted Owen's help in London. On 26 February 1635, Owen wrote that he had asked Rice Williams 'concerneing the placeinge of my brother with Mr Grymes', but Rice Williams said 'that he liketh not the man'.[55] Instead, on 27 June 1635, John was apprenticed to Charles Lloyd for seven years.[56] Lloyd was an experienced draper who completed his own nine-year apprenticeship in 1622. Although John began his apprenticeship in June, he was already in London by 9 March because Owen reported home that they had spoken to each other.[57] When John joined Charles Lloyd's household, Lloyd already had two other apprentices: Peter Thelwall, son of Simon Thelwall of Plas Newydd, Denbighshire, who began an eight-year apprenticeship in 1632, and Henry Cressey, son of Everingham Cressey of Birkin, Yorkshire, who began an eight-year apprenticeship in 1634. The presence of a Thelwall suggests there was a Welsh connection to William's choice of apprenticeship, and Charles Lloyd himself was kin of some degree to the Salesburys: John reported that his master's only niece, 'my cosen Penelope', died on 30 November 1635.[58] This, along with Owen's inquiries about a suitable master, replicated the Welsh network experienced by Owen during his education. John

---

[54] Patrick Wallis and Cliff Webb, 'The education and training of gentry sons in early modern England', *Social History*, 36/1 (2011), 52.

[55] NLW, Bachymbyd Letters 25.

[56] All apprenticeship details are taken from *Records of London's Livery Companies Online: Apprentices and Freemen 1400–1900*, available at *https://www.londonroll.org/home* (accessed 17 September 2021).

[57] NLW, Bachymbyd Letters 26.

[58] NLW, Bachymbyd Letters 32.

was a competent apprentice and Charles Lloyd trusted him to be in charge of receiving and disbursing money on his behalf. John took his responsibilities seriously, telling his father, 'God forbid I should disburse out the least farthinge [without instruction]'.[59] However, John did not always enjoy the work. The household was small with only a bookkeeper and two maids in addition to the three apprentices. As a result, the apprentices also acted as servants in the household. John said that they 'do waite at the table and wee make fiers in the parloure and many other necessary occasions . . . [too] tedious to be perused'. However, the successful completion of the apprenticeship would have established John in a prosperous trade and enabled him to look after himself without any reliance on his older brother for financial security. Unfortunately, John died in 1639, four years into his apprenticeship, and he never had the opportunity to establish himself as a cloth merchant.

Commonly, the youngest son of a gentry family was apprenticed in London and thus John's career choice was unusual.[60] However, families could choose to make different choices for their children and the provision of education based on birth order was not uniform. It is possible that William's sons helped to decide on their chosen careers. For example, William's youngest son, Charles (d.1666), became a student at Gray's Inn on 1 August 1642.[61] Charles's time at Gray's Inn, however, was disrupted by the outbreak of the Civil War and it is unlikely he spent much time there.[62] There is far less information about the education of the third son, Robert, who died in 1646. Like his brothers, he spent time living in London. On 3 April 1635, Owen wrote to his father, 'I have turned away Robert for his offence wherewill I hope you will be pleased for I should be lothe to harbour a thought that would seem offensive unto you'.[63] Sadly, he does not give any further details about Robert's actions, but

---

[59] NLW, Bachymbyd Letters 31.
[60] Wallis and Webb, 'The education and training of gentry sons', 52–3.
[61] Foster, *Admissions to Gray's Inn*, p. 237.
[62] Griffith, 'Welsh Students', 554–5.
[63] NLW, Bachymbyd Letters 27.

they were clearly a source of discontent between Robert and their father. Nevertheless, it shows that all four of William's sons lived in London as young men, partaking in a standard practice for the sons of the country gentry.[64] By the mid-seventeenth century, there was a large Welsh population in London, and sons in London helped to consolidate existing relationships.[65] For example, many of the letters between William and his sons include regards to various cousins and acquaintances, both back home in north Wales and away in England. On 19 January 1635, William told Owen that bad weather had prevented him from travelling to Chester to meet Harry Vaughan, Owen's uncle. On 10 February, Owen replied that Harry Vaughan had come to London and he still wanted to meet William to discuss a marriage between Roger Kynaston of Hordley and William's daughter, Margaret. William's conversation with Harry Vaughan, postponed from Chester, thus went via Owen in London. It demonstrates the number of Welsh gentry gathered in London for various reasons and the ease with which they maintained their social connections in the city, as well as their motivation to maintain them.

The focus thus far has been on the education of sons. The education of a gentry family's daughters developed competent wives, capable of running a busy household. However, wives could easily become widows, and widows of prosperous gentlemen could receive substantial amounts of land or money. Thus, any sensible education of daughters needed to account for the possibility that she might one day require a level of education to manage her own affairs. Depending on the type of widowhood provision arranged for her marriage, it was perhaps more likely that a daughter would control her own land in the future than would a younger son, reliant on his eldest brother for annuities. The formal education of daughters in England was, per annum, more expensive than the education of sons. Linda Pollock gives the example of Sarah and Martha Worsley, whose education cost their grandfather £10 a

[64] Jones, *Welsh Gentry*, pp. 52–3.
[65] Griffith, *Learning, Law and Religion*, p. 144.

year each, compared to their brother, Ralph, whose education cost between £6 and £7 a year; Pollock notes that parents were willing to pay the extra money for their daughters.[66] The competency of the Salesbury wives and daughters as widows suggests their parents, formally or informally, did prepare their daughters to run estates. For example, Elizabeth Salusbury of Lleweni (d.*c.*1584), John Salesbury's wife, was executrix of his will in 1580, along with their daughter, Margaret (d.1650). This required literacy and numeracy, the ability to read documents, manage claims on the estate, and ensure bequests went to the intended recipients. Equally, Elinor Bagnall (d.1656), wife of Sir Robert (d.1599), astutely managed her estate in widowhood and she could read, write and keep account of her money: on 14 January 1653, for instance, Elinor wrote to her brother-in-law, William Salesbury, and complained that she had yet to receive the rent owed to her at Michaelmas.[67]

The daughters of gentry families rarely attended even local schools and usually studied under tutors at home.[68] It is likely that this was the case for the Salesbury wives and daughters, particularly before the mid-seventeenth century. William Salesbury, however, who valued education highly, sent his daughters to boarding schools. For example, Katherine Salesbury, his second daughter, attended a boarding school in Shrewsbury. This detail for Katherine only survives because she died at school, a fact recorded by John Salisbury of Erbistock in his additions to the Painted Book of Erbistock, the seventeenth-century collection of north Wales pedigrees started by Owen Salesbury.[69] Katherine, like her brother Owen, went to school in England. Shrewsbury, the county town for Shropshire, had various educational establishments, but they went largely unrecorded until a census of 1817 and there are very few records of seventeenth-century schools for girls in

---

[66] Linda Pollock, '"Teach her to live under obedience": The making of women in the upper ranks of early modern England', *Continuity and Change*, 4/2 (1989), 239.
[67] NLW, Bachymbyd Letters 45.
[68] Norma McMullen, 'The education of English gentlewomen 1540–1640', *History of Education*, 6/2 (1977), 91.
[69] DRO, DD/WY/6674, f. 74r.

Shrewsbury.[70] However, dating from before 1672, there was a finishing school run by Esther Chambre and Barbery Saxfield.[71] In the 1690s, Celia Fiennes described it as 'a very good Schoole for young Gentlewomen for learning work and behaviour and musick'.[72] There were eighteen girls in total at the school and six were the daughters of gentlemen.[73] Given Katherine was born in the late 1610s or early 1620s, she did not attend the Chambre-Saxfield finishing school. However, it gives an idea of the sort of school Katherine might have attended: small, well-respected, targeted at the daughters of gentlemen, and providing a suitable education in deportment and music, as well as 'learning'. To send Katherine to school forty miles away in Shrewsbury suggests that William wanted to invest in her education and endeavoured to find a highly regarded institution, although it is important not to forget the role that William's wife, Dorothy Vaughan (d.1627), played in the education of her children while she was alive: mothers often made key decisions about their daughters' schooling.[74]

Owen Salesbury (d.1658) and his wife, Mary Goodman (d.1676), also sent at least one of their daughters to school, although, again, this is only recorded because she died there. Margaret was their second-born child, and second daughter, and John Salisbury of Erbistock recorded that she 'died young at school in Ruthyn'.[75] Ruthin was the county town for Denbighshire and thus, like Shrewsbury, it had a range of schools, which were better recorded in the eighteenth century.[76] In the mid-

---

[70] Judith Everard, 'Education c.1600–2000', *Victoria County History Shropshire*, vol. 2 draft (March 2017), http://www.vchshropshire.org/drafts/ShrewsburyPart2/7_1_Education.pdf (accessed 15 February 2022).

[71] Angus McInnes, 'The emergence of a leisure town: Shrewsbury 1660–1760', *Past and Present*, 120/1 (1988), 64.

[72] C. Morris (ed.), *The Journeys of Celia Fiennes* (London, 1947), p. 186.

[73] McInnes, 'Emergence of a leisure town', 64.

[74] Deborah Youngs, '"For the preferement of their marriage and bringing upp in their youth": The education and training of young Welshwomen, c.1450–c.1550', *WHR*, 25/4 (2011), 480.

[75] DRO, DD/WY/6674, f. 74r.

[76] D. G. Evans, *The Foundations of Ruthin 1100–1800* (Wrexham, 2017), pp. 76–7, 114. I am grateful to D. G. Evans for providing me with a copy of his book.

seventeenth century, educational provision evidently included at least one finishing school for young ladies, again probably small and run by women. The death of a second Salesbury daughter at school suggests that formal education for daughters was accepted practice in the Salesbury family by the mid-seventeenth century and that all the daughters received schooling outside the home. The Salesbury daughters were certainly not educated to the same level as the Salesbury sons. Neither the universities of Oxford and Cambridge nor the Inns of Court were open to women, and arguably they did not provide the sort of education required to be a successful, marriageable woman in this period. Women needed to cultivate feminine attributes, rather than detailed knowledge of the law. They could learn to be good wives and mothers at home, with their own mother providing an example of how to run a household. William Salesbury's wife, Dorothy, died in 1627 and William might have sent his daughter to school because she no longer had an exemplar at home. However, William's son, Owen, also sent his daughter to school even though his wife, Mary (d.1676), outlived him. Thus, there were other advantages to educating daughters away from the home, even when the costs were higher than educating sons. There was evidently a seventeenth-century market in educational establishments for the daughters of gentlemen, which implies some degree of normality and expectation. Ultimately, the Salesburys wanted to educate their daughters to be capable wives and competent widows and they were willing to spend money on formal provision outside the home.

The Salesburys were a well-educated gentry family. Their sons predominantly attended local grammar schools or, later, English public schools and, after the mid-sixteenth century, many went on to higher education at the universities and the Inns of Court. Their education, increasingly humanist in focus through the sixteenth century, gave the Salesburys a solid grounding in at least Latin and English, and probably Greek too. By the mid-seventeenth century, and possibly earlier, daughters also received a level of formal schooling. In properly educating their children according to their status, the Salesburys demonstrated that they were a gentry family who had the means and interest to provide for their children's future. Education was a vital part of the Salesburys' identity as a Welsh gentry family, enabling them to administer their own affairs and run their estates and to expand their social and business networks. However, it also enabled them to engage in the pursuit of scholarship and maintain their engagement with Welsh culture, because the family still possessed a high level of Welsh literacy. It is very likely that the Salesburys' Welsh literacy came from study in the family home and the use of Welsh in religious settings. Their knowledge and use of Welsh was not negatively affected by schooling in England: Owen Salesbury (d.1658) studied at Winchester College, the University of Oxford and Gray's Inn, all English institutions, but he was also, as we shall see, an enthusiastic scholar in Welsh and English.

SCHOLARSHIP

The early modern Welsh gentry were crucial to the continued survival of Welsh scholarship.[77] Their humanist education emphasised the importance of vernacular culture and the gentry became enthusiastic collectors of medieval manuscripts, building on an older tradition of collecting in medieval Welsh gentry culture.[78] By the late seventeenth century, gentry houses across England and Wales kept book collections, although not yet in the libraries which became fashionable in the eighteenth century.[79] When Owen Salesbury died in 1694, the inventory of his estate

[77] John Gwynfor Jones, 'Scribes and patrons in the seventeenth century', in Philip Henry Jones and Eluned Rees (eds), *A Nation and its Books: A history of the book in Wales* (Aberystwyth, 1998), p. 89.
[78] Graham C. G. Thomas, 'From manuscript to print – 1. Manuscript', in R. Geraint Gruffydd (ed.), *A Guide to Welsh Literature*, vol. 3 (Cardiff, 1997), p. 243.
[79] Susie West, 'Looking back from 1700: Problems in locating the country house library', in Matthew Dimmock, Andrew Hadfield and Margaret Healy (eds), *The Intellectual Culture of the English Country House, 1500–1700* (Manchester, 2015), pp. 178–91.

included over 600 books in the study.[80] There are no surviving catalogues of the Salesburys' collection, but there are over twenty early modern manuscripts connected to the Salesburys scattered in archives across England and Wales, primarily in the National Library of Wales and the British Library.[81] These represent only a fraction of the Salesburys' collection by the end of the seventeenth century and they comprise mainly contemporary copies of older manuscripts, rather than original texts. As a result, the Salesburys' manuscripts have attracted little attention from scholars of Welsh literature. However, the range of manuscripts is sufficiently broad to reconstruct the family's scholarly interests, revealing that they enjoyed Welsh history and genealogy and religious or moral works. Almost all the surviving manuscripts are Welsh-language texts, demonstrating a strong and sustained interest in Welsh culture. Education conveyed entry into the community of gentlemen scholars and the Salesburys were active members in north Wales.

The Salesburys were also patrons of Welsh scholarship, surviving most visibly in the collection of praise poetry written for the family.[82] Professional poets originated in the royal courts of Wales, providing poetry for ceremonial occasions as well as entertainment. However, after the Edwardian Conquest decimated the Welsh aristocracy, gentry families gradually began to act as patrons to poets.[83] Bardic patronage thus reinforced the gentry's identity as the inheritors of the cultural and social roles of the Welsh aristocracy. Praise poetry was an opportunity to hear about the brilliance of a Welsh gentleman and his family, the quality of his hospitality, his beautiful home and his distinguished ancestry. However, it also helped to define Welsh gentility and it set the

---

[80] TNA, C 6/474/15.

[81] See Huws, *RWMS*, pp. 66, 68, 72, 81, 88, 92, 95, 109, 125, 156, 185, 224–5, 245, 250, 289, 304, 306–7, 381–2, 401, 429, 456, 523, 540, 545, 618, 619, 626–7, 629, 676–7, 747–8.

[82] For praise poetry composed for the Salesburys of Rhug and Bachymbyd, see Hughes, 'Noddwyr y beirdd', 559–634.

[83] Ceri W. Lewis, 'The content of poetry and the crisis in the bardic tradition', in A. O. H. Jarman and Gwilym Rees Hughes (eds), rev. Dafydd Johnson, *A Guide to Welsh Literature 1282–c.1550*, vol. 2 (Cardiff, 1997), pp. 88–9.

standards of how the Welsh gentry were expected to behave.[84] In the later sixteenth and seventeenth centuries, poets complained that their patrons had lost interest in poetry, although Gruffydd Aled Williams warns that we should not always believe what they say, while allowing that the inflation of the period reduced the gentry's spending power.[85] John Gwynfor Jones has convincingly argued that bardic patronage continued to be a defining feature of the Welsh gentry into the seventeenth century, although it became rather more tokenistic as cultural and literary tastes shifted away from strict-metre poetry.[86]

Arwyn Lloyd Hughes's edition of Salesbury praise poetry demonstrates that the Salesburys continued to patronise poets throughout the family's existence. However, the largest collection of poems written for the family date to the sixteenth century. In Hughes's edition, there are five *marwnadau*, or elegies, for Robert Salesbury (d.1550), written by some of the leading poets of the day, including Lewys Morgannwg and Gruffudd Hiraethog. There are eleven poems in total for John Salesbury (d.1580), five *moliannau*, or praise poems, and six *marwnadau*, again by leading poets such as Siôn Tudur, Simwnt Fychan and William Cynwal. John Salesbury's eldest son, Sir Robert (d.1599), has five poems in the edition, but although the middle son, John Salesbury (d.1611), also has five poems, four of them were composed by the same poet, Ieuan Llwyd Sieffrai. In the seventeenth century, there is a definite decline in the number of Salesbury poems: just one for William Salesbury (d.1660), three for Owen (d.1658), four for William (d.1677) and one anonymous poem for Roger Salesbury (d.1719). Hughes's edition is not complete and it excludes, for example, any poetry written for wives, daughters and younger sons. Equally, there may be poems written for the family which

---

[84] For an exploration of this aspect of praise poetry, see John Gwynfor Jones, *Concepts of Order and Gentility in Wales 1540–1640* (Llandysul, 1992).

[85] Gruffydd Aled Williams, 'Bibles and bards in Tudor and Stuart Wales', in Geraint Evans and Helen Fulton (eds), *The Cambridge History of Welsh Literature* (Cambridge, 2019), p. 244.

[86] Jones, 'The Welsh poets and their patrons', 271–7.

did not survive. However, the range of poetry in Hughes's edition supports John Gwynfor Jones's argument that the Welsh gentry continued to patronise poets in the seventeenth century, but with less enthusiasm as their literary interests changed. In fact, as this chapter will demonstrate, the Salesburys of the seventeenth century had a vibrant interest in Welsh-language scholarship, including history and literature. They may have engaged less with bardic patronage, but they began to be enthusiastic scholars in their own right, producing and preserving Welsh texts.

In the sixteenth century, when bardic patronage remained strong, there is limited evidence for the Salesburys' interest in books and manuscripts. Towards the end of the sixteenth century, Siôn Conwy translated Leonard Wright's *A Summons for Sleepers* (1589) from English into Welsh and dedicated it to his first cousin, Sir Robert Salesbury (d.1599).[87] In his dedication, Conwy, the son of John Conwy of Bodrhyddan, Flintshire, and Jane Salesbury, described Sir Robert as esquire of the body to Elizabeth I, lord of Glyndyfrdwy and keeper of peace and good rule in Merioneth and Denbighshire. The book may never have been kept in the Salesbury household, but there was evidently status in an association with scholarship. The Conwys of Bodrhyddan are thought to have been a Catholic recusant family, but *A Summons for Sleepers* was a Protestant text which defended the state's bishops and clergy, situating it at one end of the Protestant spectrum in opposition to Puritanism.[88] This sort of literature opposed challenges to reform the English Church, associating Puritanism with the same threat to the state posed by Catholicism.[89] As Sally Harper has suggested, it is possible that Siôn Conwy wanted to demonstrate religious conformity with his translation and this would include his dedication to Sir Robert, the respectable head of a Protestant family and his first

---

[87] BL, Add. MS 14920.
[88] J. Sears McGee, 'Wright, Leonard', *ODNB* (2004).
[89] Joseph Black, 'The rhetoric of reaction: The Martin Marprelate tracts (1588–89), Anti-Martinism, and the uses of print in early modern England', *The Sixteenth Century Journal*, 28 (1997), 716–17.

cousin.[90] Sir Robert's younger brother, John Salesbury (d.1611), also received a dedication in a manuscript. Hugh Gruffudd, a minor officer from Maelor, collected an anthology of *englynion* for 'the heroicall-mynded' Captain John, 'the wish of all good fellows [and] honest gentlemen and kind consorts'.[91] Gruffudd intended to give John the first English versions of the poems and he made some attempt at translating them in the margins, but the project is largely incomplete. It is possible that John Salesbury never received the poems because Gruffudd never finished the project. Nevertheless, the two surviving dedications to Sir Robert and John Salesbury suggest that the family was developing an association with scholarship from the end of the sixteenth century.

The family's interest in scholarship became properly established in the seventeenth century. Sir Robert and John's younger brother, William Salesbury (d.1660), was a keen scholar with a particular interest in religious texts and poetry. Despite his disrupted education, William was confident in his learning. For instance, in an increasingly hostile exchange of letters between William and Bishop Godfrey Goodman in the early 1650s over the division of the Salesbury estates, William cited multiple religious and historical examples to support his actions.[92] He began by referencing Luke 12: 13–14, writing that Goodman knew how Christ responded when a man asked Him to tell his brother to share his inheritance: Christ refused to intervene because no one appointed Him judge or executor, an implicit criticism of Goodman's intervention. William added that Emperor Constantine divided his empire between two sons, 'Brutus divided this Island between his three sonnes', and Cadwallader, 'the Last King of the Britaynes' divided 'Southwales, Northwales, and Powis amongest his three sonnes'.[93] William then referred

---

[90] Sally Harper, *Music in Welsh Culture Before 1650: A study of the principal sources* (Aldershot, 2007), p. 333.

[91] Ca. MS 2.39, f. 4. For the background of the manuscript, see Huws, *RWMS*, p. 545.

[92] NLW, Bachymbyd Letters 44.

[93] William gave an unusual interpretation of the tripartite division of Wales which early modern historians commonly associated with Rhodri Mawr (d.878). See, for example, David Powel, *The Historie of Cambria, now called Wales* (London, 1584), pp. 35–6.

to partible inheritance in Welsh law, 'by which every son was to have equall share with the eldest, but the youngest was to have the prime stead', and said that his right to divide his estates was also supported by 'Statute Lawe'. William's defence of his decision is a microcosm of a gentleman's learning: William knew the Bible, he knew history, both classical and British, and he knew the law.

The bishop responded in kind.[94] He refuted William's reference to Luke 12 by arguing that Christ 'left one Church not many Churches and as the Roman Catholics say he left only one Governoure to prevent Schism'. Goodman was also dissatisfied with William's examples from history and religion. He responded that Constantine's empire was large, but 'this is farre from your condition'; the division of the island of Britain between Brutus' three sons was a punishment from God; and partible inheritance 'was brought into Wales for the weakning and distraction of that Contry'.[95] He added,

> In truth I had thought you had mocked me by producing such Like examples: it should seeme that a man must read Antiquities, peruse the Roman histories, or at least consult with the Welsh Bards, before he is fit to treate with you or to iudge of your actions.

Goodman intended to be scornful, but this seems a fair assessment of what William expected from his correspondents. Goodman continued his attack by saying that he had known William a long time and 'when I consider your carriage, your habit, your present imployment, I wonder how you should have such aspiring thoughts as to propose unto your selfe only such Greate examples, certainly you had them not from Prince Rupert'. This comment ridiculed William's status after the Civil War, when William had supported the losing, Royalist side. The bishop, desperate to secure his niece Mary Goodman (d.1676) and her husband a larger inheritance,

---

[94] NLW, Bachymbyd Letters 47.
[95] Similar views on partible inheritance were expressed by other early modern Welsh scholars; see, for example, Powel, *Historie of Cambria*, p. 21.

mocked William's learning, but the two men were the product of the same education, understood the same references, and were willing to use their knowledge to support their arguments. This is less surprising in a bishop, but perhaps more so in the youngest, posthumous son of a north Wales gentleman. It demonstrates William's devotion to scholarship and the confidence in his command of it.

It is probable that William Salesbury was responsible for the early development of a library at Rhug, in the sense of a collection of books rather than a dedicated book-room. From the surviving manuscripts connected to the family, this collection was varied. The family had texts which were consulted by genealogists, including heraldry books.[96] They also had a Latin copy of the medieval laws of Hywel Dda, and Robert Vaughan of Hengwrt used the manuscript to make a comparison with one of his own copies, itself a copy of NLW, Peniarth 28.[97] Another copy, Trinity College Cambridge, MS O.5.22, also references additions and corrections made using the Salesbury manuscript.[98] William Salesbury's main interest, however, as demonstrated by surviving works in his own hand, was Welsh-language poetry. For example, he owned a manuscript of later medieval poetry, mainly by Tudur Aled, the leading poet in the first half of the sixteenth century, and it contains William's annotations, including poetry headings such as 'Cowydd [Cywydd] Howel ap Griffyth ap Res'.[99] A *cywydd* is a particular type of strict-metre Welsh poetry. William's handwriting also appears in a mid-sixteenth century collection of *cywyddau*; William signed his name on fol. 1 and added free-metre poetry to the blank numbered pages at the end.[100] William also retained an interest in material relating to his early career as a sailor: in 1635, William received a book about Virginia which cost 2s. 2d from his son, Owen, in London.[101] In

---

[96] BL, Harley MS 1971, f. 63r.
[97] Hywel David Emanuel, *The Latin Texts of the Welsh Laws* (Cardiff, 1967), p. 99.
[98] Trinity College Cambridge, MS 1303 [O.5.22]; Emanuel, *Latin Texts*, pp. 102–3.
[99] NLW, Peniarth 110D, p. 61.
[100] Ca. MS 2.114, f. 1, pp. 940–63.
[101] NLW, Bachymbyd Letters 26.

addition, there are four surviving manuscripts written in William's own hand: BL, Add. MS 14974; BL, Add. MS 14973; NLW, Llanstephan 37B; and NLW, Llanstephan 170. They all include prose extracts and complete poems by other authors, usually with a religious theme. Three primarily contain copies of other texts, but NLW, Llanstephan 170 includes William's own poetry compositions. Coupled with eclectic material such as medicinal recipes and lists of tenants, the manuscripts resemble commonplace books, which were important repositories for early modern scholars, containing extracts and notes from their reading material.[102] William rarely named his sources, but he probably relied on the manuscripts owned and borrowed by his circle of friends and family. His main interests were religious poetry and Welsh antiquarian material, and the manuscripts provide an insight into how a seventeenth-century country gentleman in north Wales engaged in scholarly activity.

BL, Add. MS 14974 is the oldest surviving collection of William's scholarship. The manuscript was first used by Elinor Bagnall, William's sister-in-law, when she was married to Sir Robert Salesbury in the 1590s.[103] William was thus repurposing an existing book in the household. As a result, this manuscript is less cohesive than William's other works and he added to it over time; his script dates from the 1610s and the 1630s.[104] It is likely that he found the manuscript in the Salesbury collection when he inherited the patrimony in 1611 and utilised it for his own scholarly interests. It is the most linguistically mixed of William's manuscripts and it includes text in Welsh, English, Greek and Latin.[105] It is primarily a collection of Welsh-language, religious poetry.[106] However, reflecting

---

[102] Fred Schurink, 'Manuscript commonplace books, literature, and reading in early modern England', *Huntington Library Quarterly*, 73/3 (2010), 453–4. For Welsh commonplace books, see Smith, 'Grammar and commonplace books', 175–84; E. D. Jones, 'Llyfr amrywiaeth Syr Siôn Prys', *Brycheiniog*, 8 (1962), 97–104.

[103] BL, Add. MS 14974, f. 46r.

[104] Daniel Huws identifies William's early and later hands in the manuscript: Huws, *RWMS*, p. 629.

[105] The manuscript also includes Italian, but these are later additions in a different hand.

[106] For a summary of the contents, see British Museum, *Catalogue of Additions to the Manuscripts in the British Museum in the Years 1841–1845* (London, 1850), pp. 50–1.

a commonplace book, the manuscript also includes a wide range of miscellaneous material, albeit almost all with a religious theme. For example, William transcribed an English-language letter purportedly written 'by Godes owne hand' and found under a stone in 1603. Writing out the letter and keeping a copy of it came with the promise that it would protect a woman in childbirth or a house from vexatious spirits, and bring 'greatnes . . . unto the house'.[107] William also transcribed the Letter of Lentulus, a medieval forgery which was alleged to be a contemporary eyewitness account of Jesus Christ in Judaea, as well as a letter believed to be from Pontius Pilate to Claudius Tiberius about Christ's resurrection.[108] At the foot of both letters, William signed his name in Greek letters. There are a limited number of poems in English in this collection, including a poem mourning a lost love: 'The heavens can witness that I loved her well / . . . I scorne all weemen only for your sake.'[109] Highlighting the variety of material in this manuscript, there is also an undated list of the tenants of Sir Robert Salesbury (d.1599) and a grant of a moiety of land.[110]

William may have written other manuscripts between the 1610s and the mid-1630s which do not survive. However, given the presence of his early and later hand in BL, Add. MS 14974, it is plausible that scholarship was not William's main focus in this period, merely an interest. Nevertheless, in the last twenty-five years or so of his life, William wrote three substantial manuscripts of poetry. William completed what is now known as NLW, Llanstephan 37B on 20 April 1637.[111] It includes multiple poems by Rhys Prichard (c.1579–1644), vicar of Llandovery, and other free-metre religious poetry, or *canu rhydd*.[112] William had a prolonged

---

[107] BL, Add. MS 14974, f. 96.
[108] BL, Add. MS 14974, f. 97; Cora E. Lutz, 'The Letter of Lentulus describing Christ', *Yale University Library Gazette*, 50 (1975), 91–7.
[109] BL, Add. MS 14974, f. 47v.
[110] BL, Add. MS 14974, ff. 88r–91v, 71r.
[111] NLW, Llanstephan 37B, p. 327.
[112] For a detailed analysis of Rhys Prichard's poems in NLW, Llanstephan 37B, see Nesta Lloyd, 'Sylwadau ar iaith rhai o gerddi Rhys Prichard', *National Library of Wales Journal*, 29 (1995–6), 257–80.

interested in Prichard's work and he also copied Prichard's poetry in his next manuscript, BL, Add. MS 14973. William's copies are now an important source as the first major collection of Prichard's work.[113] It is possible that William knew Rhys Prichard from their overlapping time at Oxford, where William and Prichard were students at Oriel College and Jesus College respectively.[114] Nesta Lloyd has hypothesised that William attended services in the chapel at Jesus College, citing the proximity of the college to Oriel, the presence of fellow Welsh speakers, and Jesus College's importance as a Protestant centre in the university.[115] Whether William knew Prichard or not, he certainly admired Prichard's poetry and recorded his own copies. Suggesting its importance to him, he kept NLW, Llanstephan 37B after he sold Rhug to his son Owen in 1640. For example, in 1649, William used a spare page to record his dream from the previous night of 8 March. This was in accord with the religious tone of William's manuscripts and suggests his religious devotion was also present in his subconscious:

> I dreamed uppon the 8th night of March 1649 that I was in a Church [with] many persons and devines and my unkle John Thelwall deceased having a [multi] coolerdd gowne uppon hym stood upp and sayed these woords Blessed bee all those that fear the Lord and walke in his wayes. I expected some devines to answer but none dyd. God of his mercy geve mee grace to remember his woords and Duly to folow to them Amen.[116]

In 1637, just after finishing NLW, Llanstephan 37B, William started the manuscript now known as BL, Add. MS 14973.[117] Like William's other manuscripts, it was a substantial undertaking with 167 folios and it must have taken a considerable amount of

---

[113] Lloyd, 'Cerddi Rhys Prichard', 270; E. D. Jones, 'Cerddi Wiliam Salesbury', *Y Dysgedydd*, 25 (1957), 69.
[114] For biographies of Rhys Prichard, see S. N. Richards, *Y Ficer Prichard* (Caernarfon, 1994) and Nesta Lloyd, 'Prichard, Rhys [Rice]', *ODNB* (2004).
[115] Lloyd, 'Cerddi Rhys Prichard', 264.
[116] NLW, Llanstephan 37B, p. 147.
[117] BL, Add. MS 14973, f. 1r.

time and energy to complete. Like the earlier collection at BL, Add. MS 14974, this manuscript resembles a commonplace book, containing prose extracts and poetry with a religious or moral theme. William recorded many religious poems by notable Welsh poets Siôn Tudur, David Johnes, Iolo Goch, Meredydd ap Rees and others. William also transcribed parts of two Welsh morality plays: *Y Dioddefaint a'r Atgyfodiad* ('The Passion and the Resurrection') and *Y Tri Brenin o Gwlen* ('The Three Kings of Cologne').[118] It includes antiquarian material such as the fifteenth-century *Englynion o Misoedd* ('Verses on the Months'), which William believed to be composed by the early medieval poet Aneirin.[119] William also transcribed the prophecies of Myrddin Wyllt and his sister Gwenddydd; these were adapted from an older oral tradition by Elis Gruffudd in his sixteenth-century chronicle, drawing on a rich history of prophetic literature in Wales. It was a localised north Wales story, set in the Conwy valley.[120] Other material in the collection includes a transcript of *Y Hoianau* of Myrddin, a prophetic poem first surviving in the thirteenth-century Black Book of Carmarthen, and *Y Gorddodau*, another prophetic poem ascribed to Myrddin.[121] William was also interested in triads, a Welsh poetic tradition grouping objects, people or events into threes, possibly for mnemonic reasons.[122] William particularly liked the *Eira Mynydd* ('Snowy Mountain') poems, transcribing multiple versions in this collection, as well as BL, Add. MS 14974 and NLW, Llanstephan 170.[123] Originating as medieval gnomic

---

[118] See Gwenan Jones, *A Study of Three Welsh Religious Plays* (Bala, 1939).

[119] For a study of the poem, see D. Tecwyn Lloyd and Nicolas Jacobs, 'The "Stanzas of the Months": Maxims from late medieval Wales', *Medium Aevum*, 70/2 (2001), 250–67.

[120] BL, Add. MS 14973, ff. 157–160r; Morfydd E. Owen, 'The prose of the cywydd period', in *A Guide to Welsh Literature 1282–c.1550*, pp. 34–5; Thomas Jones, 'The story of Myrddin and the five dreams of Gwenddydd in the Chronicle of Elis Gruffudd', *Études Celtiques*, 8/2 (1959), 313–45.

[121] BL, Add. MS 14973, ff. 162v–166r.

[122] BL, Add. MS 14973, ff. 126v–128r; BL, Add. MS 14974, ff. 8v–9v; Ceri W. Lewis, 'The content of poetry and the crisis in the bardic tradition', in *A Guide to Welsh Literature 1282–c.1550*, pp. 76–7. See also Rachel Bromwich, *Trioedd Ynys Prydein* (3rd edn: Cardiff, 2006).

[123] BL, Add. MS 14973, ff. 24v–26v, 108r–109r. Other examples occur in BL, Add. MS 14974, ff. 5r–8v, and NLW, Llanstephan 170, pp. 137–44.

poems focused on nature, the *Eira Mynydd* poems later acquired a religious tone only nominally connected to nature.[124] William's collection features both early and later examples of the *Eira Mynydd* tradition, highlighting his particular interest in the poems.

William began his final manuscript, NLW, Llanstephan 170, in 1655 and finished it in 1658.[125] Composed during the interregnum, this was a difficult period for William. Along with his younger son Charles, William had compounded the Salesbury estate and Charles had taken responsibility for paying his father's debts, incurred during William's tenure as governor of Denbigh Castle.[126] Neither William nor Charles was involved in local or national offices. Nevertheless, William still occupied himself during retirement by composing poetry. Although Charles Salesbury received the Bachymbyd estate in return for paying William's debts, William still lived on the estate: a Latin heading notes that the manuscript belonged to William Salesbury, armiger, of Bachymbyd, Denbighshire.[127] William's compositions were primarily religious in tone and followed the work of Rhys Prichard in metre and subject matter.[128] There is, however, debate as to whether William purposefully imitated Prichard or whether William's poetry naturally reflected a style he liked and admired. Brynley F. Roberts, for example, argues that William's poetry produces a different effect in the reader from Prichard's *Cannwyll y Cymry* ('The Welshman's Candle').[129] In addition to his own compositions, William still made transcriptions of other works. For instance, he included the medieval poem *Ymddiddan Arthur a'r Eryr* ('A Dialogue between Arthur and the Eagle'), which William also copied into BL, Add. MS 14973.[130] Although Arthurian in nature, the *englyn* poem has a religious theme: the eagle provides Arthur

---

[124] Kenneth Jackson, *Studies in Early Celtic Nature Poetry* (Cambridge, 1935), pp. 144–7.
[125] NLW, Llanstephan 170, pp. 3, 181.
[126] See above, pp. 91–2.
[127] NLW, Llanstephan 170, p. 3.
[128] Jones, 'Cerddi Wiliam Salesbury', 70.
[129] Brynley F. Roberts, 'Defosiynau Cymraeg', in T. Jones (ed.) *Astudiaethau Amrywiol a Gyflwynir i Syr Thomas Parry-Williams* (Cardiff, 1968), p. 108.
[130] NLW, Llanstephan 170, pp. 149–56; BL, Add. MS 14973, ff. 27v–29v.

with Christian instruction.[131] William also retained his enjoyment of free-verse religious poetry, transcribing, for example, Welsh-language *carolau* on the Virgin Mary and an allegorical tale of the four daughters of the Trinity.[132] At the end of NLW, Llanstephan 170, William included medicinal recipes 'for the stone' and 'for the plwresyr [pleurisy]'. These pages are written upside down and thus they are not a connected part of the poetry collection.

William's manuscripts are a wonderfully rich source for his scholarship. They demonstrate that he retained his interest in poetry and antiquarian material throughout his life, possibly sparked by his studies at Oxford at the same time as Rhys Prichard. William completed NLW, Llanstephan 170 just two years before he died in 1660. He read widely, but he primarily enjoyed texts with a moral or religious tone. With very few exceptions, William's manuscripts suggest his scholarly interests were predominantly Welsh language, but that he could also read in Greek, Latin and English. The manuscripts represent a great deal of work, demonstrating that William had the leisure to commit himself to such substantial projects, particularly from the 1630s onwards when William was in his fifties. It is possibly relevant that William held few offices after 1629, when he was no longer a Justice of the Peace. His early work in BL, Add. MS 14974 demonstrates that scholarship was not a new interest for William, but he evidently had the time and motivation for reading texts, making transcripts and composing his own poetry in later life. Retained by William at Bachymbyd, the manuscripts became part of his son Charles's inheritance, forming part of William's moveable goods in his last will and testament.[133]

However, the Salesburys at Rhug still retained a collection of books and they inherited William's love of scholarly pursuits. Although William and Owen struggled to repair their relationship

---

[131] Patrick Sims-Williams, 'The early Welsh Arthurian poems', in R. Bromwich, A. O. H. Jarman and Brynley F. Roberts (eds), *The Arthur of the Welsh: The Arthurian legend in medieval Welsh literature* (Cardiff, 1991), pp. 57–8.
[132] NLW, Llanstephan 170, pp. 156–60, 173–6.
[133] TNA, PROB 11/302/545.

after Owen's illicit marriage in 1635, William clearly inculcated in Owen an appreciation for scholarship. For example, Owen owned a manuscript anthology of early modern poetry, which includes various poems written in praise of the Salesbury family, both Owen and his ancestors.[134] Owen also made additions to the manuscript, copying poems such as a *cywydd* to Edward Vaughan of Llwydiarth, Montgomeryshire, by Rowland Vaughan.[135] Owen dated one of his contributions 'y 17 o fis Ebrill 1654' ('17 April 1654') and thus the manuscript may have been at Rhug when Owen received the estate in 1640 or Owen may have bought the manuscript himself.[136] Although clearly interested in poetry, Owen was a genealogist rather than a poet. Reflecting the seventeenth-century Welsh gentry's continued interest in genealogy and heraldry, Owen's most impressive work of scholarship is now known as the 'Painted Book of Erbistock'.[137] The manuscript is a collection of the pedigrees and arms of north Wales families, similar in style to the Book of Edward Puleston (NLW, 2098E). It is richly decorated and detailed, written in Owen's own hand and completed by his friend and kinsman, the noted genealogist John Salisbury of Erbistock (*fl.* 1650).[138] Owen also made additions to the Book of Edward Puleston, so he may have owned it himself.[139] However, Owen did not expand the Salesburys' own pedigree in the collection, which ended with his cousin, John (d. 1608), the son and heir of Sir Robert Salesbury, who died as a child.[140] Owen also owned a manuscript containing two folios of poetry, written on flyleaves taken from Thomas Stanley's *The History of Philosophy* (1655). Gifted to him by one of his children, the first folio includes the dedication 'For my very loving father Owen Salesbury Esq 1655 [1656] Feb 10th'.[141]

[134] NLW, 6499B.
[135] NLW, 6499B, pp. 626–9.
[136] NLW, 6499B, p. 638.
[137] DRO, DD/WY/6674.
[138] Huws, *RWMS*, p. 748.
[139] NLW, 2098E, ff. 90v, 100v, 115v.
[140] NLW, 2098E, f. 105v.
[141] NLW, 9857C, f. 1r.

William had his own interest in scholarship. In 1659, for example, he commissioned Robert Jones, curate of Cyffylliog, to translate *The Balm of Gilead* (1646) by Joseph Hall, bishop of Norwich, from English into Welsh.[142] William's own son, Owen (d.1694), is one of multiple names included on a copy of the *Brut y Brenhinedd* ('Chronicle of the Kings').[143] This was a Welsh translation of Geoffrey of Monmouth's *Historia Regum Britanniae* ('History of the Kings of Britain'), copies of which first survive from the thirteenth century.[144] It remained an important and popular work in early modern Wales, as well as a vehicle for understanding Welsh identity in a British context, and suggests Owen, like other Welsh gentry of the period, dismissed humanist critiques of the text by scholars such as Polydore Vergil.[145] The scholarly pursuits of William Salesbury (d.1660) thus reverberated down the generations to his great-grandson. Scholarship became an important part of the Salesburys' lives, and it is notable that even Owen Salesbury (d.1694) retained an interest in Welsh antiquarian material. This is, however, perhaps unsurprising, given the shared nature of the family's scholarly interests and access to literary material in the collection at Rhug.

Shared scholarship was not limited to within the family. The Salesburys were part of a community of gentlemen scholars in north Wales, one of the multiple strands of interests that connected the north Wales gentry. Robert Vaughan of Hengwrt's transcription of various medieval Welsh records names some of his sources, and he obtained records of Edeirnion and Dinmael 'through the hande of Wor William Salusbury [d.1660] of Rûg Esq'.[146] The records addressed who had liberties and privileges in the commotes, including the right to hold a court, hang a gibbet,

---

[142] NLW, Llanstephan 110B, p. 148.
[143] NLW, 13B.
[144] Owen, 'The prose of the cywydd period', pp. 322–3.
[145] For surviving seventeenth-century manuscript copies of the *Brut y Brenhinedd*, see Owain Wyn Jones, 'Historical writing in medieval Wales' (unpublished PhD thesis, Bangor University, 2013), 432–3.
[146] NLW, Peniarth 236B, p. 151.

and claim goods and chattels of anyone who died intestate.[147] As Robert Vaughan was a Justice of the Peace in Merioneth, he knew the Salesburys through their offices, as fellow gentry as well as scholars. In 1650, Owen asked to be remembered as Vaughan's 'bedfellow' as well as his cousin, identifying that they once shared sleeping quarters and suggesting they were old friends. In a postscript, Owen thanked Vaughan for recommending his new tenant, Jonet; the two gentlemen evidently sought and trusted each other's advice.[148] Equally, Owen worked closely with his kinsman, John Salisbury of Erbistock. John sometimes included references to his sources, and he utilised the books at Rhug. In material compiled in 1661, for instance, John transcribed the Hanmer of Hanmer pedigree from a source at Rhug.[149] In 1664, he also used books at Rhug, among other sources, to compile the genealogy of various branches of the Puleston family.[150] In John Salisbury's notes for his additions to the Painted Book, he took the model for his pedigrees, including the symbols used, 'Ex libris Gulielmi Salesbury de Rûg armiger'('from the books of William Salesbury of Rhug, esquire' (d.1677)).[151] The Salesburys were clearly content for fellow gentry to use their collection and make transcriptions; another paper included in John's notes was entitled 'Allan o lyfr Thomas ap Evan yn Rug' ('Out of Thomas ab Evan's book in Rhug').[152]

The Salesburys of Rhug and Bachymbyd were an active part of the early modern Welsh cultural renaissance in the Vale of Clwyd. From the end of the sixteenth century, the Salesburys demonstrably engaged in scholarship, primarily in Welsh. Sir Robert and John Salesbury received dedicated works, highlighting that scholarship was considered a valuable gift. However, William, their younger brother, was an enthusiastic scholar and gathered a

[147] NLW, Peniarth 236B, pp. 151–2.
[148] NLW, Peniarth 326E Part II, p. 165.
[149] NLW, 11058E, f. 1r.
[150] Uncatalogued MS, Gwysaney Hall, Flintshire. I am grateful to Shaun Evans for this reference.
[151] DRO, DD/DM/1647, f. 8r.
[152] DRO, DD/DM/1647, f. 46r.

collection of material. The surviving manuscripts in William's own hand show that he read widely and he was particularly interested in religious poetry and Welsh antiquarianism. The Salesburys remained interested in Welsh material, both original texts and translations, throughout the seventeenth century. The Salesburys also continued to receive praise poetry, despite modern criticism that the seventeenth-century Welsh gentry moved away from the patronage of professional poets. The family's engagement with scholarship required time, money and effort; they needed to purchase or borrow texts as well as read the literature and sometimes copy material into other manuscripts. They also discussed their collections with other gentry and received visitors who engaged with their books. It is reasonable to assume that the Salesburys also travelled to see collections in other houses. In this way, scholarship reinforced the Salesburys' identity as a Welsh gentry family, expressing their level of education and their willingness and enthusiasm to engage with Welsh culture, as well as strengthening their ties with other gentry families.

RELIGION

William's interest in religious poetry gives a rare insight into a Salesbury's beliefs. Religion is largely absent from the Salesbury archives, with the exception of their scholarly activities. The sixteenth and seventeenth centuries, however, were a period of turbulent religious change where religion could be a family's downfall or the key to its success. After the Henrician Reformation in the early 1530s, success required, at the very least, outward compliance with the state religion. It is unclear to what extent and how quickly the Reformation took hold in Wales. Welsh Protestant scholars, such as William Salesbury of Plas Isaf, Richard Davies (*c.*1501–81) and Matthew Parker (1504–75), promoted the government's interpretation of the Reformation as a return to an ancient British, and therefore Welsh, Christianity, and the

Reformation was a stimulus for an interest in Welsh history.[153] Among Welsh scholars, there was a close relationship between the Welsh language, Welsh identity and Protestantism, encapsulated in the idea of a true British Church. The lexicographer John Davies (c.1567–1644) of Mallwyd believed, as translated by Ceri Davies, that the Welsh language would not have survived 'in the face of so many disasters for the nation . . . had [God] not also ordained that his name should be called upon in this language'.[154] In contrast, Catholicism lacked a similar level of government support for scholarly promotion and it was more difficult to spread Catholic messages.[155] On the other hand, the Elizabethan government held real fears that Wales would aid a Catholic invasion, supporting the view that the Reformation was still largely incomplete in Wales by the end of the sixteenth century.[156] At parish level, Wales may have been reformed slowly and the populace remained inclined to conservative practices, which they or may not have seen as Catholic in the fluid religious landscape of the sixteenth century.[157] The gentry, however, with some exceptions, recognised the advantages of political power which came with government conformity.

Before the break with Rome in 1534, the Salesburys were a Catholic family. However, they quickly adjusted to the changing religious landscape of the 1530s and recognised that wielding state power required adherence to the state religion. For example, in 1537, Robert Salesbury (d.1550) brought a traitorous priest before

[153] See Brendan Bradshaw, 'The English Reformation and identity formation in Wales and Ireland', in Brendan Bradshaw and Peter Roberts (eds), *British Consciousness and Identity: The making of Britain, 1533–1707* (Cambridge, 1998), pp. 73–83.
[154] Ceri Davies, 'Introduction: John Davies and Renaissance Humanism', in Ceri Davies (ed.), *Dr John Davies of Mallwyd: Welsh Renaissance Scholar* (Cardiff, 2004), pp. 15–16.
[155] Lloyd Bowen, 'The Battle of Britain: History and Reformation in early modern Wales', in T. Ó hAnnracháin and R. Armstrong (eds), *Christianities in the Early Modern Celtic World* (Basingstoke, 2014), p. 150.
[156] Alexandra Walsham, 'The Holy Maid of Wales: Visions, imposture and Catholicism in Elizabethan Britain', *EHR*, 132/555 (2017), 274–6; Glanmor Williams, *Renewal and Reformation: Wales c.1415–1632* (Oxford, 1987; repr. 2002), pp. 327–9.
[157] Katharine K. Olson, 'Slow and Cold in the True Service of God': Popular Beliefs and Practices, Conformity and Reformation in Wales, c.1530–c.1600', in Ó hAnnracháin and Armstrong (eds), *Christianities in the Early Modern Celtic World*, pp. 92–107.

the Council in the Marches on behalf of his father, Piers, the steward of Ruthin.[158] An unnamed witness accused the priest, Sir Robert ap Roger Heusten, parson of Llanelidan, Denbighshire, of saying that 'the king's grace was about to pull down all the churches in the lordship of Ruthyn, except Llanlledan [Llanelidan], Llanonys [Llanynys], and Llandornock [Llandyrnog]'. Another witness claimed that the priest said it did not matter whether they went to church or not, 'for the King's grace hath robbed us, and now he robbeth the saints'. In total, six deponents testified against Sir Robert at the Ruthin court and then confirmed their depositions before the Council. One deponent said that Sir Robert's 'paramour', Margaret, his mistress and possibly his household servant, offered him a bribe of £100 if he refused to confirm his testimony. Three other deponents spoke for the priest and refuted the accusations against him, and one of them, Llywelyn ap David ab Ieuan, was 'reputed for an honest true man by Pers Salysbury'. Piers thought the priest was innocent, but he still sent him before the Council in the Marches. Piers and his son Robert had been Catholics until three years earlier in 1534, but they enforced the law, and any remaining devotion to Catholicism was outweighed by their responsibilities to the Crown.

The Salesburys quickly understood the importance of cultivating a Protestant public image, although by the end of the sixteenth century, their public image also reflected their private beliefs. Following the state religion enabled the family to hold positions of authority in their local community. This was a common, pragmatic approach by the gentry: Sir Thomas Mostyn (*c.*1542–1618) of Mostyn, Flintshire, similarly prioritised the importance of his officeholding and the need to maintain public order above religious beliefs.[159] Flintshire remained a focus for Catholicism at all social levels, and a sizeable minority of gentry families across

---

[158] *LP*, vol. 12, part 1, pp. 552–3.
[159] Shaun Evans, 'St. Winifred's well, office-holding and the Mostyn family interest: Negotiating the Reformation in Flintshire, *c.*1570–1642', *Journal of the Flintshire Historical Society*, 40 (2015), 63–6.

north Wales had members who retained their Catholic faith.[160] It is easy to see families as homogenous entities, but they comprised individuals who had different influences on their belief systems. The Salusburys of Lleweni, for example, were tainted by the participation of their Catholic heir, Thomas Salusbury, in the 1586 Babington Plot, but Thomas's younger brother, Sir John, was loyal to the Crown, and thus the Crown's religion. In the wider Salusbury kindred, one John Salusbury of Merioneth became a Jesuit priest and founded the College of St Francis Xavier, a Jesuit missionary district which covered the whole of Wales and some English border counties.[161] As a result, it is unsurprising that historians have traditionally believed that the Salesburys of Rhug and Bachymbyd were also a Catholic recusant family.[162] Many of their allies and friends were Catholics, including the Conwys of Bodrhyddan, who married twice into the Salesbury family. Sarah Ward Clavier argues that the conservative Welsh gentry had some respect for Catholic recusants who preserved the 'old faith' and saved their ire for dissenters and Puritans, a new and potentially more destabilising influence. This dislike of Puritans only intensified after the Civil Wars and the subsequent Puritan reforms of the Interregnum; for the Welsh gentry, Puritans were rebels and traitors who threw the realm into chaos.[163] The Welsh gentry prioritised stability and they inclined towards moderate religion.

For the Salesburys of Rhug and Bachymbyd, the religious flexibility of the sixteenth century brought the ability to hold power. This meant obeying the laws of the land when a priest was accused of treason. However, it was also a useful skill in the

---

[160] Walsham, 'The Holy Maid of Wales', 250–85.

[161] Geraint Bowen, 'John Salisbury', *National Library of Wales Journal*, 8 (1953–4), 387–98. Bowen confuses this John with John Salesbury (1575–1611) of Rhug and Bachymbyd, but the Jesuit priest died much later.

[162] See, for example, P. S. Edwards, *HPO (1509–1558)*: 'Salesbury, John (1533–80)'; John Gwynfor Jones, 'Government and society 1536–1603', in J. Beverley Smith and Llinos Beverley Smith (eds), *History of Merioneth: Vol. II – The Middle Ages* (Cardiff, 2001) p. 681; E. D. Evans, 'Politics and Parliamentary Representation in Merioneth, 1536–1644: Part 1', *Journal of the Merioneth Historical and Record Society*, 15 (2006), 18.

[163] Clavier, *Royalism*, pp. 115–16.

turbulent religious politics of the sixteenth century. In 1553, John represented Merioneth in Mary I's Parliament, when Mary expressly requested Catholic MPs to support the reintroduction of Catholicism. John was not a natural supporter of Mary: his master at the time was William Herbert, earl of Pembroke, who had supported Lady Jane Grey's claim to the throne and a man who preferred the state to maintain its supremacy over the Church.[164] John may have professed Catholicism during Mary's reign, although there is no surviving evidence that he did, beyond the tentative conclusions which can be drawn from his time in the Commons. However, it was almost certainly a calculated, political decision to protect himself and his family in unstable times, not long after his lord had made a serious misstep by actively working against the new queen. From the mid-1560s, John was a loyal servant of Ambrose Dudley, earl of Warwick, and his wife, Anne, countess of Warwick, who were both deeply committed Protestants. Ambrose Dudley supported Puritan writers and ministers and the Dudley family had also supported Lady Jane Grey against Mary I, a link with John's earlier service to the earl of Pembroke.[165]

John, head of the Salesbury family, moved in Protestant circles and he was rewarded with power and influence by his noble patrons. John was also an associate of Gabriel Goodman (1528–1601), dean of Westminster, who was part of the Goodman family of Ruthin. The two men were close in age and status and probably knew each other from childhood. In 1580, the Catholic recusant Richard Gwyn (c.1537–84), otherwise known as Richard White, was imprisoned in Ruthin Castle. He was eventually executed for treason in 1584 and he later became a Catholic saint. The anonymous author of a sixteenth-century manuscript purporting to give an account of Richard Gwyn's life says that Gabriel Goodman was out walking with John Salesbury

[164] Narasingha P. Sil, 'Herbert, William first earl of Pembroke', *ODNB* (2009; first pub. 2004).
[165] Simon Adams, 'Dudley Ambrose, earl of Warwick', *ODNB* (2008; first pub. 2004).

when they caught sight of Richard Gwyn in the prison.[166] John Salesbury loudly denounced Gwyn and his beliefs. Rather strangely, this incident has been used as proof that John had Catholic sympathies and needed to gain Goodman's approval, but the most straightforward explanation is that John, perambulating with an old friend, expressed his genuine condemnation of a recusant whom he believed to be traitorous.[167] John was steward of Ruthin and Richard Gwyn was a criminal in his jurisdiction. John was a loyal servant of the Crown and his noble patrons; he did not hold treasonous, Catholic beliefs.

Of John's children, William was the most demonstrably pious and a committed Protestant. During the Puritan reforms of the Interregnum, he was also the first Salesbury paterfamilias to refuse to follow the state religion, giving some indication of the strength of his beliefs. Religion was of central importance in William's life. In addition to his several manuscripts of religious poetry, his legacy also includes a chapel he built on the Rhug estate in his brief period of financial stability after repaying the mortgage on Bachymbyd and before the outbreak of the Civil War.[168] The existence of the chapel demonstrates William's devotion and his desire to worship regularly without visiting the parish church at Corwen. It also provided opportunity for his servants, labourers and tenants to worship at the chapel, emphasising the shared community of William's estate. On 3 January 1641, William and his son Owen endowed the chapel with a chaplain, who earned a salary of £12 a year.[169] It was a serious financial investment, not just building the chapel but ensuring that it was prosperous into the future. The chapel's interior, although restored, survives

---

[166] For a transcription of the manuscript (Holywell MS), see D. Aneurin Thomas (ed.), *The Welsh Elizabethan Catholic Martyrs: The trial documents of Saint Richard Gwyn and of the Venerable William Davies* (Cardiff, 1971), pp. 85–131. John Salesbury's walk with Gabriel Goodman is at pp. 88–9.

[167] Evans, 'Politics and parliamentary representation', 18; Jones, 'Government and society', p. 681.

[168] For a history of the chapel, see D. B. Hague, 'Rug Chapel Corwen', *Journal of the Merioneth Historical and Record Society*, 3 (1958), 167–83.

[169] NLW, Bachymbyd 322–3.

remarkably well. The walls are elaborately decorated: on the north wall, for example, there is a painting of a skeleton lying in its tomb with objects, including a skull, an hourglass, lighted candles, and a timepiece, representing humanity's inevitable death, above it. The decoration in the chapel invites viewers to contemplate their own mortality. Interestingly, given William's Protestantism, one of the quotations on the walls is taken from a poem by Richard Gwyn.[170] However, William had eclectic tastes, as seen in the discussion of his poetry collection, and the tone of the poem reflected the theme of mortality. On the surface, William's chapel can be mistaken for Catholicism, but, in reality, it is the opposite of recusancy; it is conservative and closely adhering to the English Church.

There is insufficient information to know whether William approved of Archbishop Laud's reforms in the 1630s.[171] Without knowing William's views on predestination and free will, it is difficult to judge whether his Protestantism was Calvinist or Arminian, but it is plausible that he was a conformist, non-Puritan Calvinist, or a Reformed Conformist.[172] In his debate with Godfrey Goodman, Bishop of Gloucester, William mentioned an acquaintance with 'Doctor Williams', very likely John Williams (1582–1650), archbishop of York, a Welshman born in Conwy and educated at Ruthin School at around the same time as William and Goodman. William received 'satisfaction' from John Williams, a moderate Calvinist, after the death of his brother John in 1611.[173] John Bridgeman (1577–1652), bishop of Chester, held similar views. Richard Cust and Peter Lake have argued that Bridgeman accepted and even promoted some of the Laudian reforms in the 1630s because of his belief in the beauty of holiness; altar rails, for example, were a feature of the Laudian reforms, but they also

---

[170] See above, p. 188.
[171] I am grateful to Richard Cust for his reflections on William's religious beliefs.
[172] For the theological tradition of Reformist Conformity, see Stephen Hampton, *Grace and Conformity: The Reformed Conformist Tradition and the Early Stuart Church of England* (Oxford, 2021).
[173] NLW, Bachymbyd Letters 47.

enhanced the order and beauty of a church.[174] The chapel at Rhug and its elaborate decoration, which includes evidence that the altar was originally railed, might suggest that William, like the bishops, believed a church should be beautiful and ordered. William's beliefs are thus not easily categorised, but they belonged to someone who had evidently thought deeply about his religion and he was very committed to it.

While under siege at Denbigh Castle in 1646, William wrote a letter to Major General Thomas Mytton and declared himself to be 'a lover of the true Protestant religion'.[175] Piety was at the heart of his service to the king: on 18 April 1646, William wrote, 'when I shall have need of reliefe I shall undoubtedly expect it from my mercifull God, who knows the justness of my cause'.[176] William, however, was quite literally fighting a losing battle, and the end of the Civil War brought religious changes across Britain: the Puritan movement espoused by Oliver Cromwell and his followers. Puritanism's effect on parish religion depended on the cooperation of local ministers, but the government enforced the removal of the prayer book and parishioners' access to the sacraments became controversial, the result of the Puritan urge to prioritise the godly.[177] For an old Calvinist like William, it was a deeply unhappy time and he abhorred the enforced Puritanism. At some point between 1655 and 1658, William composed a poem lamenting the state of the realm. He wrote:

> Och Dduw, pa beth a ddaw o'r byd
> Sy ers ennyd wedi ynfydu? . . .
> Mae'r bobol yn terfysgu.

---

[174] Richard Cust and Peter Lake, *Gentry Culture and the Politics of Religion: Cheshire on the eve of Civil War* (Manchester, 2020), pp. 200–6. For railed altars as a feature of Laudianism, see Kenneth Fincham, 'The restoration of altars in the 1630s', *Historical Journal*, 44/4 (2001), 919–40.

[175] NLW, Bachymbyd Letters 36, p. 43.

[176] NLW, Bachymbyd Letters 36, p. 15.

[177] Bernard Capp, *England's Culture Wars: Puritan Reformation and its Enemies in the Interregnum, 1649–1660* (Oxford, 2012), chapter six.

> Gwyliau'r Nadolig oedd gynt yn barchedig
> Gan bob rhyw garedig o Gristion;
> Nid oes heddiw ronyn bri,
> Ni droesom ni'n Iddewon.[178]

> [Oh God, what will become of the world which has, since a short while, become insane? ... The people are rioting. Christmas festivals used to be respected by every loving Christian; today there is absolutely no honour, we have been turned into Jews.]

The Puritanism of Cromwell's Commonwealth was too opposed to William's religious beliefs. His unwillingness to adapt to the new regime contrasts starkly with his grandfather and great-grandfather, Robert and Piers Salesbury, who abided by the reforms introduced by Henry VIII in the 1530s. William's forefathers had depended on the government for their authority. However, as a Royalist, William held no offices during the Commonwealth and he had nothing to lose by refusing to adjust his religious beliefs. William was also in his seventies by the 1650s and he was a devoutly religious man. Until William's refusal to accept the Commonwealth's Puritanism, the Salesburys followed the state religion, whether Catholic or Protestant. They were a conservative family who rarely questioned the established order. However, as the example of William Salesbury demonstrates, their religion could also be their sincerely and deeply held beliefs, not merely a facade to maintain power and influence. William is the only member of the family with any significant evidence for his devotion, but between the Reformation and the Civil Wars, the Salesburys of Rhug and Bachymbyd accepted that holding power required compliance with the Crown's prescribed interpretation of Christianity.

After the Civil War, the family was less conformist. For example, William Salesbury's great-grandson, Owen (1663–94),

---

[178] Jones, 'Cerddi Wiliam Salesbury', 71.

converted to Catholicism, the first confirmed Catholic in the Salesbury family since the early 1530s.[179] This was still a period of intense anti-Catholic prejudice and Catholics struggled to hold positions of political power and social influence due to discriminatory legislation, even if they were able to live relatively harmoniously with their Protestant neighbours.[180] Perhaps, like his great-grandfather, Owen was a particularly devout man, and his religious beliefs may have been influenced by his friends or possibly even his wife, Elizabeth Bateman, daughter of an Oxfordshire gentleman, about whom little is known. Women played an important role in the religious education of a gentry household and, as a result, it is likely Elizabeth had an influence over her family's religion.[181] However, Owen and Elizabeth's elder daughter, Elizabeth, married Rowland Pugh (d.1724) of Mathafarn, Montgomeryshire, and the Pughs of Mathafarn are not known as a recusant family.[182] Margaret Salesbury, the younger daughter, married Richard Tracy (d.1734) of Coscombe, Gloucestershire, a junior branch of the Tracys of Toddington.[183] The Tracys of Toddington were a committed Protestant family predating the Reformation and proud of their early sacrifices in the name of the Protestant cause, although admittedly this may not have been reflected in the cadet branch of the family.[184] Any Catholic beliefs among the owners of Rhug did not extend far beyond Owen Salesbury; Elizabeth and Rowland's daughter, Maria Charlotta Pugh, who inherited Rhug, married Reverend John Lloyd after the death of her first husband.

---

[179] NLW, 7008E; Mostyn, MS 9069E, nos 27; 28; 32, cited in Clavier, *Royalism*, p. 118.
[180] Hannah Cowell Roberts, 'Re-examining Welsh Catholicism, *c.*1660–1700' (unpublished PhD thesis, Swansea University, 2014), 204–7.
[181] Heal and Holmes, *Gentry in England and Wales*, p. 76.
[182] I am grateful to Melvin Humphreys and Murray Chapman for their reflections on the Pughs of Mathafarn.
[183] TNA, PROB 11/665/105.
[184] Heal and Holmes, *Gentry in England and Wales*, pp. 356–7.

CONCLUSION

The early modern Welsh gentry acted as the preservers of Welsh culture. Although bardic patronage declined in the early modern period, it was replaced by an intense interest in other forms of Welsh-language scholarship. The Salesburys of Rhug and Bachymbyd were influenced by the location of their estates at the centre of the Welsh renaissance and by the changing shifts in indicators of gentility across England and Wales. Scholarship emphasised that a family was learned and could afford to educate their children, which was certainly true of the Salesburys, who sent their daughters, as well as their sons, to boarding schools in the seventeenth century. Scholarship also enabled the Salesburys to develop and maintain connections with other gentry families, building on their kinship and friendship links, which, as the previous chapter showed, were the source of so much strife in the sixteenth and early seventeenth century. The family were not without strife in the later seventeenth century, but there is far less evidence of violent altercations. The impact of different religious beliefs had also changed by the end of the Salesburys' period. Owen Salesbury's conversion to Catholicism was a source of controversy, but it did not bring with it a risk of death and, perhaps worse, a loss of status, which caused so many problems for the conservative Welsh gentry in the sixteenth and early seventeenth centuries.

By the end of the seventeenth century, the Salesburys had a collection of over 600 books at Rhug and they still retained an interest and an awareness in Welsh culture, including their continued passion for genealogy. At the same time, however, they were not insular or restrictive in their approach to scholarship. Welsh scholars were conscious of a European community of scholarship and the gentry collected manuscripts and print works from beyond England and Wales. William Salesbury, for example, included Dutch material in his commonplace book and his son sent him a book on Virginia. This reflects the focus of the next chapter, which considers the international involvement of the Salesburys in foreign wars and early British colonialism. The Welsh gentry, particularly their younger sons, needed to look beyond Wales for employment, and soldiering, sailing and merchant trade were lucrative opportunities. Engagement with scholarship was a key part of the Welsh gentry's identity and they played an important role as collectors and copyists of Welsh-language works, but this did not prevent them from cultivating an international outlook and retaining broader interests beyond Wales.

5
THE WIDER WORLD

The Welsh gentry did not restrict their activities to England and Wales. Echoing the international outlook of their scholarship, they were active participants in Britain's burgeoning global expansionism in the late sixteenth and seventeenth centuries. For example, the 1585–1604 naval war with Spain encompassed Spanish holdings in the Americas and a land war in the Low Countries and France, providing ample opportunities for enterprising Welshmen to find employment as soldiers and sailors. Equally, the Elizabethan conquest and settlement of Ireland in the 1590s recruited substantial numbers of Welshmen, capitalising on Wales's geographical proximity to Ireland. The gentry's motivations to fight in international wars varied. As ever, status remained important and war provided the opportunity to achieve martial glory. Money was a key driver for younger sons with little expectation of inheriting the family estates. There is also a distinct sense that some gentlemen enjoyed the adventure of campaigning with their friends. However, the Welsh gentry did not leave Wales only to fight in wars. Grand Tours in Europe became popular from the seventeenth century and the sons of the Welsh gentry began to participate in them; for example, John Wynn, the eldest son and heir of Sir John Wynn (1553–1627), of Gwydir died while visiting Italy in 1614.[1] There is no evidence that the Salesburys of Rhug and Bachymbyd embarked on Grand Tours, but there is significant evidence that they went overseas as soldiers and sailors. This chapter focuses in particular on the three

---

[1] John Gwynfor Jones, 'Educational activity among the Wynns of Gwydir', *Transactions of the Caernarvonshire Historical Society*, 42 (1985), 40.

sons of John (d.1580) and Elizabeth (d.c.1584). All three sons, Sir Robert, John and William, had international connections, and all three inherited the patrimony and had an impact on its long-term security. There is, perhaps unsurprisingly, little mention of Welsh gentlewomen and it is clear that they did not have the same opportunities to engage in war or trade.

EARLY CONNECTIONS

The early Salesburys did not have substantial dealings beyond England and Wales. However, through their extended kinship networks, the sixteenth-century Salesburys of Rhug and Bachymbyd were part of a bigger European society which took them out of Wales and gave them contacts and experience on the continent. For example, the wife of John Salesbury (d.1580), Elizabeth Salusbury of Lleweni, was sister-in-law to Katherine of Berain through Katherine's first marriage to Elizabeth's brother, John Salusbury. John Salusbury died young in 1566 and the newly widowed Katherine married Sir Richard Clough, a Welsh merchant from Denbighshire who worked with Sir Thomas Gresham and advised him on the establishment of the Royal Exchange in 1562.[2] Before his marriage to Katherine, Sir Richard lived in Antwerp and he drew directly on his knowledge of the Antwerp bourse, or exchange market, for the creation of the Royal Exchange. Thus, through Katherine of Berain, the Salesburys were connected to a powerful and wealthy Welsh merchant who dealt in international markets from the mid-sixteenth century. Helen Williams-Ellis has proposed that, when Sir Richard Clough was dying in Hamburg in 1570, John Salesbury of Rhug travelled to Germany with his brother-in-law, Robert Salusbury, to ensure that Sir Richard provided for his Salusbury stepchildren.[3] Sir

---

[2] John Guy, *Gresham's Law: The life and world of Queen Elizabeth I's banker* (London, 2019), pp. 142–7.
[3] Williams-Ellis, 'Delweddu Catrin o Ferain Mewn Llun a Gair', 527.

Richard wanted to leave everything to his new infant son, but he made a codicil to his original will on 15 February 1570 and bequeathed £20 each to his stepsons. The Salesburys were not an insular family and they engaged in the world beyond Wales.

The next generation of Salesburys, particularly Sir Robert (d.1599), John (d.1611) and William Salesbury (d.1660), the three sons of John and Elizabeth, were internationally active as soldiers and sailors who participated in conquest and colonisation, as well as trade. This was mostly clearly expressed through their involvement in the Elizabethan conquest and settlement of Ireland. Leading Welsh gentry families, including the Bulkeleys of Baron Hill, the Trevors of Trevalyn, the Bagnalls of Plas Newydd, the Herberts of St Julian's and the Mostyns of Mostyn, all fought in Ireland and, in total, over ten thousand Welshmen were levied to go to Ireland between 1558 and 1625.[4] It is possible that only a percentage of the levied Welshman actually arrived in Ireland; mustered men could bribe their way out of conscription or run away to avoid it.[5] However, geographical proximity alone, particularly the convenience of the port at Chester, made Wales a target for recruitment.[6] Welsh captains preferred to lead Welshmen, which had the additional benefit for the government of preventing a language barrier between captain and troops, although Welshmen did captain non-Welsh recruits if numbers from Wales were limited.[7] Rhys Morgan has argued that Welsh gentlemen fought in Ireland because of the geographical convenience, a desire for martial honour, and because they were generally poorer than their English counterparts.[8] Equally, the earls of Leicester and Essex were active patrons in Wales and they had some responsibility over recruitment for the war in Ireland, encouraging Welsh participation.[9]

---

[4] Rhys Morgan, *The Welsh and the Shaping of Modern Ireland, 1448–1641* (Woodbridge, 2014), table 1.1.

[5] Vincent Carey, '"As lief to the gallows as go to the Irish wars": Human rights and the abuse of the Elizabethan soldier in Ireland, 1600–1603', *History*, 99/336 (2014), 477–9.

[6] Morgan, *The Welsh*, p. 45.

[7] Morgan, *The Welsh*, pp. 33–5.

[8] Morgan, *The Welsh*, p. 39.

[9] Morgan, *The Welsh*, p. 41.

Early modern Wales had little sense of a cultural connection to Ireland; the Welsh were an ancient British people with close ties to England, and theoretically Scotland, as fellow inhabitants of the island of Britain.[10] Welsh participation in the Elizabethan conquest of Ireland reflected a longer history of anti-Irish sentiment in Wales visible, for example, in the twelfth-century writings of Gerald of Wales.[11] Although Gerald probably wrote for an English audience, he supported the hybrid Cambro-Norman marcher lords of south-west Wales, including his own brothers, who were prominent in the late twelfth-century conquest of Ireland.[12] As Rhys Morgan has discussed, Meredith Hanmer (1543–1604) claimed in his *Chronicle of Ireland* (1633) that the Welsh had been prominent in the Anglo-Norman conquest of Ireland, presenting England's activities in Ireland as a common British endeavour.[13] The shared British identity of England and Wales goes some way to explain the differing attitudes of the Tudor monarchs to Wales and Ireland. For example, the 1537 'Act for the English Order, Habite, and Language' ordered that English should be used in Ireland, initially to prevent the Gaelicisation of Anglo-Irish settlers, but it developed into an Elizabethan desire to establish English monolingualism and eradicate Irish, beginning with the anglicisation of the Irish lords.[14] In Wales, however, the Acts of Union (1536–43) were never intended to promote anglicisation, notwithstanding the much-debated language clause, and they did not develop under the Elizabethan government into a desire to eradicate the Welsh language; indeed, an Elizabethan parliament passed the 1563 Act for the translation of the Bible into Welsh, a

---

[10] See, for example, George Owen Harry, *The Genealogy of the High and Mighty Monarch, James, by the Grace of God, king of great Brittayne, &c. with his lineall descent from Noah, by diuers direct lynes to Brutus, first inhabiter of this Ile of Brittayne, and from him to Cadwalader, the last king of the Brittish bloud; and from thence, sundry wayes to his Maiesty . . .* (London, 1604).

[11] See, for example, Gerald of Wales, *The History and Topography of Ireland*, trans. John O'Meara (London, 1982).

[12] Robert Bartlett, *Gerald of Wales 1146–1223* (Oxford, 1982), pp. 20–5.

[13] Rhys Morgan, *The Welsh*, pp. 131, 143–52.

[14] Patricia Palmer, *Language and Conquest in Early Modern Ireland* (Cambridge, 2001), pp. 136–47.

publication credited as the saviour of Welsh as a living language.[15] The role of religion was key. In converting to Protestantism, Wales had returned to what its humanist propagandists termed an ancient British, and therefore Welsh, Church.[16] The Protestant view of the early British Church, independent from Rome, was predicated on hostility to Catholicism. Ireland was still Catholic, and so the military enterprise of England and Wales in Ireland during the sixteenth and early seventeenth centuries was also a war of religion, endeavouring to prevent papal influence in Ireland and a potential Catholic invasion into the British realm, an invasion which would almost certainly begin on Welsh shores. Demonstrating this link between religion and the war in Ireland, Richard Davies, bishop of St David's and author of the prefatory Epistle to the 1567 Welsh translation of the New Testament, was fiercely anti-Catholic and supported the conquest of Ireland; he gave the funeral sermon for Walter Devereux (1541–76), 1st earl of Essex, who was active in the colonisation of Ulster.[17] It is no surprise then that the Welsh gentry, tasked with protecting Wales's coastline as deputy lieutenants, were enthusiastic participants in the Irish wars, and John Gwynfor Jones has suggested that the Welsh gentry valued their status as protectors of the realm, preventing Catholic incursion.[18]

SIR ROBERT SALESBURY

Sir Robert, John and William Salesbury all fought in Ireland. Sir Robert, who inherited the patrimony at thirteen years old, was

---

[15] Glanmor Williams, 'Unity of Religion or Unity of Language? Protestants and Catholics and the Welsh language 1536–1660', in Geraint H. Jenkins (ed.), *The Welsh Language before the Industrial Revolution* (Cardiff, 1997), pp. 213, 231–2.

[16] See Brendan Bradshaw, 'The English Reformation and identity formation in Wales and Ireland', in Brendan Bradshaw and Peter Roberts (eds), *British Consciousness and Identity: The making of Britain, 1533–1707* (Cambridge, 1998), pp. 43–111.

[17] Gruffydd Aled Williams, '"Ail Dewi Menew": golwg newydd ar Richard Davies', *Y Traethodydd*, 174/229 (2019), 94–112.

[18] Jones, *Welsh Gentry*, pp. 143–6.

already the head of the Salesbury family when he volunteered to fight in Ireland. Sir Robert's father-in-law, Sir Henry Bagnall (1556–98), had close links to Ireland. He was Marshal of Ireland and a wealthy landowner with estates in Newry, as well as Staffordshire and Anglesey. Sir Robert married Sir Henry's daughter, Elinor, before December 1594 and kinship with Sir Henry enabled Sir Robert to participate in the Irish campaign.[19] The marriage was part of a longer-term plan by Sir Henry, a Welsh speaker raised partly on Anglesey, to establish himself in north Wales, a more stable prospect than Ulster.[20] The marriage was mutually beneficial for Sir Henry and Sir Robert; Sir Robert was the head of a prosperous north Wales family with useful connections for Sir Henry. For example, he provided security for a loan to Sir Henry from Sir Thomas Myddelton (*c.*1556–1631) of Chirk.[21] In return, access to the Irish campaign enabled Sir Robert to cultivate the martial reputation which brought valuable status in Welsh gentry society.

The kinship link with Sir Henry was crucial to Sir Robert's engagement in Ireland. Sir Henry Bagnall had a long-standing rivalry with Hugh O'Neill (*c.*1550–1616), earl of Tyrone, who revolted against English rule in the 1590s. Indeed, Tyrone married Sir Henry's sister in secret, invoking Sir Henry's ire and increasing the tension between the two men; S. J. Connolly notes that Tyrone once claimed that his marriage to Mabel Bagnall prompted Sir Henry to outlaw him and caused the rebellion.[22] Tyrone's Rebellion was thus a personal matter for the Bagnall family as much as a political one, and Sir Robert Salesbury was part of the Bagnall kindred through his marriage to Elinor. In early 1595, Sir Robert travelled to Dublin and, after he arrived, he sent a letter on 3 March 1595 to Lord Burghley. Ostensibly, this letter updated Lord Burghley on Sir Henry Bagnall's progress, but Sir Robert also asked if he could 'have some imployment in

---

[19] TNA, SP 63/177, f. 156.
[20] Morgan, *The Welsh*, pp. 113–14.
[21] TNA, SP 63/177, f. 156.
[22] S. J. Connolly, *Contested Ireland: Ireland 1460–1630* (Oxford, 2007), pp. 229–30.

her highness service'.[23] Sir Robert emphasised his father-in-law's hard work in Ireland, telling Lord Burghley that Sir Henry 'spares neither pain nor charge to fortify the Newry'. Lord Burghley evidently granted Sir Robert's request and, by spring 1595, Sir Robert commanded a section of Sir Henry's company. In May 1595, Sir Henry's company fought in the Battle of Clontibret, County Monaghan. At Monaghan Castle, the British garrison was under siege by the earl of Tyrone and Sir Henry's company were sent to relieve them. However, they were attacked by the earl of Tyrone's large and well-trained army, resulting in heavy casualties for Sir Henry's company and highlighting the inefficiencies of the British forces.[24] On 3 June 1595, Sir Robert wrote to Lord Burghley from Newry to inform him of the ambush. He pleaded with Lord Burghley to send recruits from Scotland because 'his end wil be soon' if they did not arrive that summer.[25] Sir Henry Bagnall struggled to provide for his company. On 6 December 1595, he formally petitioned Lord Burghley for the more than £2,000 owed to him and complained that his company 'is in great penury for want of pay'.[26]

Sir Robert did not participate in a successful campaign and he was only in Ireland for a limited period. Sir Robert's time in Ireland coincided with a series of military losses by the British in a campaign which was largely being won by the earl of Tyrone. Sir Robert was at his estates in Wales when he died on 15 July 1599, a time when both his younger brothers were fighting in Ireland as part of the earl of Essex's campaign against Tyrone. Possibly the death of Sir Henry Bagnall in action on 14 August 1598 ended Sir Robert's military adventuring or he may have been forced home by the illness which later killed him. Nevertheless, Sir Robert's brief foray into soldiering was financially disastrous for the Salesbury patrimony, the beginning of the rot which was cured only by the

---

[23] TNA, SP 63/178, f. 168.
[24] Hiram Morgan, *Tyrone's Rebellion: The Outbreak of the Nine Years' War in Tudor Ireland* (Woodbridge, 1993), p. 179.
[25] TNA, SP 63/180 f. 5.
[26] TNA, SP 63/185, f. 8.

diligence of William Salesbury. To fund his campaign, Sir Robert borrowed money from Sir Thomas Myddelton, who also lent money for the same reason to Sir Robert's younger brother John.[27] By 12 January 1595, Sir Robert owed Sir Thomas £865, at an interest rate of ten per cent.[28] Sir Robert was a wealthy, landed gentleman. His estates were not lavish compared to many gentry families in England, but the Salesburys lived comfortable lives surrounded by luxury goods, including wall-hangings, framed pictures and books. Unlike his younger brothers, Sir Robert did not have to worry about his prospects or negotiate the complicated status that came with being a gentleman and a younger son. Sir Robert was the paterfamilias of the Salesbury family. Yet, he was also willing to incur significant debts in order to go to war and participate in the Irish campaign. When he died in 1599, he owed £1,000 to his creditors according to his younger brother William, who also criticised Sir Robert for selling land worth £100 per annum to Sir Thomas Myddelton.[29] Sir Robert's soldiering threatened the stability of the Salesbury patrimony, as well as the financial security of his infant son and heir. As discussed elsewhere, Sir Robert was young when he died, just thirty-two years old, and with sound financial management, and no more soldiering, he might have repaid the debts eventually.[30] Nevertheless, Sir Robert's willingness to borrow significant amounts of money and threaten his family's security highlights his drive to volunteer as a soldier.

The financial cost stresses the cultural and social pressure to engage in martial activities. There is also, of course, the possibility of familial pressure from his father-in-law, but Sir Robert clearly wanted Lord Burghley to find him employment in Ireland. The elegies to Sir Robert after his death praised his martial abilities, building on the stereotypical images of the Welsh gentry which offered a pro-forma portrayal of their lives. Sir Robert was 'orau

---

[27] NLW, Chirk F12540, p. 86.
[28] NLW, Chirk F12540, p. 178.
[29] NLW, Bachymbyd Letters 48.
[30] See chapters one and two.

un llew o Rug' ('the very best lion of Rhug'), 'or fowart faith' ('of the long distant vanguard'), and 'Y marchog ir mawr ywch gwaed' ('The thriving knight, great is your blood').[31] Although stereotypical, these images demonstrate the social expectations that Welsh gentlemen were brave warriors who could fight and lead their men into battle. Sir Robert could also legitimately claim that he had fulfilled the martial expectations of the Welsh gentry. Campaigning brought significant social reward for Sir Robert because, while on campaign, he was knighted by the Lord Deputy of Ireland, William Russell, achieving an important symbol of status in gentry society.[32] As John Gwynfor Jones has explored, knighthood was a rare honour in early modern Wales, with only nine of the hundred Welsh members of the Council in the Marches knighted during Elizabeth's reign, and it neatly combined the Welsh gentry's love of martial valour and public service.[33] Unlike his younger brothers, Sir Robert had no need to go to war for money; in fact, war was financially disastrous for him. Nevertheless, volunteering as a soldier gave him a knighthood, a priceless honour in the status-driven world of the Welsh gentry, and it meant that the eulogies about him were true: Sir Robert was a brave warrior and he did lead his men into battle against Wales's enemies, the Irish. For the Welsh gentry, their participation in early modern British expansionism was not necessarily about money, but fulfilling cultural and social expectations.

JOHN SALESBURY

Sometimes, it was also about money. John Salesbury, Sir Robert's younger brother, was a career soldier. John was a second son who inherited a fraction of the Salesbury estates: his father bequeathed him the township and park of Segrwyd, Denbighshire, which

---

[31] Hughes, 'Noddwyr y beirdd', pp. 593, 594, 601.
[32] TNA, SP 63/173, f. 29. See also Morgan, *The Welsh*, p. 114.
[33] Jones, *Concepts of Order and Gentility*, pp. 128–30.

previously belonged to Piers Salesbury, John's great-uncle and another second son of the Salesbury family. Younger sons of the gentry were particularly attracted to military service in Ireland; it had the potential to bring them honour, a good reputation and, more practically, financial gain.[34] John Salesbury was known as Captain John long after his retirement from campaigning and after his inheritance of the Salesbury estates. For example, he received a book of Welsh-language poems from Hugh Gruffudd dedicated to the 'heroical-minded' Captain John Salesbury.[35] When John died in 1611, the elegy on his tomb celebrated his 'martial spirit':

> And if that any Brittain passing by
> aske thee what worthie in this yard doth lie
> Say there's interr'd Captain John Salisbury
> & say no more, since far his fame is spred
> as well elswhere as where this Brave was bred [36]

In his elegy, John Salesbury was a soldier of international repute worthy of being listed among such heroes as Achilles, Hercules and Hannibal. Like his older brother, he achieved the Welsh gentleman's goal of a strong, martial reputation. Unlike Sir Robert, however, John captained a company. It was a position that conveyed respect and it was certainly a job with considerable responsibility for looking after his men, who numbered between one hundred and two hundred.[37] His company comprised fellow Welshmen; one Richard Puleston, for example, was a younger son of the Pulestons of Hafod-y-wern, Caernarfonshire, themselves a cadet branch of the Pulestons of Emral.[38] John also continued to provide for some of his men after he ended his soldiering career. For example, Harry Salusbury, a former soldier,

[34] Morgan, *The Welsh*, pp. 47–9.
[35] Ca, MS 2.39, f. 4.
[36] DRO, DD/DM/1647, f. 21.
[37] R. A. Roberts (ed.), 'Cecil Papers: April 1599', in *Calendar of the Cecil Papers in Hatfield House: Volume 9, 1599*, pp. 126–50. *British History Online*, available at http://www.british-history.ac.uk/cal-cecil-papers/vol9/pp126-150 (accessed 3 August 2022).
[38] A. H. Dodd, 'North Wales in the Essex Revolt of 1601', *EHR*, 59 (1944), 362, n.5.

remained one of John's servants after his return to Wales. Harry's surname suggests that some of John's company were part of the wider Salusbury kindred. John also continued to maintain close relationships with men throughout his life and he was loyal to his friends, regardless of the personal or financial cost. Through his role as captain, John was fulfilling a Welsh gentleman's cultural obligation to be a leader of his community.[39]

In 1599, John followed the earl of Essex to Ireland. Newly appointed as Lord Lieutenant, Essex led a large army in a bid to quell the continued revolt of the earl of Tyrone.[40] Although Essex had some early military successes, he realised he was unable to take control of Ulster and accepted a truce with Tyrone, a decision which eventually led to his downfall as he never regained the queen's favour. While in Ireland, John was closely associated with another member of the Salusbury kindred: his cousin, Captain Owen Salusbury (d.1601) of Holt. It is possible that Owen Salusbury was John's introduction to soldiering. A. H. Dodd inferred that John Salesbury went with Sir William Stanley of Hooton in the earl of Leicester's 1586 expedition to aid Sir Philip Sidney in the Dutch Revolt, but John was born in 1575 and would have been only about eleven years old in 1586.[41] Owen Salusbury, however, is a plausible Salesbury candidate. Sir William Stanley notoriously betrayed the earl of Leicester's English expedition in the Netherlands and surrendered the city of Deventer to the Spanish, promptly joining the Spanish side of the Anglo-Spanish war. The authorities feared Sir William had Catholic leanings before the expedition began and he was suspected of colluding in the Babington Plot, which involved another of Owen Salusbury's cousins, Thomas Salusbury, the Lleweni heir.[42] On the other hand, the link may have been through the earl of Leicester, whose patronage was the source of so much factionalism in north Wales. In any case, Owen Salusbury ended up in Sir William Stanley's

[39] Jones, *Welsh Gentry*, p. 143.
[40] Connolly, *Contested Ireland*, chapter six, esp. pp. 243–4.
[41] Dodd, 'North Wales in the Essex Revolt', 357.
[42] Rory Rapple, 'Stanley, Sir William', *ODNB* (2008; first pub. 2004).

service and became an associate of Hugh Owen (1538–1618), a Catholic Welsh gentleman in Brussels who managed a network of informants on behalf of the Spanish Crown.[43] Hugh Owen was from the Catholic enclave of the Llŷn Peninsula in north Wales, an area where the gentry stubbornly clung to the Old Faith long after the Protestant Reformation.[44]

In 1588, one Thomas de Barney confessed about the activities of British Catholics in the Low Countries, naming the ringleaders as Sir William Stanley, Hugh Owen, Antoine de Goignies, alias La Motte, the Spanish governor of Gravelines, and an unnamed Spaniard described as 'a tall black man'.[45] When Hugh Owen received intelligence from England, he talked about it with 'one Salbery, his very familiar', almost certainly Owen Salusbury. In another confession, Ithel ap Parry reported that Sir William Stanley told ap Parry to take a letter from him, 'Captaine Salysburie', Peter Wynne, 'and the rest' to a Lieutenant Pugh in Ostend.[46] At first ap Parry resisted because he did not want to travel through an unfamiliar country, but Sir William promised that he could have Salusbury and Wynne as guides. The next day, Salusbury, Wynne and ap Parry went to Bridges and met with Hugh Owen, who talked with ap Parry in Welsh and persuaded him to carry the letter. If ap Parry could not find Lieutenant Pugh, he was told to find Pugh's cousin, John Edwards. From the surnames of the men involved, there was evidently a coterie of Welshmen in the Low Countries, fighting on the Spanish side of the Dutch Revolt and trying to keep the British Catholic cause alive from the continent. Religious persecution encouraged Welsh Catholics to travel abroad, not just to fight in wars, but also to pursue their religion. They included one John Salusbury from Merioneth, not, as Geraint Bowen believed, the middle Salesbury brother who inherited the Salesbury patrimony in 1608, but a

---

[43] Francis Edwards, 'The first Earl of Salisbury's pursuit of Hugh Owen', *British Catholic History*, 26 (2002), 2.
[44] See, for example, Glanmor Williams, *Wales and the Reformation* (Cardiff, 1997), pp. 64–5.
[45] *CSP For., Jan–June 1588*, pp. 79–80.
[46] *CSP For., Jan–June 1588*, pp. 81–2.

member of the wider Salusbury kindred. This John Salusbury of Merioneth travelled to Valladolid, Spain, where he trained as a Jesuit priest before returning to Britain and establishing the College of St Francis Xavier.[47]

It is possible that Owen Salusbury was driven by religious belief to support the Catholic cause in Europe, but he was also a gentleman of limited financial means, and soldiering provided an income and a chance to prove his martial abilities. By 1590, Owen Salusbury regretted his actions in the Low Countries and wrote to Sir Francis Walsingham, the queen's private secretary, asking for employment that could prove Owen's loyalty to the queen.[48] Owen complained to Walsingham that another gentleman had maligned his honour by calling him a traitor. However, Owen argued that he did not fight to betray his country, but because he needed employment. In a separate letter to the gentleman who insulted him, Owen wrote, 'you knewest full well how my condycon resteth having nothinge els to maynteyn my lyfe but warre'.[49] Owen did not have the convictions of men like Hugh Owen, who stayed in exile for over fifty years and loyally served the Catholic Spanish cause. This was also true of some of Owen Salusbury's associates: Captain Peter Wynne, for example, found a patron in John Egerton (1579–1649), 1st Earl of Bridgewater, and the Egertons were a committed Protestant family.[50] The willingness of Egerton and Walsingham to overlook the involvement of gentlemen such as Owen Salusbury and Peter Wynne in the Dutch Revolt suggests a degree of understanding that they fought primarily for financial reasons rather than from a fervent desire to support the Catholic cause. As a result, the religion of their paymasters might well have been irrelevant, with no bearing on their own beliefs.

By the latter half of the 1590s, Owen Salusbury was serving the earl of Essex, another committed Protestant. Indeed,

---

[47] Geraint Bowen, 'John Salisbury', *National Library of Wales Journal*, 8 (1953–4), 387–98.
[48] BL, Lansdowne MS 99, f. 256.
[49] BL, Lansdowne MS 99, f. 258.
[50] Paul E. J. Hammer, 'A Welshman Abroad: Captain Peter Wynne of Jamestown', *Parergon*, 16 (1998), 59–92.

gentlemen soldiers tended to cluster around powerful military men and, in the 1590s, Sir William Stanley lost much of his company, English and Welsh, to Sir Francis Drake and the earl of Essex.[51] It is thus difficult to draw conclusions about the religious loyalties of Stanley's soldiers, who depended on campaigning for money and status. Like others in Sir William Stanley's company, it is possible that Owen Salusbury joined Sir Francis Drake for what transpired to be his final voyage, in 1595–6, to Panama with Sir John Hawkins.[52] This expedition, an extension of the Anglo-Spanish war, was intended to thwart Spain's acquisition of gold from the West Indies; the expedition partially succeeded in limiting the amount of gold sent to Spain by its West Indies fleet, but overall it was a dismal failure, costing the lives of Drake, Hawkins and many of their men. A Captain Salusbury was listed among Drake's company and Kenneth Andrews believes he was a land captain who commanded a company of men, which fits with Owen Salesbury's career, but it could have been Owen, John, or neither of them. It certainly would have provided valuable experience for the earl of Essex's 1596 expedition to Cadiz and there were other Welshmen on the voyage: one of the ship captains, for example, was William Myddelton (d.1596), a cousin of Sir Thomas Myddelton of Chirk, moneylender to the Salesbury family, who also provided significant funds for the expedition to Panama.[53]

The presence of Welshmen on the expedition, as well as in the Low Countries, highlights that the Welsh were engaging in the wars on the continent and travelling far beyond Wales to the New World. This was not new: medieval Welsh soldiers had made their living by fighting in wars, seeking to repair damaged reputations or to claim favour from noble patrons and improve

---

[51] A. H. Dodd, 'The Spanish Treason, the Gunpowder Plot, and the Catholic refugees', *EHR*, 53 (1938), 628.
[52] Kenneth R. Andrews (ed.), *The Last Voyage of Drake & Hawkins* (Cambridge, 1972), p. 47. I am grateful to Gruffydd Aled Williams for this reference.
[53] Andrews, *Last Voyage*, p. 51.

their situations.[54] While abroad, the gentry remained part of their networks in Wales and they were influenced by noble patrons and other leading figures in their local communities. For instance, Owen Salusbury fell in with Sir William Stanley because Owen followed the earl of Leicester as part of his expeditionary force to the Low Countries and the earl of Leicester was the major noble active in north Wales in the 1580s. Even when Owen defected to the Spanish side with Stanley, he remained part of a network of Welshmen who spoke Welsh to each other and trusted each other with communication lines. In the 1590s, when Owen returned to north Wales, he became a follower of the earl of Essex and once more followed him in his overseas military campaigns, this time accompanied by his younger cousin, John Salesbury of Rhug and Bachymbyd. The Welsh gentry were buffeted by the currents of influence which emanated from the nobility.

However, they were also caught up in their own disputes and factions. In 1593, Owen Salusbury lost a duel to Sir John Salusbury (1567–1612) of Lleweni. The duel caused great consternation among the professional poets, who rued the rift in the Salusbury kindred.[55] Lloyd Bowen sees Owen's challenge to Sir John as part of an effort to assert his gentility, particularly the martial qualities expected of Welsh gentlemen, after a period when Owen had received little glory as a Catholic traitor.[56] A. H. Dodd hypothesises that the duel arose because Owen attempted to draw Sir John Salusbury into a Catholic plot to overthrow the monarchy.[57] Whatever the circumstances, Owen was extending a feud which saw the Salusburys of Lleweni in opposition to their cousins at Rhug and Bachymbyd, and Owen was firmly in the Rhug and Bachymbyd faction. Owen, as suggested by his

[54] Adam Chapman, *Welsh Soldiers in the Later Middle Ages, 1282–1422* (Woodbridge, 2015), pp. 188–91.
[55] For transcripts of poems on the duel by Simwnt Vychan and Siôn Tudur, see John Rowlands, 'A critical edition and study of the Welsh poems written in praise of the Salusburies of Llyweni' (unpublished PhD thesis, University of Oxford, 1967), 406–7, 440–2.
[56] Bowen, *Anatomy of a Duel*, p. 76.
[57] Dodd, 'North Wales in the Essex Revolt', 358.

association with Hugh Owen, had Catholic sympathies, and Sir John Salusbury was a Protestant who remained very conscious of his elder brother's execution for participating in the Babington Plot. Bowen suggests that Owen Salusbury's defeat in the duel, and the subsequent publication of this fact by the Welsh poets who praised Sir John Salusbury's victory, encouraged Owen to partake in overseas military adventuring in order to bolster his martial reputation.[58] John Salesbury, around eighteen years old when the duel took place, followed Owen in his later soldiering, and thus the factionalism in north Wales indirectly encouraged John Salesbury to fight in Spain and Ireland.

The earl of Essex was central to John's ability to make a career as a soldier. Essex patronised a number of north Wales gentry families and had considerable support in the local area. In 1596, John and his cousin Owen received a commission from Essex to muster men for Essex's expedition to Cadiz, and John was later accused by Robert Thelwall of abusing the commission.[59] This is the earliest evidence for John's involvement with Essex, although Owen Salusbury may have been involved with him from the early 1590s.[60] The defeat of the Spanish Armada in 1588 had been a major victory for England in its war with Spain, but Spain was still a large, wealthy and powerful enemy. England's naval engagements with Spain after the Armada resulted in English defeats, not helped by the poor quality of England's conscripted soldiers.[61] The earl of Essex, however, collected experienced soldiers and gentlemen volunteers who followed their noble patron to war. Their obsession with honour made them, in Paul E. J. Hammer's words, 'the boldest soldiers in the army'.[62] This is the context for John Salesbury's involvement with Essex and gives some indication of John's attitude to fighting, as well as that

[58] Bowen, *Anatomy of a Duel*, p. 77.
[59] TNA, STAC 5/T7/31.
[60] Dodd, 'North Wales in the Essex Revolt', 357–9.
[61] Paul E. J. Hammer, 'The earl of Essex and England's expeditionary forces', in Hester M. Thomas, Jeanne Shami and Dennis Flynn (eds), *The Oxford Handbook of John Donne* (Oxford, 2011), pp. 436–9.
[62] Hammer, 'Essex and England's expeditionary forces', p. 441.

of other Welsh gentlemen soldiers, including John's two brothers and his cousin Owen. In addition to being bold soldiers, however, Essex's gentlemen volunteers also had the power to bring their own recruits to war, capitalising on their positions of authority in their local communities to muster men. As the example of Sir Richard Trevor of Trevalyn and Sir John Salusbury in the 1601 Denbighshire election demonstrated in chapter three, gentlemen were not adverse to using their commissions to blackmail the followers of their enemies or pressure people to act in certain ways. As a captain, John's company comprised local men whom he recruited to the expedition using his mustering commission, possibly not always in the best faith if Robert Thelwall's accusation was true. The Welsh gentry thus took other Welshmen with them to fight overseas and the earl of Essex benefited from the power and influence of his gentlemen volunteers.

Unlike Ireland, Cadiz was generally a success, although Essex came into conflict with the commanders of the naval fleet for allowing his land army to pillage the city. It was a successful endeavour for the Salesbury cousins, who would have partaken in looting the city and obtaining spoils of war. In the aftermath of the capture of Cadiz, a contemporary account celebrated the destruction of the king of Spain's 'shippes of greatest fame in the which all the pryde and Confidence of the Spanyards were reposed'.[63] It was portrayed as a great naval victory for England, harking back to the defeat of the Spanish Armada and preventing the launch of a second invasion fleet by Philip II of Spain: he 'was now disarmed by sea and being discovered to be so weake by lande and at home'. The land army remained at Cadiz for a fortnight and the 'men of war both souldiers and mariners ar made ritch and fitt to goe into any action of service as well with more ability as with greater charge'. Thus, not only did war bring plunder for the queen's soldiers, it also gave them experience which could be used to fight the queen's wars. For John Salesbury, it was the start of a relatively short, but important military career. For the rest of

[63] National Maritime Museum, HSR/A/1.

his life, he was Captain John Salesbury, a gentleman of martial skill and reputation and a leader of his men.

However, John Salesbury's soldiering career ended abruptly after the 1601 Essex Revolt. As discussed in chapter three, the Essex Revolt was a failure and John Salesbury found himself imprisoned in the Marshalsea for around ten months. Owen Salusbury, John's cousin and partner-in-soldiering, was in charge of the musketeers guarding hostages at Essex House, and Owen died in the gallery. Although John Salesbury continued to brawl and riot after the events of the Essex Revolt, these were primarily local affairs, mainly the result of significant factionalism among the gentry in Denbighshire. In fact, it seems that John settled down after the revolt. This was partly the result of changing circumstances: his elder brother, Sir Robert, was dead and the Salesbury estates belonged to Sir Robert's infant son, who would himself later die in 1608, leaving the estates to John. During his nephew's minority, John became heavily involved in the administration of the Salesbury estates and the wardship. This cannot be the only reason for John's decision to stop soldiering because his brother died in 1599, two years before the Essex Revolt. Perhaps John's imprisonment had some effect on him and he decided to settle down back home in north Wales. However, it is also worth considering the impact of the death of Owen, his adventurous cousin, who betrayed Deventer with Sir William Stanley, possibly sailed to Panama with Sir Francis Drake, fought with John in Cadiz and Ulster, and was killed by a musket shot in a thwarted and badly planned attempt at rebellion on 8 February 1601. In thinking about why John became a soldier, what pulled him to international campaigns, it is possible that he enjoyed it, that he liked fighting alongside his cousin, and that Owen's death meant that John would have to campaign without him and John preferred to go home instead and make money from the opportunity presented by his nephew's minority.

WILLIAM SALESBURY

Arguably, the most successful soldier in this generation of Salesburys was the youngest brother, William. John Salesbury and Owen Salusbury were both captains, but William had the honour of being a colonel and governor of Denbigh Castle, the commander of a regiment rather than a company. William's youngest son, Charles, was a captain in William's regiment, presumably commanding his own company of men. William's third son, Robert, may also have been a soldier: he died in 1646, the year that William was defending Denbigh Castle and the final phase of the First English Civil War. The conditions of the 1640s were unusual, requiring the considerable mobilisation of men and holding a mirror up to the Welsh gentry's adulation of martial prowess by forcing them to take sides in the conflict between king and Parliament. It is possible that William's sons would never have become soldiers without the pressures of civil war; Charles, for instance, was studying law at Gray's Inn when war broke out and Owen Salesbury, William's eldest son, may not have fought at all.

A staunch Royalist like most of the Welsh gentry, William remains most famous for holding Denbigh Castle for the king in the Civil War. Charles I appointed William governor of Denbigh Castle in 1643, which William proceeded to keep for the king until Charles personally commanded him to surrender it.[64] William spent £1,905 of his own money on the upkeep of the castle, equating to two-thirds of the £3,000 Bachymbyd mortgage which had consumed William's finances for twenty years.[65] In 1646, the castle was besieged by Parliamentary forces for five months and William exchanged a series of letters with their leader, Major General Thomas Mytton (1597–1656). He was a former associate of William, signing his letters to William, 'Your ould friend'.[66] William

---

[64] For the history of William's defence of Denbigh Castle, see N. Tucker, 'Denbigh's Loyal Governor', *Transactions of the Denbighshire Historical Society*, vol. 5 (1956), 13–33. The biographical information at 7–13 is based on antiquarian literature and not reliable.
[65] TNA, C 5/550/32.
[66] NLW, Bachymbyd Letters 36, various.

went further, describing himself as Mytton's 'poore Kinsman and old Play fellow'; they had known each other since they were youths, although there was a seventeen-year age gap between them.[67] The Myttons were a prominent gentry family in Shropshire and there was considerable intermixing between the gentry of north Wales and the English border counties. Unlike William Salesbury, however, Mytton did not have any significant military experience when he joined Parliament's cause in the Civil Wars.[68]

William's correspondence, as well as his actions, emphasised his loyalty to the king. When Mytton requested that William surrender the castle, William refused until 'I am commanded by my King and Parliament . . . for noe other cause, I have armed myself, as well as God did enable me . . . [but] for the service of my King and Countrey'.[69] William prioritised his duty to the king above his own personal desires: he wrote to Mytton, 'Sir I have bin, and am dayly robbed and spoyled contrary to the Law of God and this kingdome for noe other Offence that I know, but for my loyalty to our King'. Emphasising that William was willing to sacrifice his life and his family estates for the Royalist effort, William swore to keep the castle for the king 'without regard of my life, lands or postirity . . . to my last gaspe'.[70] Honour, loyal service and a good name were more important to William than the success of his own family and estate, despite his determination to recover his ancestors' lost lands when he became head of the Salesbury family. The eventual surrender of Denbigh Castle was a good-natured affair and the garrison were permitted to leave peacefully.[71] William received the king's command to surrender Denbigh Castle on 13 September 1646 and, a month later, William and Mytton agreed the Articles of Surrender.[72] It was a gentlemanly affair between kinsmen.

[67] NLW, Bachymbyd Letters 36, p. 10.
[68] Stephen K. Roberts, 'Mytton, Thomas', *ODNB* (2004).
[69] NLW, Bachymbyd Letters 36, p. 44.
[70] NLW, Bachymbyd Letters 36, pp. 10–11.
[71] A. H. Dodd, 'The Civil War in east Denbighshire', *Transactions of the Denbighshire Historical Society*, 3 (1954), 72.
[72] NLW, Bachymbyd Letters 36, p. 38; *CSP Dom., 1645–1647*, pp. 477–8.

When civil war broke out in 1642, William was able to draw on his significant experience as a soldier. His eldest brother, Sir Robert, became a soldier for the glory and perhaps to please his father-in-law, Sir Henry Bagnall. His middle brother, Captain John, made his living as a soldier, attracted by the patronage of powerful men like the earl of Essex. William was a more reluctant soldier, or at least he did not look back on his need to fight fondly. For William, it was a symbol of his position in the world as a younger son, born after his father's death, and treated badly by his older brothers, particularly Sir Robert, who withheld the annuity granted to William in their father's will. In the 1670s, Eubule Thelwall recalled William saying, on more than one occasion and over an extended period of time, that he was a younger son 'left destitute of a porcion and forced to serve as a Souldier by Sea and land for a maintenance'.[73] Thelwall also said that William fought in Ireland, where he 'refused to serve souldier under Capt John Salesbury but lifted himself under Capt Owen Salesburys company'. William was not a captain in his youth, lacking the prestige of his brother's and cousin's status. Thelwall's language, however, suggests that William fought to improve his own condition: he 'lifted himself' in Owen's company. William was one of many younger sons of the gentry who saw profit in soldiering, and Ireland was an obvious choice: there was an active war zone in the 1590s; his eldest brother, Sir Robert, had already participated in the fighting there; and his middle brother and cousin had their own companies. William did not draw on his nuclear family connection, however, and Thelwall's testimony suggests that there was no love lost between William and his older brothers.[74]

William Salesbury was able to pay substantial sums to reclaim the family patrimony when he inherited from his brother John. One campaign in Ireland in 1599 would not be enough to justify William's repeated claim that he was 'forced to serve as a

[73] CRO, XD2/463.
[74] See pp. 39–40, 119, 158.

Souldier by Sea and land for a maintenance', given that he did not inherit the Salesbury estates until 1611, nor would it explain his financial situation upon inheriting them. During the siege of Denbigh Castle, William complained to Thomas Mytton that the prisoners released by William were being used in the fight against him, but prisoners released by Mytton were not able to join William in the castle, even though some of them were taken while serving in his garrison. To justify his argument, William told Mytton, 'I assure you I offer you noething but reason for in the Low Countries (the best scoole of warre of these times) soldiers exchanged or ransomed may goe to what Garrison they make choise of'.[75] According to Eubule Thelwall, William fought in Ireland, but William's letter might also imply that he fought in the Low Countries too, where he acquired first-hand knowledge of prisoner exchange. William's description of the campaign in the Low Countries as the 'best scoole of warre of these times' could suggest that he himself learnt how to fight a war there. It reflects the common terminology used by contemporaries to describe the war; soldiers such as the Welshman Sir Roger Williams ($c.$ 1539–95) regarded it as useful training for Europe's armies.[76] As the example of Owen Salusbury has demonstrated, Welsh soldiers were active in the Low Countries at the end of the sixteenth century. William was firmly not Catholic, but he could well have fought on the Dutch side of the war, supporting the Protestant cause. William would have been one of the eight thousand men from England, Scotland and Wales fighting in the Low Countries by 1605, formidable training for the Civil War thirty years later.[77]

After fighting in Ireland, William did not join John and Owen in the Essex Revolt and it is likely that he was not one of Essex's men. William studied briefly at Oxford, but left after a year, possibly due to the expense.[78] According to Thelwall, William 'served at sea for diverse yeares' and the description of William

---

[75] NLW, Bachymbyd Letters 36, p. 17.
[76] Hugh Dunthorne, *Britain and the Dutch Revolt 1500–1700* (Cambridge, 2013), p. 62.
[77] Dunthorne, *Britain and the Dutch Revolt*, p. 66.
[78] See above, pp. 38, 158.

as a 'Souldier by Sea' suggests he spent time in the navy. In 1602, his older brother John received word from the Norfolk gentleman Sir John Townshend that Townshend had bought a quarter share in a barque, a three-masted sailing ship, called *Wylloby*. Sir John Townshend was an old friend of John, addressing him as 'my Deare and worthy friend . . . Jack'.[79] It was an unusually enduring association, given that they held opposing views on the earl of Essex. It is probable that Townshend and John Salesbury met while soldiering, possibly on Essex's Cadiz campaign. Townshend was a close and trusted associate who held the lease for the third part of the Salesbury estates when Sir Robert Salesbury's son was a minor, until Townshend's death in 1603.[80] Soldiering abroad provided lasting contacts for the Salesbury men. Another share in *Wylloby* was held by John Trevor (1563–1630), almost certainly the future Sir John Trevor, second son of John Trevor of Trevalyn, who was knighted in 1603. Sir John Trevor's older brother, Sir Richard Trevor of Trevalyn, was another close associate of the Salesburys, and John Salesbury was caught up in Sir Richard's campaign to prevent Sir John Salusbury's election as MP for Denbighshire in 1601. The Trevors had connections to the navy: Sir Richard was Vice-Admiral of North Wales from 1596, while Sir John was Surveyor of the Queen's Ships from 1598.[81] Sir John Trevor was thus well placed to advise on the purchase of a barque and knowledgeable of the money to be made in international shipping. Drawing out the connections further, the youngest Trevor son, Sir Sackville Trevor, captained ships in the navy and married Sir Henry Bagnall's widow, Elinor; Sir Robert Salesbury was married to Sir Henry and Elinor's daughter. The Salesburys thus had close ties to a seafaring Welsh gentry family who made substantial reputations for themselves at sea.

Sir John Townshend reported that he and his fellow investors wanted to send *Wylloby* 'to the Indys', captained by Sir Thomas

---

[79] NLW, Bachymbyd Letters 6.
[80] See above, p. 42.
[81] H.G.O., *HPO (1558–1603)*: 'Trevor, Sir Richard (1558–1638)'; 'Trevor, John (1563–1630)'.

Button.[82] Sir Thomas Button (d.1634) was the fourth son of a Welsh gentleman, Miles Button of Worleton, Glamorgan, who forged a successful career in the navy and received a knighthood from James I after exploring the Hudson Bay in Canada.[83] When Sir Thomas was not officially serving in the navy, he was a privateer, part of the fleet of licensed pirates who extended the war with Spain across the Atlantic. Townshend told John Salesbury that 'Will Salesbury I heare will go if you be contented he shall learne the arte of pyracy'. Thelwall's testimony that William had served at sea adds verisimilitude to the claim that William did learn the art of piracy and served on a privateer vessel, preying on Spanish ships in the West Indies. William was a long way from his home in north Wales, but he retained a Welsh connection, serving under a Welsh captain. According to Townshend's letter, William was already determined to go to the West Indies, so he had heard about the voyage and evidently had his own connections to learn about new opportunities for a younger son looking to make his fortune. A Welsh captain of a ship, possibly owned by at least one Welshman from a family who had strong connections to the Salesburys, suggests that William remained part of a close-knit Welsh community while abroad from Wales.

It is unclear how long William served under Sir Thomas Button, but he was at sea long enough to live later 'on that fortune he had by his owne industry'. Although Eubule Thelwall portrayed William as a struggling younger son who never would have chosen his seafaring life if he had been supported properly by his father and elder brothers, William was extremely proud of his career at sea. In 1632, William commissioned a portrait of himself. Above his left shoulder, as seen by the viewer, there is the Salesbury coat of arms and William's personal motto, 'A vynno Dew dervid', or 'As God wills, so it will be'. Above his right shoulder, there is the date of the painting, 1632, William's age, fifty-two, and a roundel displaying a three-masted sailing ship, possibly the barque called

[82] NLW, Bachymbyd Letters 6.
[83] Andrew Thrush, 'Button, Sir Thomas', *ODNB* (2008; first published 2004).

Wylloby. William thus considered his youth as a sailor to be a vital part of his identity, proudly displaying a ship opposite his coat of arms. The portrait was painted during a brief time of financial stability for William's estates, not long after he finally paid off the mortgage on Bachymbyd. While John Salesbury, who had the good fortune to be older than his brother, almost ruined the Salesbury patrimony with his profligacy, William Salesbury worked hard as a sailor to make his own fortune. William's career enabled him to repurchase alienated Salesbury lands and engage in expensive court cases to restore his ownership of disputed titles. By the time William had his portrait painted, he felt he was, as he later declared in a letter to Godfrey Goodman, bishop of Gloucester, 'worthy to dispose of my lands as I please'; his estates, geographically similar to the Salesbury patrimony, were virtually of his own making.[84]

As a result, the Salesbury family's wealth after 1611 was directly connected to Britain's growing global expansionism in the early seventeenth century. William's youth as a sailor, and the money he accumulated, provided the basis for the family's estates and income. William evidently travelled to the West Indies, where he worked as a privateer attacking Spanish ships. However, it is also possible that William spent time in the colonies of North America. On 9 March 1635, Owen Salesbury sent his father a book about 'the state of Virginia', which might reflect William's interest in the North American colonies. There was a local connection to Virginia through Owen Salusbury (d.1601) and John Salesbury (d.1611); one of Owen's confidants in the Low Countries was Captain Peter Wynne, who became a close friend of John Salesbury too and fought with both men in the Essex Revolt.[85] By 1608, Peter Wynne had emigrated to live in Jamestown, Virginia. Wynne told his patron, the earl of Bridgewater, that 'I was not so desirous to come into this

---

[84] NLW, Bachymbyd Letters 48.
[85] Roberts, 'Cecil Papers: February 1601, 21–28', in *Calendar of the Cecil Papers in Hatfield House: Volume 11, 1601*, pp. 75–100. See above, pp. 123–7.

Country, as I am now willing here to end my dayes for I finde it a fare more pleasant and plentyfull country than any report made mencion of'.[86] Given the level of trade between Virginia, the Caribbean and Britain, it is not unreasonable that William may have travelled there too. If he stayed in the service of Sir Thomas Button, William may have been involved in preventing pirate activity in the Irish Sea and along the south coast of England and Wales, highlighting the blurred line between piracy, privateering and naval activity.

The Salesburys were also part of the developing international consumer culture which depended on Britain's global expansionism. In 1629, for example, Owen Salesbury sent his father some tobacco and promised to send more if William wanted it.[87] Smoking tobacco was a fashionable and novel activity for the early seventeenth-century gentry, one which they quickly adopted as a marker of gentry sociability, but it was also an activity associated more with urban centres like London than the countryside of north Wales.[88] However, it has been demonstrated elsewhere that the Welsh gentry retained strong commercial and familial connections to London, and it is thus unsurprising that status-conscious consumer items, like tobacco from Virginia, made their way to north Wales. William himself had been part of the transatlantic trade in European and American goods and he had the potential to have been an early adopter of tobacco practices, themselves adapted from the Powhatan people in North America. When William was an MP in the 1621 Parliament, he was involved in the examination of a petition from Virginian planters, possibly reflecting his own experience in the colonies, and discussed tobacco import quotas.[89] He also participated in a debate on 'the inordynate use of Tobacco' and he 'spake well', though frustratingly there is no record of what he said or whether

---

[86] THL, EL MS 1683.
[87] NLW, Bachymbyd Letters 21.
[88] Lauren Working, 'Tobacco and the social life of conquest in London, 1580–1625', *Historical Journal*, 65/1 (2022), 30–48.
[89] Simon Healy, *HPO (1604–1629)*: 'Salesbury, William (1580/1–1660)'.

he thought the law should restrict the use of tobacco.[90] Country gentlemen were thus active in the regulation of new goods and confident enough to express opinions on it. William Salesbury was the first of the Salesburys of Rhug and Bachymbyd to speak in the House of Commons and he spoke on issues that he knew well and that reflected his own life experience.

THE LATER SALESBURYS

There is little evidence of the later Salesburys engaging in travel or developing careers as soldiers in overseas wars. Of course, this does not mean that the Salesburys never left Britain, but perhaps reflects the increased financial stability for the Salesburys' younger sons, who found careers as lawyers and merchants, rather than soldiers and sailors. They still participated, however, in an increasingly international economy and took an interest in world news. In 1673, for example, Eubule Thelwall wrote to Sir Walter Bagot and included an account of the Battle of Schooneveld, part of the Third Anglo-Dutch War, a naval battle where England lost, according to Thelwall, a thousand men including five captains, and Sir John Hanmer's man lost a leg. The Hanmers of Hanmer, Flintshire, were another prominent Welsh gentry family, and Sir John Hanmer (d.1701) was Commissioner of the Navy under Charles II. Thus, members of the Welsh gentry were still active soldiers towards the end of the seventeenth century, even if the Salesburys restricted their military activity to serving as deputy lieutenants. As a result, there also remained local connections to international affairs, providing opportunities for families back home to stay informed. Equally, as with Owen Salusbury and the Welsh Catholics in the later sixteenth century, continental Europe remained a refuge for people wanting to escape hostile circumstances in Britain. Notably, Gabriel Salesbury, younger

---

[90] W. Notestein, F. H. Relf and H. Simpson (eds), *Commons Debates 1621* (New Haven and London, 1935), p. 344.

son of Owen Salesbury (d.1658) of Rhug, fled to Paris when the court of Great Sessions ruled that he had commissioned a forged document during the 1670s dispute over Bachymbyd between his brother William Salesbury (d.1677) and their cousin, Jane (d.1695).[91] This was a forced exile, however, the result of a crime which saw his mother, Mary Goodman, disinherit him from her will, persuaded, according to Gabriel, by his 'angry sister', either Dorothy or Sioned.[92] Perhaps Dorothy or Sioned did not approve of their brothers' actions towards their cousin Jane, or they believed Gabriel's actions harmed the family's reputation. On 28 November 1681, from Paris, Gabriel begged Sir John Trevor, from a cadet branch of the longstanding Trevor of Trevalyn allies of the Salesburys, and a fellow lawyer, to intervene in the dispute because 'I doe not enioy one penny out of my fathers estate which iniustice I look uppon as permitted by God for my Indirect Proceedings towards Sir Walter Bagot and his Lady'. Sir John Trevor was a close associate of the Salesburys of Rhug; later, he was one of the trustees of the estate of Owen Salesbury (d.1694).[93]

However, Sir John was not willing to act as an intermediary between Gabriel and Jane without some benefits for himself. By the time that Gabriel wrote a second letter to Sir John, on 20 January 1682, he was in Amsterdam and he may have gone there at Sir John's request. Gabriel told Sir John that he had 'searched all the Booksellers shopps in town for Bartholinus de Usu Nivis but cannot find it'.[94] *De nivis usu medico observationes variae* (1661) by Thomas Bartholin, a Danish physician and scholar, was a medical text with the early observation of refrigeration anaesthesia as a surgical technique. Gabriel said that he would try to find a copy of the book in Leyden and The Hague. Sir John also apparently requested books by Robert Boyle and Gabriel told him that 'I believe yew will take litle satisfaction in that Author who abounds

[91] TNA, C 10/173/11; NLW, Bachymbyd Letters 130.
[92] NLW, Bachymbyd Letters 179.
[93] CRO, XD2/41.
[94] NLW, Bachymbyd Letters 180.

in notionall problems . . . and speaks not of Ice and snow but other refrigerating ingredients'. Robert Boyle conducted early experiments on intravenous anaesthesia, but Gabriel evidently did not think much of Boyle's approach compared to Bartholin's refrigeration.[95] Clearly, Sir John had an interest in anaesthetic techniques and wanted to use his contact on the continent to source books from different scientists. However, Sir John was not only interested in books: Gabriel said that he had asked a friend in Paris 'about the stockings yew mencioned, as also about french paper'. This presumably meant the highly finished white paper used for books which was produced to a better quality and at a lower cost in France, compared to England.[96]

In the end, Gabriel was exiled abroad for ten years.[97] In his reply to Gabriel, it seems that Sir John warned him that Jane Salesbury was not happy about the possibility of his return to Britain; Gabriel wrote in his second letter to Sir John on 20 January 1682 that

> the Ladyes Anger may be qualified when she understands that I doe not desire to return without her good leave and permission, which I cannot hope for without such submission and acknowledgment as will be more advantagious and honorable to her then the continuance of my exile.[98]

Jane, not her husband, Sir Walter, thus controlled whether Gabriel could go home. Gabriel did not want to be abroad, where it was difficult to contest his inheritance, though he had clearly had some level of income while in France for ten years, possibly through his profession as a lawyer. By 18 November 1682, Gabriel was in London, pardoned by his cousin. He wrote

---

[95] K. L. Dorrington and W. Poole, 'The first intravenous anaesthetic: how well was it managed and its potential realized?', *British Journal of Anaesthesia*, 110/1 (2013), 7–12.
[96] John Bidwell, 'French paper in English books', in Barnard and McKenzie, *The Cambridge History of the Book in Britain*, vol. 4, p. 583.
[97] NLW, Bachymbyd Letters 181.
[98] NLW, Bachymbyd Letters 180.

to thank Jane for her clemency and allowing him to return to England 'where I shall make it my Bisnes to Proclaym your Goodnes and my own Unworthines'.[99] This letter included a full confession of Gabriel's crimes and it may have been a caveat to his return from exile; Gabriel's letter was enclosed with another from Sir John Trevor who said that Gabriel would provide 'fuller satisfacsion . . . as the most repenting Sinner in the world'.[100] Upon returning to England, Gabriel resumed his practice at Gray's Inn. In 1695, years after his exile ended, he wrote to his nephew, Roger Salesbury, newly paterfamilias of the Salesbury patrimony after Owen Salesbury's death in 1694, and enquired whether Roger was going to marry one of Sir Walter Bagot's daughters. Roger replied that he had never met any of the Bagot daughters and he would never meet them with the intent of arranging a marriage.[101] The Salesburys of Rhug remembered that they once owned Bachymbyd and that their ancestors' estate now belonged to the Bagots. Roger's reply suggests that he would never countenance a marriage with the Bagots and that the two families remained permanently estranged. After returning from exile, Gabriel lived in London and Roger Salesbury remonstrated with him in his letter of 1695 for not writing more often; Gabriel generally kept away from north Wales. Gabriel's 1711 will highlights London's international consumer culture: he bequeathed his Italian boots and French books to fellow Gray's Inn lawyers Edward Bedingfield and Basil Fitzherbert, respectively.[102] Gabriel had not wanted to spend ten years in exile and apparently regretted his crime against his cousin, but it made him well-travelled with a good knowledge of European markets.

[99] NLW, Bachymbyd Letters 181.
[100] NLW, Bachymbyd Letters 182.
[101] CRO, XD2/41.
[102] TNA, PROB 11/519/108.

CONCLUSION

The Salesburys of Rhug and Bachymbyd, a gentry family from rural north-east Wales, were an active part of Britain's growing global expansionism in the sixteenth and seventeenth centuries. Like other Welsh gentry families, they were fully engaged with Europe and the developing colonial world of the British Atlantic. For the Salesburys, this manifested itself most obviously in their careers as soldiers in Ireland, Spain and the Low Countries, but they were also part of international trade markets and a new consumer culture. William Salesbury, the stalwart defender of Denbigh Castle in the Civil War, celebrated his youth as a privateer in the Caribbean, preying on Spanish ships, and he used his experiences to contribute to parliamentary debates as a middle-aged, respectable landowner. Without William's expansionist activity, he could never have reclaimed the Salesburys' estates, which were re-founded on William's privateer fortune. On the one hand, the Salesburys' engagement with British expansionism was financial. John and William were younger sons who had an economic drive to find employment as soldiers. However, they remained part of a wider Welsh community. The Welsh gentry retained their Welshness when they were far from home and sought each other out, speaking the same language and understanding the same cultural norms. The example of the Salesburys suggests that the Welsh diaspora gathered together and continued to recognise their shared Welsh identity. When they returned home, as William Salesbury did to become the head of his family, the Welsh gentry celebrated their international experiences and incorporated them into their sense of identity. An early modern Welsh gentleman was a man of the world.

EPILOGUE

In a 1697 collection of north Wales pedigrees, there is a list of the 'Saith gamp a ddlai fod ar wr bonheddig' or 'Seven qualities needed to be a gentleman'.[1]

1. bod yn fardd ar ei fwrdd:
2. bod yn oen yn ei ystafell:
3. bod un feudwy yn ei eglwys:
4. bod yn baen yn yr heol:
5. bod yn ddoeth yn ei ddadl:
6. bod yn llew ar y maes:
7. bod yn athraw yn ei dy.

[1. to be a poet at his table:
2. to be a lamb in his chamber:
3. to be a hermit in his church:
4. to be a peacock in the road:
5. to be wise in his conversation:
6. to be a lion on the field:
7. to be a teacher in his house.]

A gentleman respected his wife and acted as the moral leader of the household. He provided good entertainment and hospitality. He was a loyal Protestant who regularly attended church. Although he was a learned man, he was also willing to be a brave fighter. He was conspicuous in public life and everyone knew his reputation. Like the concept of gentility itself, these qualities presented an

[1] NLW, 7008E, p. 12.

ideal. The example of the Salesburys of Rhug and Bachymbyd suggests that Welsh gentlemen often had their own understanding of gentility which prioritised their personal ambitions and the need to defend their status. If any of the Salesburys came even close to achieving these standards, it is perhaps William Salesbury (1580–1660), the resolute paterfamilias who reconstructed his family estates, engaged in scholarship, built his own chapel, and was commended for his bravery in war by the king himself. Yet William Salesbury was a youngest son who spent the first thirty years of his life with no household of his own to lead and little expectation of inheriting the family patrimony, a gentleman in name only with an intense awareness of his precarious position in early modern gentry society.

This book has largely focused on the paterfamilias and his engagement with gentility. Where possible, it has tried to include the experiences of younger sons and brothers, as well as women. The status of individuals changed during their lifetimes, and the slings and arrows of fortune injured or improved their lot. The birth of a healthy baby knocked a younger brother further down the line of inheritance. The death of a husband transferred control of the household from his wife to his son. A daughter inherited the family estates after all her brothers died. In early modern Wales, gentility was a matter of fact, the condition of possessing distinguished ancestry, but it also required active performance; it was a cultivated image of status and reputation. The brief insights permitted here of the experiences of widows and younger sons in the Salesbury family suggest that they had a keen sense of their own gentility, but they lacked the same mechanisms of the paterfamilias to perform it. They claimed the same descent from Welsh nobility and Norman conquerors, but they did not hold offices, control the patrimony, or cultivate extensive relationships with tenants and servants. Instead, they fiercely defended their honour and privileges: Dame Elinor Bagnall (d.1656), the widow of Sir Robert Salesbury, reminded her brother-in-law that she had yet to receive the rent due as her jointure; a twenty-year-old William Salesbury caused a brawl in a Ruthin churchyard when the younger son of a rival family cast aspersions on his family's reputation. Gentility was a matter of fact, but it was also a nebulous concept; the members of a gentry family knew they possessed it and they had to fight to keep it.

Like the fortunes and status of individuals, gentility was not static. At the beginning of the eighteenth century, the Salesburys were an Anglican family who kept hundreds of books and lived in houses filled with luxury goods from across the world. Welsh society had changed considerably during the Salesburys' three centuries of prominence, and the Salesburys changed with it. When John Salesbury began purchasing Bachymbyd in the 1470s, he inhabited a divided society where Welsh laws restricted the gentry's ability to develop estates, and they worked hard to circumvent them. Although they had English ancestors in the paternal line, the family held only low-level offices, such as the constabulary of the commote of Edeirnion in 1534.[2] John and his family were Catholics. His sons attended the local grammar school where they received an education sufficient to run their estates or take up a career in the Church. The Salesburys were enthusiastic patrons of the bardic order and they received praise poetry celebrating their estates and ancestors. They were well-established as one of the elite families of north Wales by the time that the Acts of Union extended English law and rights across the realm. This opened up a range of offices and the gentry quickly coveted the prestigious county positions of MP and JP. The legal system also provided a novel means of engaging in rivalries with other gentry families, and the gentry slowly transitioned from disputes with weapons to disputes with lawyers. However, although violence and disorder decreased in the decades after the Acts of Union, internecine conflict between gentry families continued into the seventeenth century. For the Salesburys, factionalism is most obvious in the later sixteenth and early seventeenth centuries.

[2] CRO, XD2/165.

A medieval Catholic family, carving out a patchwork of landholdings throughout the Vale of Clwyd, quick to defend its land and reputation with violence, became an early modern Anglican family with vast estates which protected itself in the law courts. Its sons went to English public schools, followed by the universities or the Inns of Court, or they gained a secure trade as apprentices in London. The Salesburys of the eighteenth century inhabited a much bigger world than their fifteenth-century ancestors. This was figuratively true and it reflected Britain's colonial ambitions, which brought opportunities for trade and settlement even to the gentry on the fringes of the British realm. However, the Welsh gentry were not an insular class; even in the Middle Ages, Welsh soldiers had fought overseas and the gentry adopted new ideas and practices. For example, the early modern gentleman-scholar was the result of humanist influences, even as the Welsh gentry clung on to their ambitions for martial glory. John Salesbury of Bachymbyd had existed within dual identities, a Welshman with English ancestors, holding both Welsh and English land. His descendants had more than one identity too: they were Cambro-Britons who served the Crown loyally; they were elite Welsh families with the ancestry to prove it; they were servants to noble patrons; they were landlords with tenants and servants of their own; they were faithful friends and dangerous enemies; they were hospitable and charitable and violent and petty. At home, they had rivals and abroad they had a growing Welsh diaspora. In short, they were characteristic of a Welsh gentry family, status-conscious and opportunistic, but never removed from their local communities which gave them historical significance and the cultural clout to claim gentility.

The Salesburys were fully integrated in north Wales society through marriage and kinship links, and thus they are plausible representations of the gentry as a social class. The family's existence spanned nearly three centuries and they maintained their position as an elite family during a period of considerable change for Wales, not least in its relationship with England. Like other Welsh gentry families, including the Pulestons of Emral, the Mansels of Oxwich and Margam, and the Thelwalls of Plas y Ward, the Salesburys were the descendants of medieval English settlers, and so they provide answers to what defined and consolidated a Welsh gentry family. Nevertheless, it is also the case that the Salesburys are just one family among many, and there are natural limitations to a case-study approach. As we explored in chapter two, gentry families had myriad ways to build up their estates and so it is also possible that they had myriad ways of conceptualising gentility. Previous research, however, suggests that the early modern Welsh gentry had a shared understanding of their position as a social class, and thus other gentry families would recognise the portrayal of gentility in the previous chapters.[3] More case studies of Welsh gentry families would build a clearer picture of how they engaged with gentility, and the range of source material for other families might allow a better knowledge of gentlewomen and younger sons. The example of the Salesburys is not intended as the final word on Welsh gentility, but to continue the conversation and encourage more work on the Welsh gentry and early modern Wales more generally.

The Salesburys of Rhug and Bachymbyd are not remembered for their prestigious manuscript collections, their exploits on the high seas, their prominent positions at court, or their contributions to scholarship. Unlike the Vaughans of Hengwrt or the Salesburys of Plas Isaf, they could not claim that one of their members saved the Black Book of Carmarthen for posterity or became the first to translate the Bible into Welsh. Few portraits of the Salesburys survive and their estates have long passed into the hands of other families. William Salesbury retains some local distinction for his defence of Denbigh Castle in the Civil War, but little is remembered about the rest of his family. In early modern Wales, however, the Salesburys were a prominent, elite family with a sphere of influence that stretched from Flintshire to

---

[3] Carr, 'The Mostyn family and estate, 1200–1642'; Jones, *The Wynn Family of Gwydir*; Evans, '"To contynue in my bloud and name"'; Clavier, *Royalism*.

Merioneth, from Anglesey to Montgomeryshire. They had friends in some of the highest places, including the Lord Chancellor and the President of the Council of the Marches. They continually engaged with the expectations and ideals of Welsh gentility and adapted to changing circumstances. The Salesburys were a family of reputation and status, embedded in the gentry community of north Wales and the borders. This book has sought to reflect a glimpse of their early modern prominence and singled them out amongst their rivals to illustrate the concept of gentility in early modern Wales. I hope they would consider it a worthy legacy for a great kindred.

BIBLIOGRAPHY

1. MANUSCRIPT SOURCES

Bangor University Archives and Special Collections:
BMSS/119.

British Library, London:
Additional MSS 14918; 14919; 14920; 14973; 14974.
Egerton MS 2586.
Harley MS 1936; 1971.
Lansdowne MS 99.
Stowe MS 669.

Caernarfon Record Office (Gwynedd Archives):
CRO, XD2/14; 38; 41; 426–8; 463; 470; 494; 498; 521; 799–800; 932; 953; 975; 1109; 1149; 1241; 1247; 1258; 1265; 1284; 1337; 1342–3; 1391; 1834; 3913.

Cardiff Central Library:
MSS 2.114; 2.39.

National Library of Wales, Aberystwyth:
MSS 13B; 1565C; 2098E; 6499B; 7008E; 9857C; 11058E.
Bachymbyd 5; 18; 39; 84; 96; 111; 113; 166; 168; 178; 251–3; 281; 301; 321–3; 351–2; 364; 426; 490–1; 514–16; 523; 527; 543–4; 549; 623; 641–3; 645; 656; 677; 693; 719–20; 729; 904; 964; 975; 983.
Bachymbyd Letters 1b; 3; 6; 9b; 18–29; 31–3; 36–9; 43–5; 47–8; 65; 70; 93; 122; 130; 179–82; 228.
Chirk F12540.
Gogerddan LB1/1; LB2/1; LB5/1.
Great Sessions 4/12/1.
Llanstephan 37B, 110B, 159, 170.
Lleweni 674.

Peniarth 110D; 236B; 326E.
Plas Nantglyn MS 1.

National Maritime Museum, London:
HSR/A/1.

North East Wales Archives (Denbighshire Record Office), Ruthin:
DD/DM/1647.
DD/WY/113; 674; 4077; 4194; 6521; 6548; 6674.
PD/90/5/9.

North East Wales Archives (Flintshire Record Office), Hawarden:
D/PT/397.

Shropshire Archives, Shrewsbury:
212/364/1.

The Huntington Library, San Marino, CA:
Ellesmere MSS 669; 1683; 1782e; 1782g.

The National Archives, London:
C 1/1385/9; 5/446/5; 5/446/195; 5/447/83; 5/550/32; 6/474/15; 8/202/58; 10/173/11; 22/185/17; 22/1005/53.
E 134/16CHAS1/EAST13; E 134/16CHAS1/TRIN7.
PROB 11/63/70; 11/96/125; 11/118/503; 11/302/545; 11/519/108; 11/665/105; 11/713/89; 11/1069/80.
SP 1/105/251a; 1/120; 1/236; 63/173; 63/177; 63/178; 63/180; 63/185.
STAC 5/Addenda 15/54; 5/A55/34; 5/L21/24; 5/L23/2; 5/L48/7; 5/S28/6; 5/S51/14; 5/S59/2; 5/T7/31; 5/T9/31; 5/T15/33; 5/T30/18; 7/4/2; 7/15/54; 8/201/24.
WARD 7/20/173; 9/66; 9/103/82; 9/108; 9/120; 9/159; 9/634.

Trinity College, Cambridge:
MS 1303 [O.5.22].

Gwysaney Hall, Flintshire:
Uncatalogued MS.

Winchester College, Hampshire:
Registrum Primum 1393–1687.

2. PRINTED PRIMARY SOURCES

A Biographical Register of the University of Cambridge to 1500, ed. A. B. Emden (Cambridge, 1963).
A Biographical Register of the University of Oxford to 1500, ed. A. B. Emden (Oxford, 1959).
A Calendar of the Register of the Queen's Majesty's Council in the Dominion and Principality of Wales and the Marches of the Same [1535] 1569–1591 from the Bodley MS. no. 904, ed. R. Flenley (London, 1916).
Acts of the Privy Council of England Volume 32, 1601–1604, ed. J. R. Dasent (London, 1907).
'Adam of Usk, *Chronicle, Part 3*', in M. Livingston and J. K. Bollard (eds), *Owain Glyndŵr: A Casebook* (Liverpool, 2013), pp. 144–9.
Alumni Oxonienses: The Members of the University of Oxford, 1500–1714, ed. J. Foster, vol. 2 (Oxford, 1892).
'A Poem of Warning to Owain Glyndŵr', in M. Livingston and J. K. Bollard (eds), *Owain Glyndŵr: A Casebook* (Liverpool, 2013), pp. 216–17.
Calendar, Committee for Compounding: Part 3, ed. Mary Anne Everett Green (London, 1891).
Calendar of the Manuscripts of the Most Honourable The Marquess of Bath, vol. 5: *Talbot, Dudley and Devereux Papers 1533–1659*, ed. G. Dyfnallt Owen (London, 1980).
Calendar of Patent Rolls (London, 1891–).
Calendar of State Papers, Domestic, ed. R. Lemon et al. (London, 1856–1998).
Calendar of State Papers, Foreign, ed. J. Stevenson et al. (London, 1863–1950).
Commons Debates 1621, ed. W. Notestein, R. H. Relf and H. Simpson (New Haven and London, 1935).
British Museum, *Catalogue of Additions to the Manuscripts in the British Museum in the Years 1841–1845* (London, 1850).
Dugdale, W., *The Baronage of England; or, An Historical Account of the Lives and Most Memorable Actions of our English Nobility* (London, 1675–6).
'Elis Gruffudd, *Chronicle*', in M. Livingston and J. K. Bollard (eds), *Owain Glyndŵr: A Casebook* (Liverpool, 2013), pp. 228–31.
Gerald of Wales, *The History and Topography of Ireland*, trans. J. O'Meara (London, 1982).
Harry, G. O., *The Genealogy of the High and Mighty Monarch, James, by the Grace of God, king of great Brittayne, &c. with his lineall descent from Noah, by diuers direct lynes to Brutus, first inhabiter of this Ile of Brittayne, and from him to Cadwalader, the last king of the Brittish bloud; and from thence, sundry wayes to his Maiesty . . .* (London, 1604).
Heraldic Visitations of Wales and Part of the Marches, ed. Sir S. R. Meyrick, vol. 2 (Llandovery, 1846).
Historical Manuscripts Commission, *Report on Manuscripts in the Welsh Language*, vol. 1 (London, 1898).

Letters and Papers, Foreign and Domestic, of the Reign of Henry VIII, ed. J. S. Brewer, J. Gairdner and R. H. Brodie (London, 1862–1932).

Newcome, R., *A Memoir of Gabriel Goodman, with some account of Ruthin School* (Ruthin, 1825).

Pennant, T., *A Tour in Wales*, vol. 6 (London, 1781).

Poems by Sir John Salusbury and Robert Chester, ed. C. Brown (London, 1914).

Powel, D., *The Historie of Cambria, now called Wales* (London, 1584).

Survey of the Honour of Denbigh 1334, ed. P. Vinogradoff and F. Morgan, vol. 1 (London, 1914).

The Register of Admissions to Gray's Inn, 1521–1889, ed. J. Foster (London, 1889).

Vita Griffini Filii Conani: The Medieval Latin Life of Gruffudd Ap Cynan, ed. P. Russell (Cardiff, 2012).

Wynn, Sir J., *The History of the Gwydir Family and Memoirs*, ed. J. G. Jones (Llandysul, 1990).

3. SECONDARY SOURCES

Adams, S., *Leicester and the Court: Essays on Elizabethan politics* (Manchester, 2002).

Andrews, K. R. (ed.), *The Last Voyage of Drake & Hawkins* (Cambridge, 1972).

Anthony, D. J., 'To Have, to Hold, and to Vanquish: Property and inheritance in the history of marriage and surnames', *British Journal of American Legal Studies*, 5 (2016), 217–39.

Barker, N., 'Editing the past: classical and historical scholarship', in J. Barnard and D. F. McKenzie (eds), *The Cambridge History of the Book in Britain*, vol. 4: *1557–1695* (Cambridge, 2002), pp. 206–27.

Batho, G., 'Landlords in England B: Noblemen, gentlemen, and yeomen', in J. Thirsk (ed.), *The Agrarian History of England and Wales*, vol. 4: *1500–1640* (Cambridge, 1967; 2011 edn), pp. 276–306.

Barrell, A. D. M. and Brown, M. H., 'A settler community in post-Conquest rural Wales: The English of Dyffryn Clwyd, 1294–1399', *Welsh History Review*, 17/3 (1995), 332–55.

Bartlett, R., *Gerald of Wales 1146–1223* (Oxford, 1982).

Bidwell, J., 'French paper in English books', in J. Barnard and D. F. McKenzie (eds), *The Cambridge History of the Book in Britain*, vol. 4: *1557–1695* (Cambridge, 2002), pp. 583–601.

Black, J., 'The rhetoric of reaction: The Martin Marprelate tracts (1588–89), Anti-Martinism, and the uses of print in early modern England', *The Sixteenth Century Journal*, 28 (1997), 707–25.

Bowen, G., 'John Salisbury', *National Library of Wales Journal*, 8 (1953–4), 387–98.

Bowen, L., *Politics in the Principality: Wales, c.1603–1642* (Cardiff, 2007).

Bowen, L., 'The Battle of Britain: History and Reformation in early modern Wales', in T. Ó hAnnracháin and R. Armstrong (eds), *Christianities in the Early Modern Celtic World* (Basingstoke, 2014), pp. 135–50.

Bowen, L., 'Information, language and political culture in early modern Wales', *Past and Present*, 228/1 (2015), 125–58.

Bowen, L., *Anatomy of a Duel in Jacobean England: Gentry Honour, Violence and the Law* (Woodbridge, 2021).

Braddick, M. J., *State Formation in Early Modern England, c.1550–1700* (Cambridge, 2000).

Bradshaw, B. and Roberts, P. (eds), *British Consciousness and Identity: The Making of Britain, 1533–1707* (Cambridge, 1998).

Bray, A., 'Homosexuality and the signs of male friendship in Elizabethan England', *History Workshop Journal*, 29 (1990), 1–19.

Bray, A., *The Friend* (London and Chicago, 2003).

Broadway, J., *'No historie so meete': Gentry culture and the development of local history in Elizabethan and early Stuart England* (Manchester, 2006).

Bromwich, R., *Trioedd Ynys Prydein* (3rd edn: Cardiff, 2006).

Butaud, G. and Piétri, V., *Les Enjeux de la Généalogie (XIIe–XVIIIe siécles). Pouvoir et identité* (Paris, 2006).

Capp, B., *England's Culture Wars: Puritan Reformation and its Enemies in the Interregnum, 1649–1660* (Oxford, 2012).

Carey, V., '"As lief to the gallows as go to the Irish wars": Human rights and the abuse of the Elizabethan soldier in Ireland, 1600–1603', *History*, 99/336 (2014), 468–86.

Carr, A. D., 'The barons of Edeirnion, 1283–1485 I and II', *Journal of the Merioneth Historical and Record Society*, 4 (1963), 187–93, 289–301.

Carr, A. D., 'An aristocracy in decline: The native Welsh lords after the Edwardian Conquest', *Welsh History Review*, 5 (1970), 103–29.

Carr, A. D., 'Appendix 2: Parishes and townships in medieval Merioneth: Edeirnion', in J. B. Smith and L. B. Smith (eds), *A History of Merioneth: Middle Ages*, vol. 2 (Cardiff, 2001), pp. 717–26.

Carr, A. D., *The Gentry of North Wales in the Later Middle Ages* (Cardiff, 2017).

Cavell, E., 'Widows, native law and the long shadow of England in thirteenth-century Wales', *English Historical Review*, 133/565 (2018), 1387–419.

Chadwick, M. and Evans, S., '"Ye Best Tast of Books & Learning of Any Other Country Gentn": The Library of Thomas Mostyn of Gloddaith, c.1676–1692', in A. Bautz and J. Gregory (eds), *Libraries, Books and Collectors of Texts, 1600–1900* (London, 2018), pp. 87–103.

Chapman, A., *Welsh Soldiers in the Later Middle Ages, 1282–1422* (Woodbridge, 2015).

Charles Edwards, T., *Early Irish and Welsh Kinship* (Oxford, 1993).

Chibnall, M., *The Debate on the Norman Conquest* (Manchester, 1999).

Connolly, S. J., *Contested Ireland: Ireland 1460–1630* (Oxford, 2007).

Cust, R., 'The culture of dynasticism in early modern Cheshire', in S. Jettot and M. Lezowski (eds), *The Genealogical Enterprise: Social practices and collective imagination in Europe (15th–20th century)* (Brussels, 2016), pp. 209–33.

Cust, R. and Lake, P., *Gentry Culture and the Politics of Religion: Cheshire on the eve of Civil War* (Manchester, 2020).

Davies, C. (ed.), *Dr John Davies of Mallwyd: Welsh Renaissance Scholar* (Cardiff, 2004).

Davies, R. R., 'The status of women and the practice of marriage in late-medieval Wales', in D. Jenkins and M. E. Owen (eds), *The Welsh Law of Women* (Cardiff, 1980), pp. 93–114.

Davies, R. R., *The Revolt of Owain Glyn Dŵr* (Oxford, 1995).

Davies, S., 'Y ferch yng Nghymru yn yr Oesoedd Canol', *Cof Cenedl*, 9 (1994), 3–32.

Dodd, A. H., 'The Spanish Treason, the Gunpowder Plot, and the Catholic refugees', *English Historical Review*, 53 (1938), 627–50.

Dodd, A. H., 'North Wales in the Essex Revolt of 1601', *English Historical Review*, 59/235 (1944), 348–70.

Dodd, A. H., 'The Civil War in east Denbighshire', *Transactions of the Denbighshire Historical Society*, 3 (1954), 41–89.

Dorrington, K. L. and Poole, W., 'The first intravenous anaesthetic: how well was it managed and its potential realized?', *British Journal of Anaesthesia*, 110/1 (2013), 7–12.

Dunthorne, H., *Britain and the Dutch Revolt 1500–1700* (Cambridge, 2013).

Edwards, F., 'The first Earl of Salisbury's pursuit of Hugh Owen', *British Catholic History*, 26 (2002), 2–38.

Emanuel, H. D., *The Latin Texts of the Welsh Laws* (Cardiff, 1967).

Erickson, A. L., 'Common law versus common practice: the use of marriage settlements in early modern England', *Economic History Review*, 2nd series, 43 (1990), 21–39.

Erickson, A. L., *Women and Property in Early Modern England* (London, 1993; 2002 edn).

Evans, D. G., *The Foundations of Ruthin 1100–1800* (Wrexham, 2017).

Evans, E. D., 'Politics and parliamentary representation in Merioneth, 1536–1644: Part 1', *Journal of the Merioneth Historical and Record Society*, 15 (2006), 4–28.

Evans, S., 'St. Winifred's well, office-holding and the Mostyn family interest: Negotiating the Reformation in Flintshire, c.1570–1642', *Journal of the Flintshire Historical Society*, 40 (2015), 41–72.

Evans, S., 'Gruffudd Hiraethog, heraldic display and the "five courts" of Mostyn: Projecting status, honour and authority in sixteenth-century Wales', in F. Robertson and P. N. Lindfield (eds), *The Display of Heraldry: The Heraldic Imagination in Arts and Culture* (London, 2019), pp. 116–33.

Fincham, K., 'The restoration of altars in the 1630s', *The Historical Journal*, 44/4 (2001), 919–40.

Fletcher, A., *A County Community in Peace and War: Sussex 1600–1660* (London, 1975).
Gajda, A., *The Earl of Essex and Late Elizabethan Political Culture* (Oxford, 2012).
Goring, J., 'Social change and military decline in mid-Tudor England', *History*, 60 (1975), 185–97.
Gray, M., 'Power, Patronage and Politics: Office-holding and administration on the Crown estates in Wales', in R. W. Hoyle (ed.), *The Estates of the English Crown, 1558–1640* (Cambridge, 1992), pp. 137–62.
Griffith, W. P., 'Schooling and Society', in J. G. Jones (ed.), *Class, Community and Culture in Tudor Wales* (Cardiff, 1989), pp. 79–119.
Griffith, W. P., *Learning, Law and Religion: Higher education and Welsh society, c.1540–1640* (Cardiff, 1996).
Griffiths, E., 'Improving Landlords or Villains of the Peace?: A Case Study of Early Seventeenth-Century Norfolk', in J. Whittle (ed.), *Landlords and Tenants in Britain, 1440–1660: Tawney's* Agrarian Problem *Revisited* (Woodbridge, 2013), pp. 166–82.
Griffiths, R. A., *King and Country: England and Wales in the Fifteenth Century* (London, 1991).
Griffiths, R. A., 'Gentlemen and rebels in later medieval Cardiganshire', *Ceredigion*, 5/2 (1964–7), 143–67.
Gruffydd, R. G., 'Wales and the Renaissance', in A. J. Roderick (ed.), *Wales through the Ages II* (1960), pp. 45–53.
Guy, B., *Medieval Welsh Genealogy: An introduction and textual study* (Woodbridge, 2020).
Habakkuk, H. J., 'The market for monastic property', *Economic History Review*, NS, 10/3 (1958), 362–80.
Guy, J., *Gresham's Law: The life and world of Queen Elizabeth I's banker* (London, 2019).
Hague, D. B., 'Rug Chapel Corwen', *Journal of the Merioneth Historical and Record Society*, 3 (1958), 167–83.
Hainsworth, D. H., *Stewards, Lords, and People: The estate steward and his world in later Stuart England* (Cambridge, 1992).
Hammer, P. E. J., 'A Welshman Abroad: Captain Peter Wynne of Jamestown', *Parergon*, 16 (1998), 59–92.
Hammer, P. E. J., 'The earl of Essex and England's expeditionary forces', in H. M. Thomas, J. Shami and D. Flynn (eds), *The Oxford Handbook of John Donne* (Oxford, 2011), pp. 435–46.
Hampton, S., *Grace and Conformity: The Reformed Conformist Tradition and the Early Stuart Church of England* (Oxford, 2021).
Harper, S., *Music in Welsh Culture before 1650: A study of the principal sources* (Aldershot, 2007).
Hays, R. W., 'Welsh Students at Oxford and Cambridge Universities in the Middle Ages', *Welsh History Review*, 4 (1968), 325–61.
Heal, F., *Hospitality in Early Modern England* (Oxford, 1990).

Heal, F., *The Power of Gifts: Gift exchange in early modern England* (Oxford, 2014).
Heal, F. and Holmes, C., *The Gentry in England and Wales 1500–1700* (Basingstoke 1994).
Herbert, A. E., *Female Alliances: Gender, Identity, and Friendship in Early Modern Britain* (London, 2014).
Hill, C., *The Intellectual Origins of the English Revolution* (Oxford, 1997).
Holt, J. S., 'The financial rewards of winning the battle for secure customary tenure', in J. Whittle (ed.), *Landlords and Tenants in Britain, 1440-1660: Tawney's Agrarian Problem Revisited* (Woodbridge, 2013), pp. 133–49.
Hoskins, W. G., *The Making of the English Landscape* (London, 1955; 1992 edn).
Houlbrooke, R. A., *The English Family 1450–1700* (London, 1984).
Howells, B. E., *The Gentry of South-West Wales, 1540–1640* (Cardiff, 1968).
Hoyle, R. W. (ed.), *Custom, Improvement, and the Landscape in Early Modern Britain* (Farnham, 2011).
Huws, D., *Medieval Welsh Manuscripts* (Cardiff, 2000).
Huws, D., *A Repertory of Welsh Manuscripts and Scribes, c.800–c.1800* (Aberystwyth, 2022).
H.W.L., 'Old Rûg', *Archaeologia Cambrensis*, 5th series, 4/13 (1887), 48–53.
Jack, R. I., 'Owain Glyn Dŵr and the Lordship of Ruthin', *Welsh History Review*, 2 (1964), 303–22.
Jackson, K., *Studies in Early Celtic Nature Poetry* (Cambridge, 1935).
Jarrett, S., 'Officeholding and local politics in early modern Wales: A study of the Salesburys of Rhug and Bachymbyd, c.1536–1621', *Welsh History Review*, 30/2 (2020), 206–32.
Jarrett, S., '"By reason of her sex and widowhood": An early modern Welsh gentlewoman in the Court of Star Chamber', in K. J. Kesselring and N. Mears (eds), *Star Chamber Matters: The Court and its Records* (London, 2021), pp. 79–96.
Jarrett, S., 'Credibility in the Court of Chancery: Salesbury v. Bagot, 1671–1677', *The Seventeenth Century*, 36/1 (2021), 55–79.
Jenkins, P., 'Seventeenth-century Wales: definition and identity', in B. Bradshaw and P. Roberts (eds), *British Consciousness and Identity: The making of Britain, 1533–1707* (Cambridge, 1998), pp. 213–35.
Johnston, D., 'Lewys Glyn Cothi: Bardd y gwragedd', *Taliesin*, 74 (1991), 68–77.
Johnston, D., 'Shaping a heroic life: Thomas Pennant on Owen Glyndŵr', in M. Constantine and N. Leask (eds), *Enlightenment Travel and British Identities: Thomas Pennant's Tours in Scotland and Wales* (London, 2017), pp. 105–21.
Jones, E. D., 'Cerddi Wiliam Salesbury', *Y Dysgedydd*, 25 (1957), 69–72.
Jones, E. D., 'Llyfr amrywiaeth Syr Siôn Prys', *Brycheiniog*, 8 (1962), 97–104.
Jones, E. G., 'Country politics and electioneering 1558–1625', *Transactions of the Caernarvonshire Historical Society*, 1 (1939), 37–46.
Jones, F., 'An approach to Welsh genealogy', *Transactions of the Honourable Society of Cymmrodorion* (1948), 303–466.

Jones, F., 'Arms of the XV Noble Tribes of North Wales', *The Coat of Arms*, 5/34 (1958), 89–94.
Jones, G., *A Study of Three Welsh Religious Plays* (Bala, 1939).
Jones, J. G., 'The Welsh poets and their patrons, *c.*1550–1640', *Welsh History Review*, 9 (1978), 245–77.
Jones, J. G., 'The Wynn estate of Gwydir: Aspects of its growth and development *c.*1500–1580', *National Library of Wales Journal*, 22/2 (1981), 141–69.
Jones, J. G., 'Educational activity among the Wynns of Gwydir', *Transactions of the Caernarvonshire Historical Society*, 42 (1985), 7–48.
Jones, J. G., *Concepts of Order and Gentility in Wales 1540–1640* (Llandysul, 1992).
Jones, J. G., 'Lewis Owen, sheriff of Merioneth, and the "Gwylliaid Cochion" of Mawddwy in 1554–55', *Journal of the Merioneth Historical and Record Society*, 12 (1994–7), 221–40.
Jones, J. G., *The Wynn Family of Gwydir: Origins, Growth and Development, c.1490–1674* (Aberystwyth, 1995).
Jones, J. G., *Law, Order and Government in Caernarfonshire, 1558–1640: Justices of the Peace and the gentry* (1996).
Jones, J. G., 'Scribes and patrons in the seventeenth century', in P. H. Jones and E. Rees (eds), *A Nation and its Books: A history of the book in Wales* (Aberystwyth, 1998), pp. 83–91.
Jones, J. G., 'Welsh gentlewomen: Piety and Christian conduct *c.*1560–1730', *Journal of Welsh Religious History*, 7 (1999), 1–39.
Jones, J. G., 'Government and society 1536–1603', in J. B. Smith and L. B. Smith (eds), *History of Merioneth: Vol. II – The Middle Ages* (Cardiff, 2001), pp. 649–701.
Jones, J. G., *The Welsh Gentry 1536–1640: Images of status, honour and authority* (Cardiff, 1998; repr. 2016).
Jones, T., 'The story of Myrddin and the five dreams of Gwenddydd in the Chronicle of Elis Gruffudd', *Études Celtiques*, 8/2 (1959), 313–45.
Jones Pierce, T., 'The Clenennau estate', in J. Beverley Smith (ed.), *Medieval Welsh Society: Selected essays by T. Jones Pierce* (Cardiff, 1972), pp. 229–49.
Jordan, J., '"To Make a Man Without Reason": Examining manhood and manliness in early modern England', in J. H. Arnold and S. Brady (eds), *What is Masculinity? Historical dynamics from antiquity to the contemporary world* (Basingstoke, 2010), pp. 245–62.
Kishlansky, M. A., *Parliamentary Selection: Social and political choice in early modern England* (Cambridge, 1986).
Knafla, L. A., 'The "County Chancellor": The patronage of Thomas Egerton, Baron Ellesmere', in F. R. Fogle and L. A. Knafla (eds), *Patronage in Late Renaissance England* (Los Angeles, 1983), pp. 33–103.

Korngiebel, D. M., 'English colonial ethnic discrimination in the lordship of Dyffryn Clwyd: segregation and integration, 1282–c.1340', *Welsh History Review*, 23/2 (2006), 1–24.

Lacey, R., *Robert Earl of Essex: An Elizabethan Icarus* (London, 1971).

Lake, P., 'Post-Reformation Politics, or on Not Looking for the Long-Term Causes of the English Civil War', in M. J. Braddick (ed.), *The Oxford Handbook of the English Revolution* (Oxford, 2015), pp. 21–40.

Larminie, V., *Wealth, Kinship and Culture: The Seventeenth-Century Newdigates of Arbury and Their World* (Woodbridge, 1995).

Lawrence, A., 'Godly grief: individual responses to death in seventeenth-century Britain', in R. A. Houlbrooke (ed.), *Death, Ritual and Bereavement* (London, 1989), pp. 62–76.

Leach, A. F., *A History of Winchester College* (London, 1899).

Lewis, C. W., 'The content of poetry and the crisis in the bardic tradition', in A. O. H. Jarman and G. R. Hughes (eds), rev. D. Johnson, *A Guide to Welsh Literature 1282–c.1550*, vol. 2 (Cardiff, 1997), pp. 72–94.

Lewis, C. W., 'The decline of professional poetry', in R. G. Gruffydd (ed.), *A Guide to Welsh Literature c.1550–1700*, vol. 3 (Cardiff, 1997), pp. 29–74.

Llewellyn, N., 'Claims to status through visual codes: Heraldry on post-Reformation English funeral monuments', in S. Anglo (ed.), *Chivalry in the Renaissance* (Woodbridge, 1990), pp. 145–60.

Lloyd, D. T. and Jacobs, N., 'The "Stanzas of the Months": Maxims from late medieval Wales', *Medium Aevum*, 70/2 (2001), 250–67.

Lloyd, J. Y. W., *The History of the Princes, the Lords Marchers and the Ancient Nobility of Powys Fadog*, vol. 3 (London, 1882).

Lloyd, N., 'Sylwadau ar iaith rhai o gerddi Rhys Prichard', *National Library of Wales Journal*, 29 (1995–6), 257–80.

Lutz, C. E., 'The Letter of Lentulus describing Christ', *Yale University Library Gazette*, 50 (1975), 91–7.

Maddicott, J. R., 'The county community and the making of public opinion in fourteenth-century England', *Transactions of the Royal Historical Society*, 5th series, 28 (1978), 27–43.

Marston, J. G., 'Gentry, honor and royalism in early Stuart England', *Journal of British Studies*, 13/1 (1973), 21–43.

Mayhew, N. J., 'Prices in England, 1170–1750', *Past and Present*, 219 (2013), 3–39.

McInnes, A., 'The emergence of a leisure town: Shrewsbury 1660–1760', *Past and Present*, 120/1 (1988), 53–87.

McMullen, N., 'The education of English gentlewomen 1540–1640', *History of Education*, 6/2 (1977), 87–101.

Morgan, H., *Tyrone's Rebellion: The Outbreak of the Nine Years' War in Tudor Ireland* (Woodbridge, 1993).

Morgan, R., *The Welsh and the Shaping of Modern Ireland, 1448–1641* (Woodbridge, 2014).

Morris, C. (ed.), *The Journeys of Celia Fiennes* (London, 1947).
Neale, J. E., 'Three Elizabethan elections', *English Historical Review*, 46 (1931), 209–38.
O'Day, R., *Education and Society 1500–1800: The social foundations of education in early modern Britain* (London, 1982).
O'Day, R., *An Elite Family in Early Modern England: The Temples of Stowe and Burton Dassett, 1570–1656* (Woodbridge, 2018).
Olson, K. K., 'Slow and Cold in the True Service of God': Popular Beliefs and Practices, Conformity and Reformation in Wales, *c.*1530–*c.*1600', in T. Ó hAnnracháin and R. Armstrong (eds), *Christianities in the Early Modern Celtic World* (Baskingstoke, 2014), pp. 92–107.
Orme, N., 'Education in Medieval Wales', *Welsh History Review*, 27/4 (2015) 607–44.
Owen, D. H., 'The Englishry of Denbigh: An English colony in medieval Wales', *Transactions of the Honourable Society of Cymmrodorion* (1975), 57–76.
Owen, D. H., 'Clans and gentry families in the Vale of Clwyd, 1282–1536', in R. A. Griffiths and P. R. Schofield (eds), *Wales and the Welsh in the Later Middle Ages* (Cardiff, 2011), pp. 145–62.
Owen, H. G., 'Family politics in Elizabethan Merionethshire', *Bulletin of the Board of Celtic Studies*, 18/2 (1959), 86–91.
Owen, M. E., 'The prose of the cywydd period', in A. O. H. Jarman and G. R. Hughes (eds), rev. D. Johnston, *A Guide to Welsh Literature 1282–c.1550*, vol. 2 (Cardiff, 1997), pp. 24–43
Palmer, A. N., 'The portionary churches of mediaeval north Wales', *Archaeologia Cambrensis*, 5th series, 3 (1886), 175–209.
Palmer, P., *Language and Conquest in Early Modern Ireland* (Cambridge, 2001).
Pearson, D., 'Patterns of book ownership in late seventeenth-century England', *The Library*, 11/2 (2010), 144–53.
Pierce, T. P., 'Landlords in Wales: The Nobility and the Gentry', in J. Thirsk (ed.), *The Agrarian History of England and Wales*, vol. 4: *1500–1640* (Cambridge, 1967; 2011 edn), pp. 357–81.
Pollock, L., '"Teach her to live under obedience": The making of women in the upper ranks of early modern England', *Continuity and Change*, 4/2 (1989), 231–58.
Prest, W., 'Legal education of the gentry at the Inns of Court, 1560–1640', *Past and Present*, 38 (1967), 20–39.
Pryce, H., 'The medieval church', in J. B. Smith and L. B. Smith (eds), *History of Merioneth: Vol. II – The Middle Ages* (Cardiff, 2001), pp. 254–96.
Richards, S. N., *Y Ficer Prichard* (Caernarfon, 1994).
Richardson, R. C., *Household Servants in Early Modern England* (Manchester, 2010).
Roberts, B. F., 'Defosiynau Cymraeg', in T. Jones (ed.), *Astudiaethau Amrywiol a Gyflwynir i Syr Thomas Parry-Williams* (Cardiff, 1968), pp. 99–110.

Roberts, E., 'The Renaissance in the Vale of Clwyd', *Flintshire Historical Society Journal*, 15 (1954–5), 52–63.

Roberts, E., 'Teulu Plas Iolyn', *Transactions of the Denbighshire Historical Society*, 13 (1964), 33–110.

Roberts, P., 'Elizabethan players and minstrels and the legislation of 1572 against retainers and vagabonds', in A. Fletcher and P. Roberts (eds), *Religion, Culture and Society in Early Modern Britain: Essays in honour of Patrick Collinson* (Cambridge, 1994), pp. 29–55.

Robinson, W. R. B., 'The Tudor revolution in Welsh government 1536–1543: Its effects on gentry participation', *English Historical Review*, 103/406 (1988), 1–20.

Schurink, F., 'Manuscript commonplace books, literature, and reading in early modern England', *Huntington Library Quarterly*, 73/3 (2010), 453–69.

Schwyzer, P., *Literature, Nationalism, and Memory in Early Modern England and Wales* (Cambridge, 2004).

Schwyzer, P., 'The age of the Cambro-Britons: hyphenated British identities in the seventeenth century', *The Seventeenth Century*, 33/4 (2018), 427–39.

Shepard, A., *Meanings of Manhood in Early Modern England* (Oxford, 2006).

Siddons, M. P., 'Welsh Heraldry', *Transactions of the Honourable Society of Cymmrodorion* (1993), 27–46.

Sims-Williams, P., 'The early Welsh Arthurian poems', in R. Bromwich, A. O. H. Jarman and B. F. Roberts (eds), *The Arthur of the Welsh: The Arthurian legend in medieval Welsh literature* (Cardiff, 1991), pp. 33–71.

Skeel, C., 'The cattle trade between Wales and England from the fifteenth to the nineteenth centuries', *Transactions of the Royal Historical Society*, 9 (1926), 135–58.

Smith, A. H., *County and Court: Government and Politics in Norfolk, 1558–1603* (Oxford, 1974).

Smith, J. B., 'Crown and community in the principality of north Wales in the reign of Henry Tudor', *Welsh History Review*, 3 (1966), 145–71.

Smith, L. B., 'The gage and the land market in late medieval Wales', *Economic History Review*, NS, 29 (1976), 537–50.

Smith, L. B., 'Tir prid: deeds of gage in land in late medieval Wales', *Bulletin of the Board of Celtic Studies*, 27 (1976–8), 263–77.

Smith, L. B., 'The grammar and commonplace books of John Edwards of Chirk', *Bulletin of the Board of Celtic Studies*, 34 (1987), 175–84.

Smith, L. B., 'Fosterage, adoption and god-parenthood: Ritual and fictive kinship in medieval Wales', *Welsh History Review*, 16/1 (1992), 1–35.

Smith, L. B., 'Family, land and inheritance in late medieval Wales: A case study of Llannerch in the lordship of Dyffryn Clwyd', *Welsh History Review*, 27/3 (2015), 417–58.

Smith, P., *Houses of the Welsh Countryside: A study in historical geography* (London, 1975).

Smith, R. M., 'Families and their land in an area of partible inheritance: Redgrave, Suffolk 1260–1320', in R. M. Smith (ed.), *Land, Kinship, and Life-cycle* (Cambridge, 1985), pp. 135–95.

Smith, W. J., 'Three Salesbury mansions in 1601', *Bulletin of the Board of Celtic Studies*, 15/4 (1954), 293–302.

Smith, W. J. (ed.), 'Introduction', in *Calendar of Salusbury Correspondence, 1553–c.1700* (Cardiff, 1954), pp. 1–13.

Stacey, R. C., 'Gender and the social imaginary in medieval Welsh law', *Journal of the British Academy*, 8 (2020), 267–93.

Tawney, R. H., *The Agrarian Problem in the Sixteenth Century* (London, 1912; repr. Oxford, 1967).

Thirsk, J., 'Younger sons in the seventeenth century', *History*, 54/182 (1969), 360–72.

Thirsk, J., 'The European Debate on Customs of Inheritance, 1500–1700', in J. Goody, J. Thirsk and E. P. Thompson (eds), *Family and Inheritance: Rural Society in Western Europe, 1200–1800* (Cambridge, 1976), pp. 177–91.

Thomas, D. A. (ed.), *The Welsh Elizabethan Catholic Martyrs: The trial documents of Saint Richard Gwyn and of the Venerable William Davies* (Cardiff, 1971).

Thomas, G. C. G., 'From manuscript to print – 1. Manuscript', in R. G. Gruffydd (ed.), *A Guide to Welsh Literature*, vol. 3 (Cardiff, 1997), pp. 242–62.

Thomas, K. M., *Ruthin School: The First Seven Centuries* (Ruthin, 1974).

Tucker, N., 'Denbigh's Loyal Governor', *Transactions of the Denbighshire Historical Society*, vol. 5 (1956), 13–33.

Tyacke, N., 'Introduction', in N. Tyacke (ed.), *The History of the University of Oxford*, vol. 4: *The Seventeenth Century* (Oxford, 1997), pp. 1–24.

Wall, A., '"The greatest disgrace": The making and unmaking of JPs in Elizabethan and Jacobean England', *English Historical Review*, 119/481 (2004), 312–32.

Wallis, P. and Webb, C., 'The education and training of gentry sons in early modern England', *Social History*, 36/1 (2011), 36–53.

Walsham, A., 'The Holy Maid of Wales: Visions, Imposture and Catholicism in Elizabethan Britain', *English Historical Review*, 132/555 (2017), 250–85.

Ward, P., 'The Idea of Improvement, *c*.1520–1700', in R. W. Hoyle (ed.), *Custom, Improvement and the Landscape in Early Modern Britain* (Farnham, 2011), pp. 127–48.

Ward Clavier, S., 'Accounting for lives: autobiography and biography in the accounts of Sir Thomas Myddelton, 1642–1666', *The Seventeenth Century*, 35/4 (2020), 453–72.

Ward Clavier, S., *Royalism, Religion and Revolution: Wales, 1640–1688* (Woodbridge, 2021).

Watt, D., *The Paston Women: Selected Letters* (Woodbridge, 2004).

West, S., 'Looking back from 1700: Problems in locating the country house library', in M. Dimmock, A. Hadfield and M. Healy (eds), *The Intellectual*

Culture of the English Country House, 1500–1700 (Manchester, 2015), pp. 178–91.
Williams, G., 'Rice Mansell of Oxwich and Margam (1487–1559)', *Morgannwg*, 6 (1962), 35–51.
Williams, G., 'Unity of Religion or Unity of Language? Protestants and Catholics and the Welsh language 1536–1660', in G. H. Jenkins (ed.), *The Welsh Language before the Industrial Revolution* (Cardiff, 1997), pp. 207–33.
Williams, G., *Renewal and Reformation: Wales c.1415–1632* (Oxford, 1987; repr. 2002).
Williams, G. A., 'The later Welsh poetry referencing Owen', in M. Livingston and J. K. Bollard (eds), *Owain Glyndŵr: A Casebook* (Liverpool, 2013), pp. 519–50.
Williams, G. A., 'Owain Glyndŵr yn ei gynefin', *Journal of the Merioneth Historical and Record Society*, 17 (2016), 229–48.
Williams, G. A., '"Ail Dewi Menew": golwg newydd ar Richard Davies', *Y Traethodydd*, 174/229 (2019), 94–112.
Williams, G. A., 'Bibles and bards in Tudor and Stuart Wales', in G. Evans and H. Fulton (eds), *The Cambridge History of Welsh Literature* (Cambridge, 2019), pp. 232–50.
Williams, G. J., 'Traddodiad llenyddol Dyffryn Clwyd a'r cyffiniau', *Transactions of the Denbighshire Historical Society*, 1 (1952), 20–32.
Williams, J., *Ancient and Modern Denbigh: A descriptive history of the castle, borough and liberties* (Denbigh, 1836).
Williams, P., *The Council in the Marches of Wales under Elizabeth I* (Cardiff, 1958).
Woolf, D., *The Social Circulation of the Past: English historical culture 1500–1730* (Oxford, 2003).
Working, L., 'Tobacco and the social life of conquest in London, 1580–1625', *Historical Journal*, 65/1 (2022), 30–48.
Youngs, D., '"For the preferement of their marriage and bringing upp in their youth": The education and training of young Welshwomen, c.1450–c.1550', *Welsh History Review*, 25/4 (2011), 463–85.

4. UNPUBLISHED THESES

Baker, M., 'The development of the Welsh country house' (unpublished PhD thesis, Cardiff University, 2015).
Carr, A. D., 'The Mostyn family and estate, 1200–1642' (unpublished PhD thesis, University of Wales, Bangor, 1975).
Evans, S., '"To contynue in my bloud and name": Reproducing the Mostyn dynasty, c.1540–1692' (unpublished PhD thesis, Aberystwyth University, 2013).

Griffith, W. P., 'Welsh students at Oxford, Cambridge and the Inns of Court during the sixteenth and early seventeenth centuries' (unpublished PhD thesis, University of Wales, Bangor, 1981).
Hughes, A. L., 'Noddwyr y beirdd yn Sir Feirionnydd' (unpublished MA thesis, University of Wales, Aberystwyth, 1969).
Jones, O. W., 'Historical writing in medieval Wales' (unpublished PhD thesis, Bangor University, 2013).
Roberts, H. C., 'Re-examining Welsh Catholicism, *c.*1660–1700' (unpublished PhD thesis, Swansea University, 2014).
Rowlands, J., 'A critical edition and study of the Welsh poems written in praise of the Salusburies of Llyweni' (unpublished PhD thesis, University of Oxford, 1967).
Williams-Ellis, H., 'Delweddu Catrin o Ferain Mewn Llun a Gair' (unpublished PhD thesis, Bangor University, 2020), 527.

5. WEBSITES

British History Online:
Roberts, R. A. (ed), *Calendar of the Cecil Papers in Hatfield House* (London, 1902–10), vols 9, 11–12, available at *http://www.british-history.ac.uk/cal-cecil-papers/*

Cadw:
Cadw, 'Reference No. 22147: T-shaped Agricultural Range at Bachymbyd Fawr', Full Report for Listed Buildings, available at *https://cadwpublic-api.azurewebsites.net/reports/listedbuilding/FullReport?lang=&id=22147*

Dictionary of Welsh Biography: https://biography.wales
Jones, E. G. and Smith, W. J., 'Salusbury, Salisbury, Salesbury family, of Lleweni and Bachygraig', *DWB* (1959).
Richards, T., 'Bulkeley family, Anglesey, etc.', *DWB (1959)*.

History of Parliament Online*: https://www.historyofparliamentonline.org*
Dodd, A. H., *HPO (1558–1603)*: 'Salusbury, Sir John (*c.*1565–1612)'.
Edwards, P. S., *HPO (1509–1558)*: 'Jones, Henry I (?1532–86)'.
Edwards, P. S., *HPO (1509–1558)*: 'Salesbury, John (1533–80)'.
Healy, S., *HPO (1604–1629)*: 'Salesbury, William (1580/1–1660)'.
H.G.O., *HPO (1558–1603)*: 'Trevor, John (1563–1630)'.
H.G.O., *HPO (1558–1603)*: 'Trevor, Sir Richard (1558–1638)'.
W.J.J., *HPO (1558–1603)*: 'Bostock, Lancelot (bef.1533–*c.*88)'.

Oxford Dictionary of National Biography: https://www.oxforddnb.com

Adams, S., 'Dudley Ambrose, earl of Warwick', *ODNB* (2008; first pub. 2004).
Baker, J. H., 'Egerton, Thomas, first Viscount Brackley (1540–1617)', *ODNB* (2004).
Clark, C. E., 'Gorges, Sir Ferdinando', *ODNB* (2004).
Clough, C. H., 'Townshend, Sir John', *ODNB* (2005).
Lloyd, N., 'Prichard, Rhys [Rice]', *ODNB* (2004).
McGee, J. S., 'Wright, Leonard', *ODNB* (2004).
McGurk, J. J. N., 'Davies [Davis], Sir John', *ODNB* (2004).
Rapple, R., 'Stanley, Sir William', *ODNB* (2008; first pub. 2004).
Roberts, S. K., 'Mytton, Thomas', *ODNB* (2004).
Sil, N. P., 'Herbert, William first earl of Pembroke', *ODNB* (2009; first pub. 2004).
Thrush, A., 'Button, Sir Thomas', *ODNB* (2008; first pub. 2004).

Records of London's Livery Companies Online: Apprentices and Freemen 1400–1900: *https://www.londonroll.org/home*.

Rhug Estate: *https://rhug.co.uk*.

Royal Commission on the Ancient and Historical Monuments of Wales:
'Rug Castle Mount and Prehistoric Funerary Monument', available at *https://coflein.gov.uk/en/site/306598?term=rug%20mound*
'Caer Drewyn', available at *https://coflein.gov.uk/en/site/95431/*

Victoria County History Shropshire:
Everard, J., 'Education *c*.1600–2000', *Victoria County History Shropshire*, vol. 2 draft (March 2017), *http://www.vchshropshire.org/drafts/ShrewsburyPart2/7_1_Ed*

INDEX

achau'r mamau, or pedigrees of the mothers 24–7
Acts of Union (1536–43) 4, 7–9, 17, 29, 33, 56, 68, 74, 111, 115, 200, 231
ancestry 10–12, 16, 21–9, 50, 57–8, 64–5, 77, 80–1, 169, 230–2
apprenticeships 44, 162–3, 232
arable crops 93

Babington Plot (1586) 116, 127, 133, 187, 207, 212
Bagnall family of Plas Newydd 199
    Dame Elinor 28–9, 36, 49, 62, 105–6, 165, 175, 219, 230
    Sir Henry 36, 202–3, 217, 219, 230
Bagot family of Blithfield Hall 14–15, 47, 50–1, 93, 101, 105–6, 108
    Sir Edward 62–3, 91
    Sir Walter 15, 49–50, 62, 92, 100, 223–4, 226
bardic patronage *see* praise poetry
books and manuscripts 13, 15, 21–2, 58, 67, 104, 107, 152, 159, 165, 168–84, 194, 204, 206, 221, 224–6, 231
Bulkeley family of Baron Hill 5, 9, 199

Cadiz, capture of 122, 126, 210, 212–14, 219
Caerwys eisteddfod (1567) 114
Cambridge, University of 153–5, 167
Cambro-Britons 8, 12, 232

Catholicism 118–19, 122, 126–7, 171, 173, 185–90, 191, 193–4, 201, 207–9, 211–12, 218, 223, 231–2
Cecil, Robert, 1st earl of Salisbury 119–20, 126–7, 137–9
Cecil, William, 1st Baron Burghley 202–4
Chancery, court of 14, 39–40, 47–8, 53–6, 62, 86–91, 93, 100, 121
Charles I 5, 92, 127, 215
Charles II 5, 223
Civil Wars (1642–51) 13, 46, 51, 56, 91–2, 127, 163, 187, 189, 191–2, 215–17, 227, 233
Clough, Sir Richard 102–3, 198
colonisation 4, 195, 197, 199, 201, 221–2, 227, 232
Conwy family of Bodrhyddan 5, 34–5, 88, 171, 187
Council in the Marches 33, 82, 90, 113–14, 129, 131, 137–8, 140–1, 186, 205, 234
country houses, or *plastai* 15, 17, 42, 58–60, 62, 67, 101–8, 152, 167, 184

debt 34–5, 38–41, 43–4, 53, 82, 85–9, 92, 94, 99–100, 141, 179, 204
de Lacy, Henry, 3rd earl of Lincoln 23, 70–1
Denbigh Castle 23, 26, 35, 92, 179, 191, 215–16, 218, 227, 233
Denbighshire Great Sessions 130, 144–6, 224

deputy lieutenant, office of 117, 201, 223
Devereux, Robert, 2nd earl of Essex 121–7, 133–5, 199, 203, 207, 209–13, 217–19
Dinmael, manor of 34, 83–4, 98, 182
Dudley, Ambrose, 3rd earl of Warwick 36, 57, 95–6, 98, 111, 114, 116–19, 188
Dudley, Robert, 1st earl of Leicester 83, 85, 111, 114–17, 122, 199, 207, 211
duels 18, 42, 145, 147, 211–12
Dutch Revolt 19, 207–9, 218

Edeirnion
 barons of 4, 17, 73–6, 80
 commote of 31, 73–4, 76, 79, 182, 231
education 18, 59–60, 167–8, 193–4
 daughters 164–7
 sons 38, 40, 44–5, 152–64, 169, 172, 174, 184, 231–2
Edward I's conquest of Wales 4, 6, 23, 69, 71, 73, 169
Egerton, Thomas, 1st Viscount Brackley 37–8, 43, 88–91, 117–21, 124–5, 143–4, 158, 209
Elizabeth I 27, 111, 127, 134, 171, 205
enclosure 68, 111
English language 24–5, 77, 132, 141, 149, 155, 167–8, 171–2, 175–6, 180, 182, 200
English settlement in Wales 4–5, 29, 70–1, 75, 233
entails 31–2, 44, 47–52, 69, 86
Essex Revolt (1601) 43, 119–21, 123–7, 133–4, 147, 214, 218, 221
estate-building 68–81
estate income 35, 44, 53, 67, 81–2, 93–101, 107

factionalism 17, 109–10, 112–18, 129–39, 145, 149, 207, 211–12, 214, 231
forgery 48–50, 176
friendship 15, 18, 21, 34, 39, 42, 44, 61, 86–9, 116–17, 119–21, 124, 128–36, 139, 156, 175, 181, 183, 187, 189, 193–4, 197, 207, 215–16, 219, 221, 225, 232, 234

genealogy 10, 13, 16, 22–9, 77, 169, 181, 183, 194
gentility, or *uchelwriaeth* 1, 3, 6–13, 16–19, 21–2, 26–9, 59, 64, 77, 81, 113, 169, 194, 211, 229–34
Glyndŵr, Owain 4, 6–7, 17, 69, 76–9, 80
Glyndyfrdwy 17, 34, 42, 74–6, 80–2, 84, 96–7, 146, 171
Goodman, Gabriel, dean of Westminster 151, 156–7, 188–9
Goodman, Godfrey, bishop of Gloucester 40, 89, 92, 157–8, 172–4, 190, 221
Goodman, Mary 45–7, 50, 92–3, 166, 173, 224
Griffith family of Penrhyn 9, 14, 87
 Piers 87–9
Gwyn, Richard 188–90

Henry IV 6–7, 78
Henry VII 30–1, 72
Henry VIII 110, 192
heraldry 1, 11, 22, 62, 174, 181, 220–1
honour 2, 10, 12, 27, 50, 77, 79, 122, 127–9, 135, 138–9, 147–8, 192, 199, 205–6, 209, 212, 215–16, 230
hospitality 10, 17, 58–60, 64, 67, 107–8, 142, 149, 169, 229
household servants 40, 67, 109, 140, 142, 148–9, 163, 186, 189

humanism 11–12, 18, 151, 153,
  167–8, 182, 201, 232

illness 36, 86–9, 203
improvement *see* estate income
inflation 95–7, 170
inheritance
  cyfran, or partible inheritance
    68–9, 72–3, 173
  primogeniture 30, 39, 49, 57
  women 28, 34, 46–7, 51–5, 57,
    72–4, 86, 93, 100, 193
Inns of Court 13, 153, 155–6, 161,
    167, 232
  Gray's Inn 44–5, 82, 116, 141,
    156–7, 161, 163, 168, 215,
    226
Ireland 19, 40, 56, 85, 121–4, 134–5,
    158, 197, 199–207, 212–13,
    217–18, 227

jointure 42, 48–9, 59, 61, 63–4, 88,
    92–3, 102, 105, 106, 230
Justice of the Peace, office of 8, 117,
    129, 131, 134, 141, 149,
    180, 183, 231

Katherine of Berain 86, 102, 198
kinship 5, 15–16, 19, 21–2, 25,
    28–34, 47, 56, 60, 64–5,
    68–73, 80, 99, 108–11,
    127–8, 132–6, 138, 141,
    152, 155, 160–2, 181, 183,
    187, 194, 198, 202, 207,
    209, 211, 216, 232

labourers 108–9, 128, 131, 141, 149,
    189
livestock 67–8, 92–4, 99, 106–7, 142,
    161
Lloyd family of Bodidris 5, 88,
    114–15, 123, 129, 133, 145

marcher lordships 4, 6, 28, 31, 33,
    36, 56, 70–3, 77, 111,
    113–14, 142, 155, 186, 200
marriage 14, 16–17, 28–32, 35–6,
    40, 42, 44, 46–51, 58–64,
    70, 72–3, 75, 86–7, 92–3,
    105, 116, 144, 164, 167,
    181, 198, 202, 226, 232
Marshalsea Prison 43, 119, 126, 214
martial valour 204–6
Maurice family of Clenennau 9, 69
Member of Parliament, office of
    113, 115–16, 135–6, 188,
    219, 222, 231
moneylending 41, 43–4, 47–8, 85–8,
    90–1, 121, 202, 210
mortgages 48, 69, 71–2, 85–8, 90–1,
    99, 159, 189, 215, 221
Mostyn family of Mostyn 2, 5, 50–1,
    70, 118, 140, 186, 199
Myddelton, Sir Thomas 41, 43, 117,
    202, 204, 210
Mytton, Major General Thomas 191,
    215–16, 218

Nine Years' War, or Tyrone's
    Rebellion 19, 122–3, 202–3, 207
noble patronage 17, 19, 109–28,
    207, 217
Norman Conquest 12, 23–4, 29, 230

officeholding 5–12, 33, 80, 109–17,
    133, 136, 149, 155–6, 172,
    179–80, 183, 186, 192,
    230–1
Oxford, University of 4, 153–5, 160,
    167–8
  Brasenose College 118, 126, 157
  Jesus College 177
  Oriel College 38, 158, 160, 177
  The Queen's College 24

Painted Book of Erbistock 21–2,
    165, 181, 183
parliamentary elections 113, 115–16,
    122, 133–9, 213, 219
paterfamilias 13, 16–17, 29–56, 43,

61, 63, 85, 88, 90, 99–100, 107, 142, 189, 204, 226, 230
Plas Issa, Wrexham 92–3
Pool Park estate 40, 42, 44–5, 49, 61, 87–8, 93, 98–9, 102, 105–7
portraiture 15–16, 51, 220–21, 233
praise poetry 5, 10–11, 13, 15, 18, 28, 58–61, 64, 77, 79–80, 151, 153, 169–72, 181, 184, 194, 204, 212, 231
Price, Dr Ellis of Plas Iolyn 114–15
Prichard, Rhys 176–7, 179–80
Principality of North Wales 4, 28, 31–2, 73
privateering 147, 220–1, 222, 227
Privy Council 134, 137–8
Protestantism 10, 118, 153, 171, 177, 184–93, 201, 208–9, 212, 218, 229
Protestant Reformation 13, 19, 33, 56, 68, 81, 118, 154, 156, 184–5, 192, 194, 208
Pugh family of Mathafarn 193
  Maria Charlotta 55, 101, 193
  Rowland 55, 193
Puleston family of Emral and Hafod-y-wern 5, 29, 32, 43, 67, 77, 118, 181, 183, 206, 233
Puritanism 118, 171, 187–9, 191–2

Ravenscroft family of Bretton 44, 61, 118
rents 37, 40, 42, 53–4, 67, 70, 76, 83–4, 93, 95–100, 114, 119, 143–4, 165, 230
reputation 5, 10, 13, 16–18, 24, 50, 74–9, 106, 116–17, 122, 127, 135, 139, 147–8, 202, 206, 210, 212, 214, 219, 224, 230–34
retinue, or *plaid* 18, 137, 139–42, 149
Rûg Chapel 15, 189–91, 230
Russell, Anne, countess of Warwick 36–7, 57, 111–12, 188

Ruthin School, Denbighshire 40, 155–9, 190, 231

Salisbury, John of Erbistock 21, 152, 165–6, 181, 183
Salusbury family of Lleweni 4–5, 23, 30–1, 35, 67, 70–1, 86, 113, 116, 118, 122, 133, 154–6, 159, 198, 211
  Elizabeth (d.*c*.1584) 28, 35, 39–40, 59–61, 113, 116, 165, 198
  Sir John (d.*c*.1578) 34, 113–15
  Sir John (d.1612) 116–17, 133–9, 152, 211–12, 219
  Thomas (d.1491) 30–1, 56, 154
  Thomas (d.1586) 116–17, 127, 187, 207
Salusbury, Owen of Holt 40, 122–5, 207–15, 218, 221
scholarship *see* books and manuscripts
soldiering 4, 10, 13, 19, 40, 43, 56, 85, 89, 100, 122–6, 135, 157–8, 195, 197, 199, 201–19, 223, 227, 232
Stanley, Sir William 207–8, 210–11, 214
Star Chamber, court of 14, 79, 122, 129–37, 140–1, 161
steward 142–3
  household 38, 99, 132, 141–9
  of Denbigh 114
  of Ruthin 33, 36, 77, 110–11, 155, 186, 189

tenants 16–18, 40, 53, 60, 68, 70–1, 76, 82–3, 92, 95–9, 100, 108–9, 111, 119, 128, 131, 140–3, 149, 161, 175–6, 183, 189, 230, 232
Thelwall family of Plas y Ward, Bathafarn, and Plas Coch 5, 35, 41, 61, 91, 134, 233
  Elizabeth 15–16, 47–8, 50, 61–4, 106–7

INDEX

Eubule 39–40, 50, 62–3, 158, 217–20, 223
timber 94, 101
tir prid, or gage land 69, 71–2
tobacco 159–60, 222–3
Tracy family of Toddington 193
Trevor family of Trevalyn 5, 133, 199, 219
    John Trevor 129–30
    Sir John 88
    Sir Richard 133–9, 213

Vaughan family of Llwydiarth 48, 62, 164, 181
    Dorothy 44, 47–8, 165
    Owen 134–7
Vaughan family of Nannau 55, 101
Virginia, Commonwealth of 174, 194, 221–2

Wards, court of 14, 34, 37, 42, 57, 129
wardship 34–7, 41–2, 95, 111–12, 117, 120–1, 143, 161, 214
Welsh diaspora 19, 124, 227, 232
Welsh language 4, 13, 15, 18–19, 24–5, 58, 141, 149–50, 153, 168–71, 174–85, 194–5, 199–202, 206, 208, 211, 227
widowhood 16, 34, 47, 50, 54, 57, 61–4, 73, 88, 99, 105–6, 130, 164–5, 167, 198, 219, 230
Winchester College, Hampshire 45, 156, 159–60, 168
Wynn family of Gwydir 67, 70, 103
    Sir John 78–9, 197